Community Action
and the Poor

Kenneth J. Pollinger
and
Annette C. Pollinger

The Praeger Special Studies program—utilizing the most modern and efficient book production techniques and a selective worldwide distribution network—makes available to the academic, government, and business communities significant, timely research in U.S. and international economic, social, and political development.

Community Action and the Poor
Influence vs. Social Control
In a New York City Community

Praeger Publishers   New York   Washington   London

PRAEGER SPECIAL STUDIES IN U.S. ECONOMIC, SOCIAL, AND POLITICAL ISSUES

PRAEGER PUBLISHERS
111 Fourth Avenue, New York, N.Y. 10003, U.S.A.
5, Cromwell Place, London S.W.7, England

Published in the United States of America in 1972
by Praeger Publishers, Inc.

© 1972 by Praeger Publishers, Inc.

Library of Congress Catalog Card Number: 72-80462

Printed in the United States of America

ACKNOWLEDGMENTS

Of the many persons who assisted the authors with their suggestions and criticisms, special mention must be made of Professors Gerald M. Shattuck, Stephen M. David, and Mary G. Powers, all from Fordham University. Gerald Shattuck, besides being the constant theoretical critic, supplied the authors with crucial insights into the problems of social control and social influence. Mary Powers provided the methodological expertise, while Stephen David, in addition to supplying constant support and encouragement, greatly aided the study with his political science perspective.

The people involved in the Tremont community action program, especially Susan Boyd and John E. Moore, deserve particular mention because of their invaluable insights and criticisms, and--more importantly--because of their continuing cooperation.

Finally, much gratitude is due to Ms. Winnie Walsh, who typed and proofread the entire manuscript.

CONTENTS

LIST OF TABLES

xiii

LIST OF FIGURES

LIST OF ABBREVIATIONS

Bronco-SIA	Bronx Community Self-Improvement Association
CAP	Council Against Poverty
CDA	Community Development Agency
ETAC	East Tremont Action Committee
ETNA	East Tremont Neighborhood Association
HRA	Human Resources Administration
NAPRA	National Association of Puerto Rican Affairs
NEED	Neighborhood Educational and Economic Development
NPB	Nonparticipant Beneficiary
OEO	Office of Economic Opportunity
P	Participant
PB	Participant Beneficiary
TCC	Tremont Community Council
THC	Tremont Housing Clinic
U	Unsuccessful
WANA	Washington Avenue Neighborhood Association
WFV	West Farms Villagers
UBP	United Bronx Parents

INTRODUCTION

This research focuses on the relationship of
the New York City community action bureaucracy to
the poor, on the neighborhood level. More specifically, this is a case study of the City's community
action program as it operated in the Tremont area
in the South-central Bronx during the 1969-70 program year. The examination of the relationship between the bureaucracy and the poor presents a difficult empirical question for social scientists
since few comprehensive theories exist for such a
concrete analysis. However, this study is based on
the contention that through utilizing the two major
perspectives of influence and social control[1] in
the evaluation of antipoverty or community action
programs, one can arrive at a fairly precise and
comprehensive view of the consequences of such programs for the urban poor. Thus, the specific object of the research is to determine whether the
poor are primarily gaining influence or being socially controlled as a result of the City's antipoverty efforts.

The study's major hypothesis may be stated as
follows: Although the stated goals of the community
action program in New York City imply that the program on the neighborhood level should be an influe-
ence output, with the community action bureaucracy
serving as an advocate of the potential partisans,
the poor, the operation in the Tremont poverty area
can best be described as a social control output,
with the community action bureaucracy functioning
as a social control agent and as another authority
with which the poor must cope.

Chapter 1 presents the setting of the study--
describing the phenomena of urban discontent, political stress, and the resulting Economic Opportunity Act of 1964--as well as a detailed description
of the major concepts and hypothesis used in the
study. Here, the community action program is reviewed in terms of outputs, with special emphasis

on the development and goals of the program in New York City. Chapter 2 presents in detail the theoretical framework utilized, along with the conceptual and operational definitions of the study's key variables.

The third chapter contains a description of the structure and functioning of the community action bureaucracy (the Council Against Poverty and the Community Development Agency) and its relationship to the 26 poverty areas in New York City. A brief sketch is given of the program in the Tremont poverty area, centering on its development, present structure, budgets, and overall functioning. Chapter 4 offers a description of the various methods employed in the research; in particular, those of observation, participant observation, and interviewing. A description of the most significant data resulting from each of these techniques is found in the next three chapters. Specifically, Chapter 5 contains analyses of the resources—funds, personnel, and technical assistance—of the neighborhood level units in the Tremont community action program and of their operation; Chapter 6 analyzes the crucial relationship between the community bureaucracy and the neighborhood level units through a detailed examination of the decision-making involved in the process through which these units are approved for funding. Chapter 7 consists of a summary of the pertinent characteristics of the respondents interviewed, and an analysis of the interview data. Finally, Chapter 8 contains a summary and interpretation of the major findings of the research.

Before proceeding into the actual study, a few brief remarks should be made concerning the question of value bias which undoubtedly finds expression in almost all social science research, but to which evaluative research of the type undertaken here is perhaps particularly vulnerable. From the outset, it should be clearly noted that one major factor influencing the content and specific formulation of this study was the authors' value position—based on the results of much recently published research,[2] as well as on several months of direct observation

of the operation of the community action program in
New York City--that the poor, and particularly the
minority poor, are generally not well served by the
antipoverty programs which claim to exist in their
behalf and for their betterment. All precautions
were taken to prevent the interference of personal
values in the data collection process, including
allowing through the interview technique the opportunity for program participants to speak for themselves and thus to serve as a check on the interpretations drawn from the observational phase of
the study. Nevertheless, in formulating conclusions on the basis of the data yielded through such
research, it is perhaps impossible to eliminate the
intrusion of one's own perspective. In spite of
this difficulty, it is hoped that the study will
accomplish the following aims:

    1. Provide a body of data on the basis of
which the community action program in New York City
may be interpreted in terms of how and to what extent the poor are being affected;

    2. illuminate present theoretical discussions
concerning the two key concepts of social control
and influence; and implicitly, the order and conflict perspectives so valuable to researchers in
studying social phenomena; and finally,

    3. clarify certain methodological problems
inherent in measuring influence and social control
through the contribution of empirical indicators of
each concept.

**THE COMMUNITY
ACTION PROGRAM:
OUTPUTS
IN RESPONSE
TO STRESS**

ORIGINS OF THE ECONOMIC OPPORTUNITY ACT

During the past decade it has become increasingly evident that the issues of poverty and the rising voices of large segments of the poor have brought about a very definite stress in the American social and political system. In various ways--through urban disorders, riots, demonstrations, invasions of official hearings, the organization of radical groups with increased reliance on violent rhetoric and tactics--the alienated poor have been articulating their grievances. And even while lamenting such events, many, both within and without the ranks of the poor, have come to agree with the recent words of Supreme Court Justice William O. Douglas: ". . . where grievances pile high and most of the elected spokesmen represent the Establishment, violence may be the only effective response."[1]

The violence and the demands, to a very large extent, have resulted in a heightened awareness of the extensiveness of the poor, and to a lesser yet significant degree, have illuminated some of the major causes of poverty. Volumes of social scientific literature have documented and described the close to one-third (or one-fourth, depending on one's definition of poverty) of the U.S. population which is at or below the poverty level, while "structural poverty"[2] or "intergenerational poverty"

3

have become hackneyed terms among sociologists in
particular. But the stress of poverty continues to
appear in the minds of many as a very real, if yet
unrealized, threat to the political system of the
country. Withdrawal of support and the advocacy of
a new revolutionary stance by the poor, many feel,
threatens not only the authorities but the political
community itself.

Perhaps it was with this perspective in view
that, early in the decade of the 1960s, academi-
cians, politicians, government agency personnel,
and foundation officials focused attention on the
issues of poverty through such undertakings as the
Grey Areas Project and President Kennedy's Committee on Juvenile Delinquency.[3] The prognosis for
poverty, in the view of those connected with such
early endeavors--David Hackett, director of the
Juvenile Delinquency Committee; Paul N. Ylvisaker
of the Ford Foundation's Public Affairs Program,
Fred Hayes, Richard Boone, Sanford Kravitz, Richard
Cloward, and Lloyd Ohlin--suggested the need for
institutional change, a shaking up of the prevail-
ing system, which led Richard Blumenthal, in his
analysis of early antipoverty developments, to
label this group "the guerrillas."[4] By the early
years of the Johnson Administration, the Grey Areas
Project and its parallels had become transformed
into community action programs, which from the beginning suffered dual interpretations at the hands
of the guerrillas and most others within the government. While the guerrillas lacked faith in the
existing institutions serving the poor and viewed
the community action programs as a method of funda-
mental redistribution of power, most government
officials, and certainly Johnson himself, looked
upon such programs as a means of channeling necessary services into poverty areas through improving
the lot of the poor, while taking care not to wire
the poor into the already overloaded political
circuits.

In early 1964 President Johnson appointed
Sargent Shriver to head a Task Force to draft the
legislation of the antipoverty efforts, including
that of the community action programs. The final

draft stated that community action should be "developed and conducted with the maximum feasible participation of the residents of areas and members of groups affected,"[5] but the definition of community action was purposely left unclear by the drafters. Adam Yarmolinsky, Shriver's assistant, stated that "the objective of the drafters was never to get the poor to think of themselves as a political force."[6] But the guerrillas, especially Boone and Cloward, saw the need for involvement and participation of the poor; they felt that the federal government should fund new and more representative political organizations that truly politically activated the poor. The Economic Opportunity Act became law on August 20, 1964 with Title II of the Act providing for the establishment of local community action programs.[7]

After the legislation was passed, many of the guerrillas became official full- or part-time members of the Shriver Task Force that was to implement Title II of the Act, with the intention of compelling local political influentials to accept the poor as co-decision-makers. Others joined the newly established Office of Economic Opportunity (OEO, the federal antipoverty agency) to administer the program. With Fred Hayes as the deputy director, the guerrillas were determined to change the past donor-donee relationship that the government's programs had fostered. They wanted to give the poor the sense of being masters of their own destiny, and aimed to see to it that the poor joined in developing, implementing, and administering the community action programs at the local level.

Thus, the guerrillas and the more traditional governmental officials began with different objectives and saw the community action program from vitally different perspectives. One of the key results was the development of a similarly dual view toward whom this new output--the community action program--was aimed. Assuming the legitimacy of the political analyst's proposition that outputs of any political system need only satisfy the "politically relevant" members of that system,[8] it can be seen that the guerrillas and the other

governmental officials differed significantly in
their assessment of exactly who was to be thought
of as politically relevant. To the guerrillas the
target of the community action program was the
poor. The program itself was seen as a vehicle for
alleviating the stress of poverty through giving
the poor the opportunity to organize themselves politically; that is, to become politically relevant
members. And the way the guerrillas saw to do that
would be to have federally funded local agencies
that would become new institutions (independent
corporations), giving rise to new attitudes among
the poor, and that would end up challenging not
only the local government but the entire local
elite structure.

On the other hand, the target of most government officials was the already traditionally politically relevant members: the mayors and other local influentials. It was their aim that the poor,
rather than being politically activated, were to
receive more services from the local political influentials, thereby maintaining and strengthening
the already existing donor-donee relationship between the local authorities and the poor.[9]

EARLY RESULTS OF COMMUNITY
ACTION PROGRAMS

But what in fact happened?[10] The mayors of
most cities opposed the involvement of the poor in
directing and administering the community action
programs. They were against the possibility of new
political groups arising in slum areas that would
challenge the mayor and his organization. The
mayors wanted to retain control over these programs
in order to use them to improve their own reputation among the poor and thereby gain their support.
Also, private welfare agencies wanted the funds
channeled into their agencies rather than into
those operated by the poor.

Thus, there developed a constant struggle between most mayors and the OEO. Whereas the OEO,
under the direction of the guerrillas, intended

that the poor develop political organizations to
represent their interests, the mayors managed to
keep control over most of the community action
boards and slowly got Congress to amend the law in
1966 and 1967 to the point that the "maximum feasible participation" clause was removed. This
meant that the mayors were given legal control over
the community action programs that were no longer
independent corporations but now became public
agencies with many restrictions on the political
activities of anti-poverty workers in the program.*

In the last analysis, then, the city halls appear to have won. Through the 1967 amendments to
the Economic Opportunity Act, they gained domina-
tion over the community action programs and thus
the ability to prevent federal funds from being
used to aid groups undertaking political activities
against the policies of the local administration.
However, between 1964 and 1967, something happened.
Granting wide regional and local variations, which
will be explored in the pages which follow, the
community action programs did provide the means for
some of the poor to gain experience in political
action and to experience a new degree of responsiveness on the part of certain local governmental
institutions. To varying degrees, then, the newly
organized poor in key municipalities created a
force that had to be reckoned with, with greater or
lesser ease, by the mayors, newly endowed with
power over the community action programs.

It has been seen, then, that the poor brought
about demands that in turn led to stress on the
political system. This stress prompted that system
to produce outputs: the Economic Opportunity Act
and Community Action (interpreted by the majority
of governmental officials as services and by the

---

*It should be noted that many mayors did not
see it as politically advantageous to make use of
the amendments. For example, see the case of New
York City's Mayor Lindsay, as cited later on in
this chapter.

guerrillas as power changes). For a time, the
power element won out and gave the poor some political experience as well as a taste for power (even
though this varied from city to city). But this
response of the poor, in turn, created another
stress: complaints from the mayors and locally
established groups. Their demands brought about
another output: amendments to the Economic Opportunity Act that placed control of community action
in the hands of the mayors.[11]

COMMUNITY ACTION OUTPUTS:
ELITIST VS. PARTICIPATORY

The key question that emerges from this analysis, and which consequently serves as the general
focal point for the present study, is the following:
What have been the consequences of the community
action programs which emerged transformed in the
late 1960s, both for the poor themselves and for
the alleviation of the stress brought about by
poverty?
     An initial answer to the question of the con-
sequences of the community action program for those
at whom they were aimed is provided by Paul E.
Peterson's comparative study of the community action programs in the cities of Chicago, Philadelphia, and New York.[12] The basic focus of Peterson's study was on the classification of community
action outputs in each of the three cities according to their impact on the structural characteristics of the political system. If the flow of demands of the poor (demand inputs) through the system was reduced, the outputs were designated elitist; if the number and capacity of the demand flow
channels of the political system in favor of the
poor was increased, then the outputs were considered participatory.
     Thus, Peterson found two main ways for a po-
litical system to alleviate stress: Through pro-
ducing either elitist outputs or participatory outputs. The elitist outputs would act to reduce the
demand inputs by diverting the gatekeepers (those

who articulate the demands of the poor) to other functions and clogging the demand flow channels of the poor, while the participatory outputs would stimulate new gatekeepers and more effective flow channels for the demands of minority groups and/or the poor.

Upon examining the community action programs, Peterson found that Chicago--controlled by Mayor Daley and characterized by a pattern of centralized political power--produced elitist outputs; Philadelphia was less controlled by the mayor and produced a combination of elitist and participatory outputs; while New York City was the least controlled by the mayor and in the pluralist tradition, produced participatory outputs.

In terms of the question of the consequences of the community action programs, his findings with regard to New York City are particularly interesting. In addition to documenting the structural change which came about as a function of the total community action program, Peterson characterized as significant the quality of the participation of the poor in three neighborhood programs: Bedford-Stuyvesant, East Harlem, and the Lower West Side. In each of these areas he noted that organized and extensive community conflict functioned to generate the articulation of demands for broad changes in governmental services to the poor. [13]   In Bedford-Stuyvesant "community action personnel had begun to generate community pressures in favor of major changes in the operation of the welfare department and the school system," while in East Harlem "a cadre of community activists continually demanded changes in welfare, housing, and educational policies in the community. Indeed, the political activity in East Harlem generated city-wide movements for drastic reorganization of the city's educational system." [14]

These findings, in contrast to those emerging from his studies of Chicago and Philadelphia, led Peterson to conclude that inter-city variation in terms of both the formation of new flow channels and the degree of formal representation of the poor was related to the dispersion of political power

and the existing electoral cleavages. In other
words, output response was determined to a great
extent by the existing political structures.

HISTORY OF N.Y.C. COMMUNITY
ACTION PROGRAM

The history of the community action program in
New York City certainly supports the conclusion
that the consequences of such programs are inte-
grally related to the political frameworks within
which they develop.[15] Immediately following the
passage of the Economic Opportunity Act in August
1964, Mayor Wagner developed a community action
structure that, while giving some appearances of
political power to representatives of the poor,
left the Mayor and appointed city officials firmly
in control of antipoverty monies. The involvement
of the poor in decision-making at the city-wide
level was minimal, and city officials, with some
assistance from the private welfare agencies, were
able to determine the shape and focus of the poverty
program. On the neighborhood level, Wagner designated 16 poverty areas in which Community Progress
Centers, tightly controlled by the City, were set
up in order to provide social services such as job
training, recreation, and Head Start programs.
The decisions that Wagner made concerning the
community action programs are to be understood in
terms of his own political stakes, which dictated
that he keep control and limit the involvement of
the poor. The maintenance of his electoral con-
stituency--which consisted of an uneasy alliance of
middle-income white ethnic groups and low-income
non-white groups--was not to be served by the political activation of the poor. As it was, splits
within the Democratic Party itself led Wagner's
candidate to lose in the 1965 primary to Abraham
Beame and ultimately to the election of John Lindsay.
Early in the first administration of Mayor
Lindsay, the community action program's main policy-
making body, the Council Against Poverty, underwent

a significant reorganization in which the representation of the poor was greatly expanded, giving
the poor the potential for dominant control. For a
time, however, the orientation of the program continued to be set by city officials, operating primarily through the Council's new administrative
arm, the Community Development Agency, and could
best be characterized as one of providing social
services. By mid-1967, there had developed considerable conflict over this orientation, with many
within the community action bureaucratic structure
pushing for the change to a political action approach. Gradually, the program appeared to shift
its emphasis to the organization and politicization
of the poor. Throughout these changes though,
Lindsay maintained a considerable degree of control, primarily through the appointment of "acceptable" representatives of the poor to key administrative positions within the community action program.

On the neighborhood level, Lindsay expanded
the number of poverty areas to 26 and set up non-
profit Community Corporations to review all proposals for funds from groups in the area and to co-
ordinate all funded programs in the community.
Election procedures were established which appear
to have identified and aided new local leadership
in assuming control of the Corporations to the
relative exclusion of the traditional institutional
leadership, who had maintained firm control of local programs under the policies of Mayor Wagner.

As was seen in the case of Mayor Wagner,
Lindsay's community action outputs reflect his own
political stakes in promoting an expanded degree of
involvement by the poor. Elected in 1965 by a most
unstable coalition of conservative Republicans and
liberal Democrats, he found it necessary to stabi-
lize his own support while drawing the support of
the poor away from the traditional Democratic ma-
chine. The large majority of blacks and Puerto
Ricans that re-elected Lindsay to office in 1969
attest to the aptness of both his analysis and
tactics.[16]

COMMUNITY ACTION PROGRAM:
GOALS AND STRATEGIES

At present, both the structure and orientation
of the community action program as last described
remains essentially intact. This is clearly reflected in the official documents of the community
action bureaucracy which describes the program's
goals and strategies with respect to individual
poverty areas. Concerning the goals of the Council
Against Poverty, such statements as the following
are made:

> The Council is committed to achieving
> maximum participation by the recipi-
> ents of services and residents of
> poverty areas. This means that the
> people who have traditionally been
> left out should be involved at every
> level of decision-making and imple-
> menting programs. . . . Another goal
> is to make the "system" work for poor
> people. This is done by encouraging
> community action in education, hous-
> ing, job training and economic devel-
> opment--that will force institutions
> that service the poor to be responsive
> to the needs of poor people.[17]

In another document, the first goal of the
Council is described as "a firm establishment of
the Council Against Poverty as a voice of the poor."
This directive continues, ". . . through Council
leadership, panels and committees, working coopera-
tively with Community Corporations, the Chairman of
the Council Against Poverty with the Community Development Agency's Commissioner will continue to
press and formalize the Council Against Poverty as
the advocate and voice of the poor."[18]
Concerning the 26 Community Corporations, we
read that:

> . . . the Community Action program
> strategy is to mobilize and enhance

the action of low-income citizens to
modify established institutional
policies and services in order to
alleviate poverty. . . . The Council Against Poverty sets the primary
program strategy for the new program
year as <u>advocacy planning and action</u>
. . . the Council Against Poverty
will give preference to those projects which develop and advocate
ways, through concerted citizen action, to alter existing institutions
to better serve the low-income communities.[19]

That The Community Corporations themselves reflect this strategy is obvious from the following
statement on goals by one particular Corporation:

Our approach is a conscious action
for change. It is our intention
to utilize all of the existing resources and services to work with all
the existing groups whose aims are to
shatter the shackles of poverty. We
will attempt to mold this community
into one voice that clamors for its
rights. We will attempt, through
community organization around specific services and community based
programs, to instill a sense of
power to those who once were powerless.[20]

In summary, the stated goals of the community
action program in New York City appear headed in
the direction of establishing the city-wide bureaucracy as an advocate of the poor and as a source of
encouragement for the establishment of action programs in the various poverty areas, aimed at bringing about institutional change in favor of the
poor. What evidence, however, exists that these
program goals are in actuality being fulfilled?[21]

THE STUDY'S THEORETICAL FRAMEWORK

In order to answer this question, it is helpful to place the foregoing discussion within a
theoretical framework, thus allowing more fruitful
conceptualization and development. Here, Peterson's
distinction between elitist and participatory outputs provides a suitable starting point. Applying
his terminology to the historical development of
the community action program in New York City, it
can be seen rather clearly that, while Mayor Wagner's decisions regarding the program can best be
termed elitist, Mayor Lindsay, primarily through
his transformation of the Council Against Poverty,
generated participatory outputs. However, it appears that two seemingly distinct stages occurred
under the Lindsay administration. While remaining
essentially participatory in terms of the relative
involvement of the poor, the early Lindsay program
emphasized the dispensing of social services to the
poor, as opposed to the encouragement of political
action and organization by the poor, which characterized the orientation of the community action
program from mid-1967 to the present.

More specifically, in his discussion of elitist and participatory outputs as the two major ways
in which a political system works to alleviate
stress, and in his application of these categories
to the community action program, Peterson implies
that elitist outputs alleviate the stress coming
from poverty primarily through the provision of social services to the poor by local political elites
--most commonly through the media of existing welfare and social service agencies. Participatory
outputs, on the other hand, imply a somewhat more
complex strategy in which primary emphasis is
placed on bringing the poor or their legitimate
representatives into the political system, thus directly or indirectly increasing their political activation. Significantly, the case of the shifting
orientations during the Lindsay administration suggests that such a participatory output may involve
the utilization of the poor themselves in the
provision of social services, as well as the

encouragement of direct and large-scale political
organization and action by the poor.

A valuable and highly applicable extension to
the line of analysis begun by Peterson is provided
by William A. Gamson in his recent work, Power and
Discontent.[22] Gamson's theoretical perspective
rests on a clear distinction between two manners in
which stress is perceived by the actors in the political system. Specifically, Gamson views stress
in two ways: (a) stress coming from the "objects
of discontent"; e.g., lack of economic opportunity
and development, poor and inadequate housing, dis-
criminatory educational policies, lack of jobs and
skills training; and, (b) stress coming from the
"sources of pressure"; e.g., the various pressures
brought to bear by low-income groups on political
structures.[23]

In most general terms, the group at whom the
political output is aimed may be said to have
gained influence, or conversely, to have been the
object of social control at the hands of the authorities, depending on which of these two stresses
is perceived and in turn motivates the production
of the output. More specifically, Gamson quite
clearly implies that two conditions must exist for
the occurrence of influence on the part of a "potential partisan" group (in the case of the community action program, the poor):[24] First, the output must provide the necessary resources in order
to allow a reasonable attempt to be made at alleviating the stress coming from the objects of discontent; and secondly, the potential partisans must
themselves be involved in such an alleviation. Any
output which does not satisfy these two conditions
cannot, in the long run, expect to alleviate the
objects of discontent--or more precisely, the conditions of powerlessness giving rise to the objects
of discontent--and thus is assumed to be aimed essentially at alleviating the stress coming from the
sources of pressure. This latter type of output
may be termed one of social control as opposed to
the influence output described above.

Here, it should be noted clearly that in addition to the quality of the output the major question

which must be asked in determining whether or not
an output is primarily one of influence or of social control, concerns those who are involved in
the alleviation of the perceived stress. This
point may be more clearly illuminated by referring
back to Peterson's distinction between elitist outputs and participatory outputs. Either of these
two types of outputs may be said to aim at the alleviation of objects of discontent; in the case of
elitist outputs, through the provision of such social services as job training or educational reme-
diation to the poor by the local political elites
or their representatives; in the case of participatory outputs, through the provision of similar
services to the poor by their own legitimate representatives, or through large-scale organization of
the poor around the objects of discontent themselves. However, elitist outputs, even where successful in terms of alleviating certain objects of
discontent on a short-term basis, imply a continuing dependency of potential partisans on authorities, which is inconsistent with the influence exercised by a partisan group as described by Gamson.
Precisely because of the maintenance of this dependency, it may be assumed that elitist outputs are
aimed primarily at alleviating the stress that political elites perceive to be coming from the
sources of pressure, thus constituting social control outputs in Gamson's terminology.

On the other hand, it should be clearly noted,
particularly in light of a growing body of literature on the concept of cooptation,[25] that participatory outputs do not necessarily constitute influence outputs. For while such outputs satisfy
the conditions of involving the poor themselves in
the alleviation of stress, the question of the goal
toward which participation on the part of the poor
is aimed, and the quality of that participation,
remain to be considered. Specifically, if the participatory output does not provide the necessary
resources in order to allow potential partisans to
make a reasonable attempt at alleviating the stress
coming from the objects of discontent, it may be
assumed that the real goal of participation of the

poor in the eyes of authorities is manipulating the
sources of pressure--in effect, maintaining their
dependency in much the same fashion as elitist outputs and thus constituting essentially a social
control output. Only where such necessary resources
are provided can a participatory output be said to
constitute one of influence.

On the basis of the above discussion, the following definitions of influence and social control
outputs, which will be used in this study to evaluate the consequences of the community action program, may be formulated:

An <u>influence output</u> is a decision or set of
decisions made by the authorities that brings potential partisans--the poor--or their legitimate
representatives into the political system, and
gives them the necessary resources to make a reasonable attempt to alleviate the stress coming from
the objects of discontent. Such an output will be
manifested either through the existence of relevant
and successful service programs, controlled and administered by legitimate representatives of the
poor, or through the occurrence of effective large-
scale organization and action by the ranks of the
poor themselves.[26]

A <u>social control output</u> is a decision or set
of decisions by which authorities primarily attempt
to alleviate the stress coming from the sources of
pressure, either through the direct provision of
social services to the poor by the authorities or
their representatives; or through allowing participation by potential partisans, but failing to provide them with the necessary resources to make a
reasonable attempt to alleviate the stress coming
from the objects of discontent. Given the participatory nature of the community action program in
New York City, such an output will most likely be
manifested in the existence of non-relevant and unsuccessful service programs under the control of
representatives of the poor, or through ineffectual
group action involving the ranks of the poor themselves.

HYPOTHESIS OF STUDY

Having defined these two key terms, we may now formulate the general hypothesis of the study, which emerged from initial research in New York City's community action program: Although the stated goals of the community action program in New York City imply that the program should be an influence output, with the community action bureaucracy serving as the advocate of the potential partisans, the poor, the program's operation can best be described as a social control output, with the community action bureaucracy functioning as a social control agent and as another authority with which the poor must cope.

Here it should be noted that a significant body of literature attests to the fact that any firm answer to the question of whether the outputs generated through the community action programs are primarily social control or primarily influence, must lie in an analysis of the actual content of the program on the neighborhood level--an analysis which would provide the type of data on which firm conclusions may rest.[27]

Most important, because of the very complexities and ambiguities of the term "participation,"[28] the stated goals of the program, especially as they appear on a city-wide level, must be clearly distinguished from actual operation of the program on the neighborhood level. Certainly, past studies[29] and, in the case of New York City, initial research for this study have suggested the existence of a very significant discrepancy between the two.

Thus emerges the central purpose of the present study: the examination of the effects of the community action program in New York City through an in-depth study of that program at a particular neighborhood level. The major theoretical framework employed rests upon Peterson's elitist-participatory conceptualization, and involves the subclassification of the participatory outputs found under Mayor Lindsay into the dual categories provided by Gamson: influence or social control.

2

CONCEPTUAL AND OPERATIONAL DEFINITIONS: INFLUENCE AND SOCIAL CONTROL OUTPUTS

DEFINITION OF TERMS

William Gamson's conceptual framework has been introduced as a means of evaluating the consequences for the poor and for the alleviation of the stress brought about by poverty of the outputs generated by the community action programs; specifically, the program in New York City, which Paul Peterson has characterized as a "participatory" output. On the basis of Gamson's distinction between the objects of discontent and the sources of pressure, definitions of influence and social control outputs have been constructed. Now it is necessary to take a closer look at the various terms used in the major hypothesis as well as the formulation of the operational definitions employed in the empirical investigation of the community action program in New York City.

Of first importance, Gamson's definitions of authorities and potential partisans should be noted, insofar as these aid in understanding the complex relationship between the community action bureaucracy and the poor. The authorities, Gamson notes, are "those who, for any given social system, make binding decisions in that system," while the potential partisans are "that set of actors who, for a given decision or set of decisions, are affected by the outcome in some significant way," the outcome being significant for potential partisans if "it

will make some difference in their lives when one
thing rather than another is decided."[1]

Secondly, it has been noted previously that
one important means of deciding whether a community
action output is primarily one of influence or of
social control involves determining whether the authorities (community action bureaucracy) have provided the potential partisans (the poor) with the
necessary resources to make a reasonable attempt to
alleviate the stress coming from the objects of
discontent. In our study, the giving of necessary
resources will be taken to mean primarily the community action bureaucracy's allocation of funds,
approval and technical assistance for such meaningful service programs or neighborhood level action
programs that aim at forcing institutions that service poor people to be more responsive to their
needs.

The last important term used in the hypothesis
that must be defined is the operation of the community action program in the Tremont poverty area.
By operation is meant the funding, program priority,
and program content decisions, along with the functioning of the Tremont Community Corporation and
its Delegate Agencies.

In considering the statement of the major hypothesis, it is clear that the key terms employed
in this study are the influence and social control
outputs. Guided by the hypothesis, the study seeks
essentially to evaluate the community action program in a particular area of New York City in terms
of whether it is functioning in keeping with its
own stated goals, constituting an influence output;
or, whether it is working rather to contain the re-
acting poor in keeping with what is best described
as a social control output.

Obviously, then, it is of crucial importance
for the study that these two key terms be specified
clearly into accurate and measurable operational
indicators. Before embarking on a discussion of
this task, it may be worthwhile to consider very
briefly the wider issue of evaluative research, especially since such research is applied to the community action program, in order that the importance

of a strong theoretical framework in this regard be
clearly seen.

REVIEW OF EVALUATIVE RESEARCH

The rather extensive amount of literature concerning the Office of Economic Opportunity, the
community action programs in various cities throughout the country, and on poverty in general, which
has been examined in preparation for this study,
makes quite clear that there is a definite need for
more substantive evaluative research in this entire
area. While official literature is generally
praiseworthy of the attempts by federal, state, and
local governments to cope with the problems of poverty through the community action programs, such
critics as Sar A. Levitan have claimed that the OEO
research staff tends to turn out "unsupported claims
of achievements and exaggerated official promises
for the federal war on poverty."[2] Levitan accuses
such official research of being intrinsically subject to political considerations, an accusation
supported by Peter H. Rossi in a recent article
concerning the evaluations of social action programs, including those of the OEO.[3] The "politics
of evaluation" in Rossi's view, have created a situation in which most often the real goals of such
social action programs are not at all the goals
evaluated in the research. Furthermore, after reviewing 170 reports coming from research on these
programs, Rossi concluded that the great majority
were merely descriptive accounts of how many people
were being reached by the program in question or
descriptions of the activities that took place
within the program. They tended, he noted, to be
written in a loosely narrative form, with "virtually
no systematic observation on the effectiveness of
the programs." While such program effectiveness
appears to be assumed by official researchers, the
opposite stance is taken by critics such as Daniel
P. Moynihan, who speaks of "the debacle of the community action program of the war on poverty: the
roaring rhetoric, the minimum performance, the

feigned constancy, the private betrayal," and summarizes the entire program as a "sell-out."[4]

But sweeping phraseology, either in praise or
condemnation of these programs, is certainly no
substitute for data on their effectiveness, of the
type which Rossi, Levitan and others call for when
they state that "evaluation is particularly important in the case of the Economic Opportunity Act
and related antipoverty programs."[5] With this in
mind, the major question--and the core problem for
any evaluative research--then becomes, "In terms of
what is such program effectiveness to be measured?"[6]
As two respected methodologists have recently noted,
answering this question involves developing yard-
sticks for measuring social behavior and community
conditions, and they state that "there is no entire-
ly satisfactory solution to the problem of developing [such] comprehensive measures."[7]

While agreeing emphatically with these authors
that "the definition of what one hopes to accomplish
with an action program, sufficiently detailed to
permit translation into observable and measureable
indices or criteria, is not a simple task,"[8] it is
the position of this study that the concepts of influence and social control outputs provide a satisfactory and valid basis for developing such concrete
indexes by which the operation of the community action program in New York City may be measured, and
consequently the effectiveness of that program as a
response to the stress of poverty. It is to this
task, then, that we must now turn.

CONCEPTS OF SOCIAL CONTROL AND INFLUENCE

A review of the literature has yielded much
material on the concepts of social control and influence, which have normally been viewed from the
perspectives of the contrasting models of social
order and social conflict, respectively.[9] However,
relatively little of this material addresses in any
concrete manner the empirical measurement of either
of these concepts.

Bredemier and Stephenson have, however, in a
very useful theoretical statement on social control,

provided some insight into the question of measurement.[10] They begin with the assumption that there are "two major kinds of processes by which people are led to conform to one another's institutionalized expectations"--the socialization process and a set of social control mechanisms. The latter are defined as "all the social arrangements that either prevent strains (in a social structure) or prevent the strains from leading to deviance."[11] With this definition, five different kinds of social control mechanisms, or five lines of defense against deviance, are outlined, as follows:

1. Those that forestall the strain itself or prevent the strain from becoming actual, including the mechanisms of segregation, insulation, and institutionalized status-priority.

2. those mechanisms of tension management that drain off or canalize responses to the strain into socially sanctioned patterns of behavior, including compensatory behavior and status alternatives.

3. those mechanisms of blockage consisting of arrangements that make socially disapproved responses either very difficult to express or very costly.

4. mechanisms that remove the deviant from the social system, such as imprisonment, banishment, excommunication, or execution.

5. therapeutic mechanisms that stress resocialization of the deviant.

While providing significant insight with respect to categories into which the concept of social control may be distributed, the relatively high level of abstraction utilized by Bredemier and Stephenson detracts from the usefulness of their various mechanisms as operational indicators of social control.

William Gamson, while concurring with many of the important ideas found in Bredemier and Stephenson's outline of social control mechanisms, has somewhat simplified the basic explanation of the social control process. Utilizing the terminology defined at the beginning of this chapter, Gamson has presented a list of four social control devices, which may be summarized as follows:

     1. <u>Insulation</u>, "an extremely
important set of controls that operates by giving potential partisans
differential access to authorities
and to positions that involve the
control of resources that can be
brought to bear on authorities."

     2. <u>sanctions</u>, which "reward the
'responsible' and punish the 'irre-
sponsible' or 'deviant.'"

     3. <u>persuasion</u>, or "attempts to
control the desire rather than the
ability to influence."

     4. <u>participation and cooptation</u>,
"the most interesting and complicated
of control mechanisms," which involves
essentially a "double-edged manipula-
tion of access" whereby certain potential partisans are brought "inside."[12]

All of these devices, Gamson claims, are normally in operation in any social control situation.
However, in describing the devices used in such a
situation, he appears to have overlooked some of
the most significant contributions of other authors,
in particular, the very important idea of resocialization as a social control mechanism.

Thus it has been to the conceptualization of
Gerald M. Shattuck[13] that this study has ultimately
turned in the quest for operational indicators of
social control. In the most comprehensive, yet
concrete manner reviewed, Shattuck presents three
strategies of social control that provide an excel-
lent conceptual framework within which observable
and measurable indices of social control may be
formulated and applied to a study of the community
action program. These three strategies Shattuck
describes in terms of the following variables:

     1. <u>Separation</u>, including the
ideas of both insulation and isolation;

     2. <u>containment</u>, including all
of the social control devices set
forth by Gamson, particularly that of
cooptation; and,

> 3. resocialization, or the at-
> tempt to "rehabilitate the deviant"
> in the manner suggested by Bredemier
> and Stephenson.

These variables will be further specified and
operationally defined in terms of their application
to this study later in this chapter. First, however, let us turn to a look at the empirical measurement of the concept of influence.

In the literature on the concept of influence,
in particular as influence operates within a social
conflict situation, even less is to be found on the
specific task of measurement than is the case with
the concept of social control. In fact, the only
systematic treatment of the concept is to be found
in the work of William Gamson, which has been previously cited.

In a rather theoretical discussion, Gamson
speaks of the nature of influence as "a shift in
the probability of an outcome." Specifically, assuming that Pb is the probability that the political system will produce outcomes preferred by a
potential partisan group before or without that
group having exercised influence attempts; and that
Pa is the new probability of obtaining the preferred outcome after the group becomes active and
does various things that alter Pb, or in other
words, after influence attempts have occurred, then
"a partisan group can be said to have exercised
influence if and only if there is a difference between Pa and Pb."[14]

Gamson then presents three specific approaches
for measuring influence conceived of in this way:
The relative frequency approach, the subjective
probability approach, and the influence attempts
approach. The first of these is based on an "operational index of influence," calculated "by sub-
tracting the frequency of obtaining a particular
outcome when a partisan group works against it from
the frequency when it works in favor of it."[15] As
Gamson himself readily admits, this approach to the
measurement of influence is beset by a number of
serious difficulties, not the least of which is the
purely practical problem of obtaining the type of

frequency data needed for the construction of the
operational index.

The second approach abandons any attempt to
calculate objective probability as a way of opera-
tionalizing influence on a single event, and con-
ceives of influence as a shift in the subjective
probabilities assigned by a set of informed observers. In other words, if, because of the occurrence
of certain relevant acts of influence, such a set
of informed observers feels that a preferred outcome
is now a better bet, influence may be said to have
occurred.[16]

The third, or influence attempts approach,
is likewise an indirect measurement of influence,
through which influence is inferred, rather than
directly measured. This involves, firstly, the
measurement of the capability of influence through
an examination of the resources possessed by the
potential partisan group. In combination with this,
a measurement of influence attempts is made by
questioning both the persons who have made such attempts and those for whom they were made, concerning
their quality and extent of use. As Gamson notes,
the central assumption made in this last approach
is that "the possession of resources plus the existence of influence attempts implies influence."[17]

While the second and third of Gamson's approaches for measuring influence are both feasible
and applicable to the study at hand, their intrinsic
indirectness, as well as the assumptions on which
they are based, point up the need for utilizing in
conjunction with such approaches a direct measurement of some concrete, operational indicators of
influence. For such indicators, we may turn back
to the work of Gerald M. Shattuck, who has formulated three comprehensive strategies of conflict,
or influence, parallel to the three strategies of
social control. These are described in terms of
the following variables:

1. _Separateness_, or the establishment by a
group of its identity within a larger society;

2. _bargaining_, or the process by which an
interest group engages a target system over a particular issue; and,

3. collaboration, or the process through which various groups unite their interests, each without losing its separate identity.

Drawing upon these three indicators of influence, as well as Shattuck's three previously mentioned indicators of social control, the following two subhypotheses may be formulated, which serve as more specific working definitions for the key terms of our study, influence and social control outputs:

1. To the extent that separateness, bargaining, and collaboration have taken place as a result of the community action program in the Tremont poverty area, this program can be described as an influence output.

2. To the extent that separation, containment, and resocialization have taken place, the program can be described as a social control output.

One important point to note in conjunction with these subhypotheses is that through any program such as the one under consideration both influence and social control may be occurring simultaneously. Thus it is the goal of the empirical research to establish whether the influence variables, or those of social control are predominant; not whether one set of variables is found to the total exclusion of the other.

CONCEPTUAL AND OPERATIONAL
DEFINITIONS OF INDICATORS

In the last section of this chapter, attention is turned to a further consideration of Shattuck's conceptual definitions of each of the six variables that will be used as indicators of the concepts of influence and social control; the application of these variables to the present study; and finally, the formulation of the operational definition of each variable.

Separateness

By separateness is meant the establishment by any group of its identity as a separate grouping

within a society. In the sense in which the concept is being utilized in this study, separateness
refers to a subjective feeling on the part of a
group of potential partisans which may be taken as
a preliminary condition for the occurrence of influence.[18] In the case of the Tremont poverty area,
the basic concept of separateness of which Shattuck
speaks may be expanded into four different types:

1. Type-one separateness: poor identity or
lower-class consciousness, whereby individuals view
themselves as a class in the sense of a status
group, opposed to the dominant groups who insulate
and exploit them;

2. type-two separateness: ethnic identity,
whereby individuals consider themselves as part of
a specific ethnic group, opposed to the dominant
exploitative groups;

3. type-three separateness: coalitional ethnic identity, whereby individual ethnic group members consider themselves as part of a coalition of
such groups, joined together in opposing the dominant groups; and

4. type-four separateness: interest group
identity, whereby individuals identify with a specific, non-ethnic interest group, opposed to the
dominant groups in control of those interests.

Applying these four types of separateness to
our study, the following operational definitions
emerge: To the extent that as a result of the community action program in the Tremont poverty area
those affected by the program, (a) have established
their identity as a separate status group of the
poor, in which type-one separateness may be said to
have occurred; (b) have established their identity
as separate ethnic groupings--blacks, Puerto Ricans,
etc.--in which type-two separateness may be said to
have occurred; (c) have established their identity
as ethnic groupings united into a broader coalition
of ethnic groups in the area; thus, type-three separateness may be said to have occurred; (d) have
established their identity as a solid interest
group, composed of the various neighborhood level
units of the community action program, specifically
the Tremont Community Corporation and the Delegate

Agencies, in which type-four separateness may be said to have occurred.

Finally, to the extent that any of these four types of separateness have taken place as a result of the Tremont community action program, separateness may be said to have occurred.

Separation

As Shattuck notes, whereas separateness is a question of group identity, separation is a social and/or geographical fact--for our purpose, a strategy of social control, which authorities may use to confer a type of "moral invisibility"[19] on potential partisans, or more significantly, to prevent the formation of significant partisan groups. Specifically, the term will be here taken to mean an individual's or a group's isolation from other individuals or groups with whom they share certain objective but latent interests.* Thus, the central question for investigation here is whether or not isolation of the type described above has been sustained or encouraged as a result of the community action program in the Tremont poverty area.

It appears that there are three different possible types of isolation, relevant to this study, which may be defined as follows:

1. Type-one isolation: non-identification, whereby individuals do not consider themselves as a part of any on-going group in the area;

2. type-two isolation: antagonistic ethnic identity, whereby individuals consider themselves

---

*It should be noted that such a definition of separation differs somewhat from Shattuck's. He defines separation as "an individual's or group's social, political, economic, or geographic isolation from the rest of society." The term "insulation" is preferred to describe that process. The concept of separation as used in this study implies a technique through which such insulation is maintained.

as a part of an ethnic group, which is opposed primarily to other ethnic groups in the area;

    3. type-three isolation: fragmented interest group identity, whereby individuals identify with a specific interest group that they see as existing primarily in opposition to other interest groups in the area.

From the above emerge the following operational definitions: To the extent that, as a result of the community action program in the Tremont poverty area, (a) those affected by the program have not established their identity in relation to any group in the area, type-one isolation may be said to have occurred or be continuing; (b) the various ethnic group members in the area, who have been affected by the program, exhibit antagonism toward other ethnic groups in the area, and do not see an ethnic coalition as possible, type-two isolation may be said to have occurred or be continuing; (c) those associated with the various Delegate Agencies in the area see themselves in competition with other Delegate Agencies, particularly for funds and other resources, and do not view the formation of all units of the area's community action program into a strong interest group as possible, type-three isolation may be said to have occurred or be continuing.

Finally, to the extent that any of these three types of isolation have taken place, or have been sustained, as a result of the Tremont community action program, separation may be said to have occurred or be continuing.*

---

*As a check on the subjective responses concerning the concept of separation, particularly those relating to type-one isolation or non-identification, Dwight G. Dean's Social Isolation Subscale, one of three independent parts comprising his Scale of Alienation, will be utilized. This will be further explained in a later chapter.

Bargaining

Bargaining, the second variable by which influence will be measured, refers to the process by
which an interest group effectively engages a target system over some specific issue in order to
bring about some kind of redistribution of power
and/or resources between the participants. For our
purposes, bargaining can be viewed in two ways:
     1. One-step bargaining, which occurs when one
particular interest group, such as a Delegate Agency,
bargains with a dominant or controlling group; and,
     2. two-step bargaining, which occurs when
several interest groups, such as two or more Delegate Agencies with a common concern, unite and bar-
gain jointly with a dominant or controlling group.
     Thus, the following operational definitions of
bargaining may be stated: To the extent that (a) an
individual Delegate Agency has, through the use of
collective action, engaged a dominant target system
over a specific issue, and has brought about a
change in power and/or resources in favor of the
partisan group (the poor), one-step bargaining may
be said to have occurred; (b) several Delegate Agencies, in particular those with similar program functions (e.g., Tenant Information or Housing Action)
have united and through the use of collective action, engaged a dominant target system over a specific issue and have brought about a change in
power or resources in favor of the partisan group,
two-step bargaining may be said to have occurred.
     Finally, to the extent that either of these
has taken place as a result of the community action
program in the Tremont poverty area, bargaining may
be said to have occurred.

Containment and Collaboration

     These two variables are considered together
here since, for empirical purposes, they are reduc-
ible to one set of objective reality.
     Containment, as an indicator of social control,
is described by Shattuck as a strategy through which

rewards are offered to "deviant" parties in return
for their acceptance of the status quo. In this
sense, programs, which purport to aim at alleviating the conditions of poverty, may well be merely
cooling-out activities, offered to potential partisans by authorities in exchange for community peace
and quiet.

Collaboration, on the other hand, may be described as a strategy of influence, involving the
unification of interests of two essentially antagonistic parties, without loss of separate identity
for either party. As applied to this study, the
concept implies a type of assimilation of potential
partisans (the poor) within a structure dominated
by authorities (the community action bureaucracy)
but in such a way that the partisan group is able
to enhance its own position and bring about desired
outcomes.

It would appear that both of these concepts
are most clearly viewed within the context of the
broader strategy of cooptation. Throughout much of
the literature on the subject, the concept of cooptation has carried a negative connotation from the
viewpoint of potential partisans. Paul Peterson,
for example, is typical of many authors when he
speaks of cooptation as "the degree to which an
organization fails to be an open channel through
which the demands of those it claims to represent
can flow."[20]

However, Phillip Selznick was one of the first
to react against such negative connotations in his
formulation of a purely neutral definition of cooptation as "the process of absorbing new elements
into the leadership or policy-making structure of
an organization as a means of averting threats to
its existence."[21] With this definition Selznick
stresses that it is only through examining the particular situation that one may decide whether the
cooptative process has had positive or negative
consequences for any specific group.

Gamson strongly supports this latter contention when he states that:

> Cooptation invariably involves some
> mixture of outcome modification

(influence) and social control, and
the exact mix is difficult to determine in advance. The authority who
opposes coopting the hostile element
fears that outcome modification will
dominate the mix; the partisan who
opposes accepting it, fears that the
social control element will dominate.[22]

And in a similar vein, Peter Bachrach and
Morton Baratz speak of the technique of cooptative
participation, which they explain as follows:
"Citizen participation is cooptative in nature when
the activities of non-elites in decision-making and
policy implementation are channeled toward the preconceived goals of higher authorities."[23] Bachrach
and Baratz contend that this technique can be made
to serve the interests either of "those who set the
objectives" (i.e., the authorities), or of the
"participants" (i.e., the potential partisans). In
the first case the primary objective of the technique of cooptative participation is the social
control of the participants; whereas in the latter,
the authorities are to be viewed as advocates of
the participants, who utilize the technique as a
means of guiding and somewhat paternalistically
manipulating them into what the authors term
"interest-oriented participation." Thus, cooptative participation may have either negative or positive consequences for the participants, depending
on what the preconceived goals of the authorities
may be.

In the sense used by these authors, as well as
by Selznick and Gamson, then, the concept of cooptation appears to be a very useful one in analyzing
the relationship between our potential partisans,
the poor, and the authorities in control of the
community action program, the community action bureaucracy. It has already been seen that the poor
were brought into the bureaucracy to an increasing
extent in recent years, satisfying the conditions
of cooptation as defined by Selznick. What remains
to be determined through the empirical investigation
at hand is whether or not the process of cooptation
has favored the poor or the authorities.

If the cooptation process favors the poor in the sense that the community action bureaucracy makes significant outcome modifications favorable to them, then the poor may be said to be exercising influence. For the purposes of the study, the term collaboration will be used to describe this outcome of cooptation.* If on the other hand, cooptation favors the community action bureaucracy in the sense that its outcomes are protective of the interests of the dominant groups who control it, and the bureaucracy is not forced to make significant outcome modifications favorable to the poor, then the bureaucracy encourages dominant groups to retain and most likely increase their social control of the poor. This outcome of cooptation will be termed containment. Thus, collaboration is the influence aspect of cooptation, while containment is the social control aspect.

The only remaining question to be decided is what will be empirically taken as significant outcome modifications favorable to the poor, as opposed to outcomes protective of the interests of dominant groups. Gamson's distinction between the objects of discontent and the sources of pressure again finds relevance here, since outcomes that work toward alleviating the objects of discontent would be favorable to the poor, while those that work toward alleviating the stress coming from the sources of pressure would be primarily favorable to the interests of dominant groups who control the poor.

Chapter 1 states that two types of programs were, for the purpose of this study, to be interpreted as aiming to alleviate the objects of discontent: Relevant and meaningful service programs, controlled and administered by legitimate

---

*It should be noted that the sense in which the term collaboration is used here implies a type of interpenetration of one unit by another, rather than unification of interests by structurally independent units, as Shattuck implies.

representatives of the poor; and effectively organized neighborhood level action programs that aim
at forcing institutions that service poor people to
be more responsive to their needs. On the other
hand, programs aimed at alleviating the stress coming from the sources of pressure would, in a participatory structure such as the New York City community action program, be evidenced in the existence of either service or action programs under
the control of the poor themselves, which, because
of a lack of necessary resources, are rendered nonrelevant, unsuccessful and ineffective.

On the basis of the above, we may formulate
operational definitions of collaboration and containment as follows: To the extent that relevant
and meaningful service programs, controlled and administered by legitimate representatives of the
poor, or effective neighborhood level action programs have been sanctioned (in the sense of either
encouragement or mere tolerance) by the community
action bureaucracy and accepted by those in the
Tremont poverty area, the poor have been positively
coopted, and collaboration has occurred. And to
the extent that nonrelevant, unsuccessful and ineffective service or action programs have been so
sanctioned and accepted, the poor have been negatively coopted and containment has occurred.

Resocialization

Resocialization, the final indicator of social
control, refers to the effort to either rehabilitate a deviant member or assimilate a nonmember as
an acceptable member of society, particularly insofar as value orientation, and consequently, behavioral patterns, are concerned.

In considering the value and/or behavioral
changes which may come about as a result of such
programs as the one under study, it appears that
resocialization in the manner described above is
only one of four distinct possibilities which may
occur, as follows:

1. Continued acceptable socialization through
which, as a result of the program, an individual

with a previously acceptable value orientation and
behavior, maintains that orientation and behavior;
     2. deviant resocialization through which, as
a result of the program, an individual with a previously acceptable value orientation and behavior,
takes on a deviant orientation and behavior;
     3. continued deviant socialization through
which, as a result of the program, an individual
with a previously deviant value orientation and behavior, maintains that orientation and behavior; and
     4. acceptable resocialization through which,
as a result of the program, an individual with a
previously deviant value orientation and behavior
pattern, takes on an acceptable orientation and behavior.

It may be noted that resocialization as described by Shattuck appears in the above classification as "acceptable resocialization." However, it
is also important to note that, insofar as the social control of potential partisans by authorities
is concerned, the process of "continued acceptable
socialization" may be just as significant--if not
more so--than acceptable resocialization. For this
would indicate that the community action program
was initially making contact with, and in a certain
sense exempting, those whose values and/or behavior
patterns were already acceptable, and was thus working to keep them that way.[24]

In order to determine which of the above four
possibilities has been achieved through the community action program in the Tremont poverty area,
it will be necessary to ascertain individuals'
views on their value orientations prior to and after
contact with the program. As a check on the expressed values, behavior patterns reflective of
various values will also be determined, since behavior is the primary indicator of the meaningful-
ness of one's values. However, we must first decide the basis on which either acceptable or deviant
value orientations and behavior is to be determined.

Since, in the context of this study, political
values and behavior would seem to be of greatest
significance, Paul Peterson's threefold typology
of politics will be utilized in this regard. This
typology is summarized below:[25]

1. Particularistic politics, or "a pattern of policy-making in which actors represent discrete individuals, in which conflict among participants is minimized as each is particularistically oriented towards the authority, and decision-making is cooptive in that the authority seeks to satisfy the claims of each individual." This pattern implies the traditional ideology of representative democracy, in which individuals vote for the candidate of their choice and leave the running of the organization or government in the hands of the officials.

2. Pluralistic politics, or "policy-making patterns in which actors speak for the interests of organizations, agencies, and organized interests broader than those of individuals but narrower than those of social strata," typically involving a multisided conflict among groups. Such a pattern implies that in order to be counted in the political process one must be a part of a specific interest group, the leader of which would then represent the group in the struggle against other groups, especially those in power.

3. Status group politics, or "policy-making which involves actors who represent--or at least claim to represent--broad social status groups," including not only social classes, but also "racial and ethnic groups, producers and consumers, and (such groups as) providers of governmental services and their recipients." This pattern is in keeping with the basic model of political conflict in which large status groups openly engage in bi-polar confrontation.

For our purposes these patterns may be taken to represent three different value positions on the question of the most effective strategy for helping the poor rise out of poverty. Agreement with any one of the three positions will be taken as reflective of a specific value orientation, and the corresponding behavior looked for in support of the individual's expressed value will be membership in organizations that espouse that particular pattern of politics.

The position taken in this study is that in the eyes of authorities, the pattern of particularistic politics, in both value orientation and

behavioral aspects is acceptable, while the pluralistic and status group patterns represent increasing degrees of deviance. The source of such deviance lies in the fact that the entrance of potential
partisans into these two forms of politics may well
be threatening to the interests of authorities, as
was previously noted by Krause.

Thus, the following operational definition of
resocialization, i.e., "acceptable resocialization,"
may be stated: To the extent that, as a result of
the community action program in the Tremont poverty
area, individuals exhibit a shift from a pluralistic and/or status group value orientation and behavior, to a particularistic value orientation and
behavior, resocialization may be said to have occurred.

Having presented the conceptual and operational
definitions of each of the six variables used as
indicators of influence and social control outputs,
it is now appropriate to view the structure and
functioning of the community action program in New
York City, at both the city-wide and neighborhood
levels, in order to gain a deeper understanding of
the situation to which the conceptual framework
will be applied.

3

THE STRUCTURE AND FUNCTIONING
OF THE COMMUNITY ACTION PROGRAM
IN NEW YORK CITY:
CITY-WIDE
AND NEIGHBORHOOD LEVELS

As has been seen in Chapter 1, the general structure of New York City's community action program underwent numerous changes during its first four years of existence. But by the fall of 1968 it existed in approximately the same form as it does today: A city-wide bureaucracy consisting of the Council Against Poverty (CAP) and the Community Development Agency, and a network of 26 Community Corporations on the neighborhood level.

COUNCIL AGAINST POVERTY

The Council Against Poverty at present has a membership of 52. Of these, 26 are representatives of the poor, with one member coming from each of the 26 designated poverty areas in the city. Seventeen CAP members are public officials or their delegates, representing such offices as that of the Mayor, the Presidents of the five City Boroughs, the Chairman of the City Planning Commission and the Commissioner of the Department of Social Services. The remaining nine members are representatives of the private welfare agencies or other city-wide organizations, including Catholic Charities of the Archdiocese of New York, Federation of Jewish Philanthropies, Federation of Protestant Welfare Agencies, Community Council of Greater New York, and the Puerto Rican Community Development Project.

The official function of the Council Against
Poverty is to serve as the major decision-making
body in the City's community action program and its
work is handled through two major types of committees: (a) those related to individual poverty
areas, called Area Panels; and (b) those concerned
with matters of policy for the entire city, called
City-wide Committees. The committee system is designed to make the work of the CAP more manageable
since any issue relating to a particular poverty
area is reviewed by its respective Area Panel before
being brought before the full membership of the
Council. Most Panels and Committees consist of ten
members: five representatives of poverty areas,
three public officials, and two representatives of
private welfare or city-wide organizations. The
representatives of poverty areas may attend their
own Area Panel meetings but are prohibited from
voting. According to official documents describing
the role of the Panels and Committees, "the power
of all Committees and Panels shall be limited to
making recommendations to the Council."[1] However,
as is shown below, their role actually is far more
significant.

COMMUNITY DEVELOPMENT AGENCY

The Community Development Agency is headed by
a Commissioner, at present, Major Owens. Directly
beneath him is the Deputy Commissioner, while the
rest of the top staff consists of three assistant
Commissioners[2]--two in Program Operations and one
in Program Planning and Budget. The Commissioner
and his top level staff supervise over 300 employees,
expanded to cover 400 in the summer, when special
programs such as Neighborhood Youth Corps are in
full operation.

The Program Planning and Budget Division is
responsible for planning and coordination with special concentration in the fields of Health, Day
Care, Head Start, and Summer Programs. The Program
Operations Division has a dual function: to provide technical assistance to those actually operating the programs on the neighborhood level by

developing programs and budgets, training personnel, monitoring elections, and determining whether or not a Community Corporation is complying with CAP and OEO guidelines. In New York City, Program Operations consists of two divisions, each supervised by an assistant Commissioner. Fourteen poverty areas in Brooklyn and Queens are covered by Program Operations I, while Program Operations II covers the twelve poverty areas of Manhattan, Staten Island, and the Bronx.

The field work for each of the Program Operations Divisions is carried out by one of its five District Offices. Each District Office is in charge of assisting and monitoring the activities of two or three Corporations, and all Community Development Agency-poverty area communications are routed through these District Offices. Each District Office is supervised by a Director who is assisted by seven staff members including two secretaries, all of whom have the dual responsibility of providing assistance and monitoring compliance with official mandates. A Community Organizer aids the District Office Director in the determination of a poverty area's needs in solving resident participation problems and in monitoring local elections. He is also responsible for evaluating the impact of the Corporation's entire operation on the area it serves. The Program Officer and Program Assistant are responsible for the development, evaluation, and coordination of a community's program. There is also an Education Action Specialist along with a Budget and Fiscal Assistant, who serves as a liaison to a Corporation's fiscal staff. He aids in the formation, interpretation, and modification of the Corporation's budget and works with CDA's Program Planning and Budget Division in its budget review.

RELATIONSHIP BETWEEN CAP AND CDA

One of the functions of the various operational units within CDA, with respect to the relationship between the Community Development Agency and the Council Against Poverty, is to make recommendations concerning such matters as budgets and program

priorities to the Panels and Committees, which in
turn present their own recommendations to the CAP.
Further, as a unit, the role of the CDA is officially described as "the administrative staff arm
of the Council Against Poverty."[3] Through an analysis of the structure of the city-wide bureaucracy
as it is described in official documents, then, the
impression is gained that the Council Against Poverty serves as the major decision-making body in
the City's community action program. The following
quotation from An Introduction to the New York City
Council Against Poverty summarizes this quite well.

> The Council is given specific powers
> to allocate among poverty areas all
> community action funds from federal
> and city sources, to decide poverty
> area boundaries, to provide for the
> creation and recognition of Community
> Corporations, to make decisions on
> program proposals and budgets for the
> use of nearly $70 million in city and
> federal funds, to hear appeals from
> applicants rejected at the local
> level, . . . and to determine overall
> program plans and priorities for the
> City's Attack on Poverty.[4]

However, at least one existing study presents
evidence that sharply conflicts with the official
view of the functional relationship between CAP and
CDA. Through a case study of the decision-making
process in the Council Against Poverty, covering
roughly the same time period as the present study
(October 1, 1969-September 30, 1970), Martin Hockbaum arrived at two major conclusions. First, that
with respect to almost all major decisions examined,
the CAP's Panels and Committees endorsed the recommendations coming from the CDA, particularly those
concerning program priorities and budgetary matters,
and served as "transmission belts," passing on to
the CAP the recommendations made primarily by the
professionals within CDA. The influence of CDA was
attributed to the fact that it is this group who,

in contrast to those within CAP, possesses the information, expertise and the time required to really
consider issues. Likewise, the Panels and Committees are able to have secondary influence as a result of the fact that their members are able to
gain some expertise and knowledge about their area
of specialization. Hockbaum's second conclusion
was that the Council Against Poverty, largely because of a system of representation that does not
allow Council members the opportunity to adequately
examine matters brought before it, is primarily a
legitimating body for the work done in its own Panels, Committees, and especially the Community Development Agency.[5]

Certainly these conclusions, which as yet remain unchallenged, point to a situation in which
the role of that branch of the city-wide bureaucracy
on which the poor themselves have the most direct
representation is seriously undermined. Such a
situation raises real questions as to the goals toward which participation of the poor is aimed, as
well as the quality of that participation in the
present community action program in New York City.
Applying Gamson's terminology, the key question
that emerges is whether or not a program officially
described and structured in terms of influence is
in actual functioning primarily one of social control.

On this point, Hockbaum's study provides more
questions than answers. In describing the significant accomplishments of the Council Against Poverty
in particular, he appears to provide evidence in
the direction of both influence and social control.
While noting that the program has provided a vehicle for participation for thousands of people, many
of whom are indigent; employment opportunities for
14,000 people, including many Blacks and Puerto
Ricans in top-level positions; and a means for de-
fusing ethnic conflict and violence, as well as for
increasing institutional sensitivity to the needs
of the poor; Hockbaum states that the major accom-
plishment has been the program's "contribution to
keeping the peace," through decreasing the possibility of major disturbance in the City's ghettos.[6]

Certainly, any of the above accomplishments could
be subjected to such a dual interpretation as that
to which Gamson's conceptualization is addressed.

Most importantly, Hockbaum concludes his study
with the note that at present there are no data
available on which to base firm conclusions concerning the nature or effects of participation by the
poor in the City's community action programs.[7]   As
has already been mentioned at the conclusion of
Chapter 1, we must look at the operation of the community action program on the neighborhood level for
these data.

POVERTY AREAS IN NEW YORK CITY

By 1968, 25 poverty areas had been designated
throughout New York City, with a twenty-sixth area,
Bronx River, in the planning stage by mid-1969 (see
Figure 1).   Early in the Lindsay administration,
the Council Against Poverty established a program
priorities and allocation formula in which each
poverty area would be allotted a proportion of the
total community action funds based upon relative
need, as determined by an index of poverty.   This
index takes into account several factors: rates of
juvenile delinquency, number of persons on welfare
and the number of live births in municipal hospi-
tals for each area, yielding a rough percentage of
New York City's poverty found in the area.[8]   For example, as can be seen from Table 3.1, Bedford Stuyvesant was assigned a poverty index of 10.8, en-
titling this area to a fair share allocation of
$3.38 million or 10.8 percent of the total funding
base of $31.30 million.   It actually obtained $5.1
million or 51 percent over its fair share.   In
every area, the discrepancy between the fair share
and actual allocations reflect political considerations, such as the degree of organization of area
residents, as well as irregularities in the total
funding process, as will be explained further in
this chapter.

FIGURE 1

Map of New York City Poverty Areas, 1969

Source: Public Affairs Office, Human Resources Administration, Community Development in New York City (New York
City: Human Resources Administration, 1969), p. 20. For
names of poverty areas, see Table 3.1.

45

TABLE 3.1

Proposed Area Allocations for 1969/70 Versatile Programs

No.	Area	Poverty Index	1968/69 Allocation	1969/70 Fair Share Allocation	1969/70 Actual Allocation	1969/70 Allocation as Percent of Fair Share
Funding Base: $31,300,000						
1.	Bedford Stuyvesant	10.8	$5,104,600	$3,380,400	$5,104,000	151.0
2.	Brownsville	9.2	2,035,000	2,879,600	2,035,100	70.7
3.	Central Harlem	7.3	5,720,300	2,284,900	4,990,850	218.4
4.	Hunts Point	7.3	1,614,800	2,284,900	1,599,430	70.0
5.	East Harlem	7.0	2,095,400	2,191,000	2,095,400	95.6
6.	Williamsburg	6.3	1,393,600	1,971,900	1,380,330	70.0
7.	Morrisania	5.6	1,238,700	1,752,800	1,226,960	70.0
8.	Lower East Side	5.5	1,731,700	1,721,500	2,190,000	126.1
9.	South Bronx	4.3	1,005,300	1,345,900	1,005,300	75.0
10.	South Brooklyn	5.1	1,128,100	1,596,300	1,117,410	70.0
11.	East New York	3.5	923,400	1,095,500	923,400	85.0
12.	South Jamaica	3.3	970,100	1,032,900	970,100	94.0
13.	Upper West Side	3.2	707,800	1,001,600	701,120	70.0
14.	Tremont	3.1	685,700	970,300	679,210	70.0
15.	Crown Heights	2.6	575,100	813,800	569,660	70.0
16.	Fort Greene	3.1	1,106,400	970,300	1,106,400	114.0
17.	Bushwick	2.6	575,100	813,800	569,660	70.0
18.	Mid West Side	2.2	511,800	688,600	482,020	70.0
19.	Lower West Side	2.0	729,000	626,000	729,000	116.5
20.	Coney Island	1.9	476,100	594,700	476,100	80.1
21.	Rockaways	0.9	199,100	281,700	200,000	70.9
22.	Sunset Park	1.0	212,200	313,000	219,000	70.0
23.	Long Island City	0.5	772,800	156,500	547,750	350.0
24.	Corona East Elmhurst	0.4	200,000	125,200	200,000	159.7
25.	Brighton Harbor	0.4	200,000	125,200	200,000	159.7
26.	Bronx River[a]					

[a]Bronx River was still in the planning stage and no monies had been allocated to this area at the time of the study.

Source: Community Development Agency, Versatile Program Guidelines 1969/70 (New York City: Community Development Agency, April 1969), p. 12.

Nevertheless, because of the wide range of actual funds allocated to the various areas (from a high of $5.1 million to a low of $200,000 in 1969/70), it is extremely difficult to speak of the City's community action program on a neighborhood level in any generalized fashion. For this reason, as well as because of limitations of time and resources, one poverty area was chosen as the focus for this study and subjected to an in-depth analysis.

In choosing this area, the primary criterion was that it be located approximately midway within the distribution of all areas, according to both poverty index and amount of funds received, since it was felt that such an area would be most illustrative of the city-wide program. After careful consideration, the Tremont area, which in 1969/70 ranked fourteenth among the 26 poverty areas according to the poverty index and sixteenth in terms of actual monies allocated, was selected for study.*
It should be noted that one additional and very important reason for deciding upon the Tremont poverty area was the fact that the administrators of that program were extremely cooperative and total access was afforded to the necessary data for the study.

For the remainder of this chapter, all information concerning the structure and functioning of the community action program on the neighborhood level will be based on data gathered from the Tremont area. In order that this information be placed in its proper context, a brief description of the area, as well as the historical development of the Tremont Community Corporation is provided here.

TREMONT POVERTY AREA

The Tremont poverty area, one of five such areas in the borough,[9] is located in the South-central Bronx and includes Health Areas 17, 19, 20, 21.10, and portions of Health Areas 10 and 18. The

---

*It may be noted that during this year, Tremont received only 70 percent of its fair share, amounting to $679,210.

boundary at the north begins at Webster Avenue and
East Fordham Road, runs east on Fordham to Hoffman
Avenue, and turns southeast on East 184th Street
into East 182nd Street and Bronx Park South. It
then turns south on Boston Road, and east on East
180th Street to the Sheridan Expressway. The east-
ern boundary is the Sheridan Expressway from East
180th Street to East 173rd Street. The southern
boundary runs west on East 173rd Street to Southern
Boulevard where it goes north, then west on East
175th Street, turning south and then west on Crotona
Park North, continuing westward along the Cross
Bronx Expressway. The western boundary runs north
on Webster Avenue from the Cross Bronx Expressway,
turning west on East Tremont Avenue, north on
Anthony Avenue and continuing north on the Grand
Concourse to East 184th Street. It turns east on
East 184th Street, north on Marion Avenue, east on
East 187th Street, north on Webster Avenue to East
Fordham Road.[10] This area is pictured in Figure 2.

The latest available population statistics
date to 1965, at which time the estimated population
of the Tremont poverty area was 116,635. A breakdown of this figure by Health Area and ethnicity is
recorded in Table 3.2.

TABLE 3.2

Population in Tremont Poverty Area,
by Health Area and Ethnicity, 1965

Health Area	Black	Puerto Rican	Other	Total
10	4,060	2,448	16,839	23,347
17	3,047	2,902	13,564	19,513
18	2,504	3,601	3,075	9,180
19	4,668	5,999	11,982	22,649
20	5,039	6,006	12,025	23,070
21.10	3,622	6,251	9,003	18,876
Total	22,940	27,207	66,488	116,876
Percent of Total	19.47%	23.33%	57.00%	100.00%

Source: Community Development Agency, Community Corporation Election Master Plan (New York
City: Community Development Agency, March 1969),
p. 55.

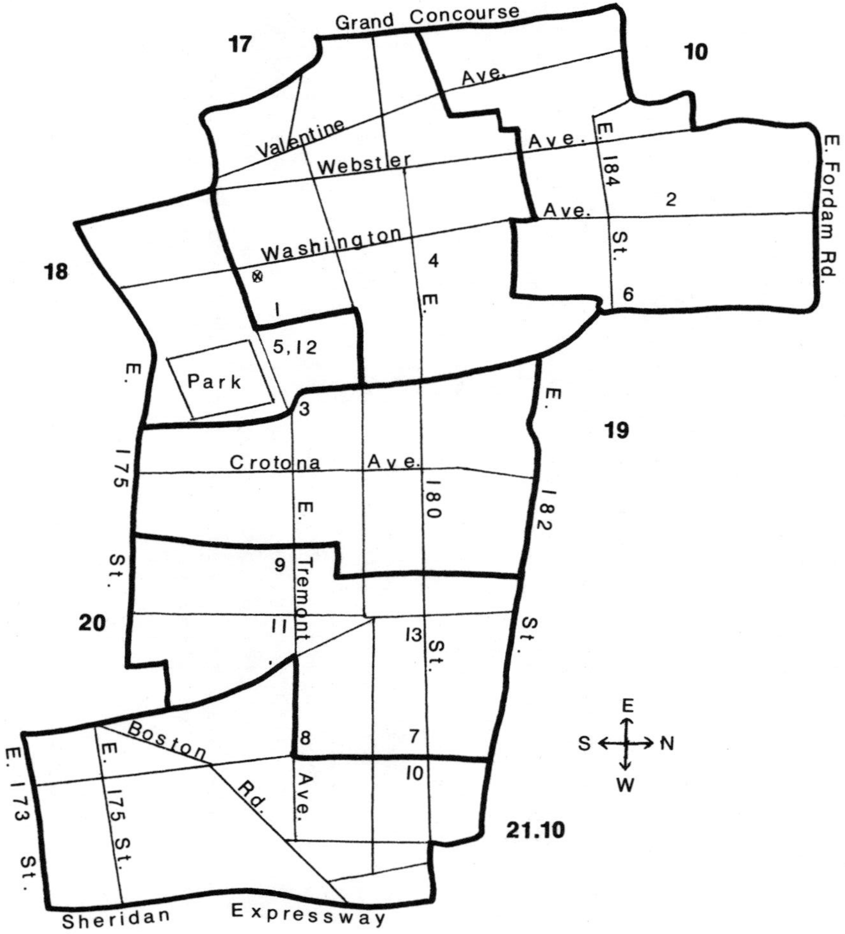

FIGURE 2

Map of Tremont Poverty Area

Health Areas 10, 17, 18, 19, 20, and 21.10

Tremont Community Corporation and Tremont Neighborhood Manpower Service Center

Delegate Agencies:

1. Tremont Community Council
2. Federation of Puerto Rican Volunteers
3. Monterey Community Association
4. National Association of Puerto Rican Affairs
5. Tremont Housing Clinic
6. Washington Avenue Neighborhood Association
7. East Tremont Action Committee
8. West Farms Villagers
9. Elsmere Tenants Council
10. East Tremont Neighborhood Association
11. Naval Cadets and Training Corps
12. United Bronx Parents
13. Bronco Self-Improvement Association

Source: Community Development Agency, Election Districts Maps for all Poverty Areas.

DEVELOPMENT OF TREMONT COMMUNITY CORPORATION

Following the usual stages in establishing a Community Corporation of the community action program,[11] the antipoverty committee of the City's Community Planning Board[12] (No. 6) in the Tremont area early in 1967 worked with the Community Development Agency in setting up orientation meetings to acquaint the people in the area with the procedures for creating a Task Force and a Planning Committee. In October of that year, 3,544 residents of the area participated in the election of the Tremont Planning Committee.[13] The most important function of the Planning Committee was to draw up a plan for a Community Corporation in the Tremont area, which would play a strong administrative role in the coordination of the various neighborhood agencies seeking funds for specific local programs, as well as in future planning for the area.[14] Serving in an interim capacity until the Corporation could be set up, the Planning Committee began almost immediately to screen various programs and formulate recommendations concerning which ones should be funded, both for the summer of 1968 and for the programs extending from October 1, 1968 until September 30, 1969. For that year, the Planning Committee, operating on a budget of $685,700, allocated funds to 13 neighborhood agencies for such activities as welfare, housing and educational action, recreation programs, and manpower outreach.[15]

Meanwhile, the Committee, utilizing the Council Against Poverty's Guidelines for the Formation of Community Corporations, which includes specifications regarding such things as election procedures, residence requirements, public meetings, and local representation,[16] proceeded to draw up a Corporation Plan and Constitution. A Tremont Area Panel and a Panel Chairman were appointed by the CAP to review the plan and to propose necessary modifications. Finally, after submitting this document to the Community Development Agency for staff evaluation and after holding a local public meeting in a Tremont area public school, the Council approved the Tremont Community Corporation Plan on November 7, 1968.[17]

The next step was the election of a Board of Directors by the residents of the poverty area, which would function as the main decision-making body of the Tremont Community Corporation. Originally scheduled for November, the election was finally held on January 11, 1969, in which 1,053 persons or 1.4 percent of the total number of eligible voters in the Tremont area, participated.[18] Twenty-four persons were elected to the Board, including 19 Puerto Ricans and 5 blacks. According to CAP guidelines concerning the composition of Community Corporation Boards, at least one-third of the elected members must be actual representatives of the poor in the area. A "poor" person is one whose annual income does not exceed the target population income as defined by CAP: $3,500 for a single individual, $4,000 for a family of two, with $500 to be added for each additional dependent.[19] According to this formula, ten of the Puerto Ricans and two of the blacks elected to the first Board of Directors in Tremont were poor, while nine Puerto Ricans and three blacks were not.

It seems plausible to infer that, in casting their ballots, most of the voters in Tremont did not know what individual candidates stood for since little actual electioneering took place. As has been the case in so much of American politics, especially in nonpartisan elections, it appears as though "ethnicity simplifies choice."[20] However, the fact that the Puerto Ricans in the area were able to capture the great majority of seats on the Board is mainly because they were the most organized group and, in contrast to other groups and individuals, made fairly heavy use of posters, leaflets, and face-to-face contact with members of the community at large prior to the election.

The 24 persons elected to the Tremont Community Corporation Board in January 1969 actually represented two-thirds of the final composition of the Board. In keeping with CAP's "Plan for Ensuring Racial and Ethnic Balance on the Boards of Community Corporations,"[21] the remaining one-third was selected by the elected members. The purpose in selecting these additional members is ostensibly to

correct any racial or ethnic imbalance resulting
from the election, the selected members being subject to the same regulations concerning income as
those elected. However, in the case of the Tremont
Board, as can be seen in Table 3.3, those selected
maintained, rather than corrected, the existing
ethnic imbalance.

TABLE 3.3

Ethnic Breakdown of Tremont Community
Corporation Board of Directors, 1969

	Puerto Ricans	Blacks	Total
Elected	19	5	24
Selected	7	5	12
Total	26	10	36

Source: Files of the Tremont Community Corporation.

Nevertheless, on April 1, 1969, this Board of
Directors was certified as the Tremont Community
Corporation by the Community Development Agency,
and the remaining structural units of the Corporation were appointed and organized shortly thereafter.

STRUCTURE OF TREMONT COMMUNITY CORPORATION

With this background, we can turn to a look at
the structure of the Community Corporation, which
is represented diagramatically in Figure 3. While
the Tremont Corporation, as it existed during program year 1969-70 is used here as a model, it should
be noted that the basic structure of the corporations in general varies only slightly from year to
year throughout the City's 26 poverty areas.

FIGURE 3

The Structure of the Tremont Community
Action Program: 1969-1970

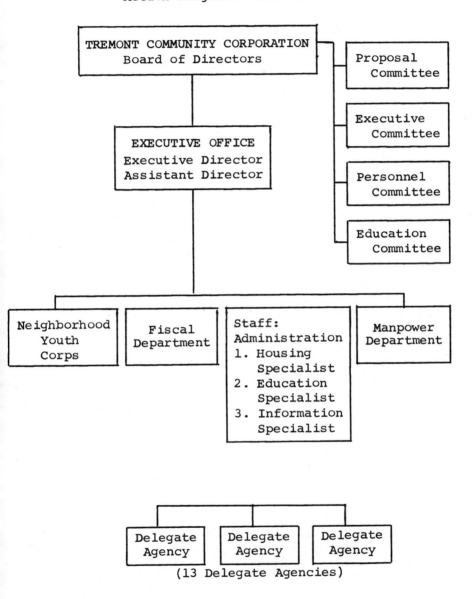

Source: Tremont Community Corporation, _Tremont
Community Corporation Year-Round Project, Program Year
"F" 1970-71_ (Bronx, New York: Tremont Community
Corporation, 1969), a modified version.

The Board of Directors is the legal representative of the Corporation and is charged with carrying out the goals described in its own Master Plan
as well as those announced by the city-wide community action bureaucracy. It employs the staff of
the total Corporation, holds all properties, exer-
cises ultimate fiscal responsibility, and alone determines Corporation policy. The Board of Directors
is supposed to meet approximately once every two
weeks to debate issues and make policy decisions,
the most crucial meetings being those concerned
with recommending to the city-wide bureaucracy on
which specific local programs to fund.

Other important functions of the Board are the
appointment of certain standing committees such as
the Proposal Committee, the Executive Committee,
the Personnel Committee, and the Education Committee, which aid in carrying out the work of the
Board; and the election of the Executive Director
and the Assistant Director, who are charged with
the daily administration of the total Corporation.
The Executive Director, who need not be a member of
the Board of Directors, nor a resident of the poverty area, is responsible for appointing all employees of the Corporation, normally in conjunction
with the Personnel Committee.

The middle level of the Tremont Community Corporation, over which the Executive Office has direct
administrative responsibility, is composed of four
major units whose main functions are outlined below.

1. Neighborhood Youth Corps Department:
Supervises the job training programs for youth in
the Tremont area, and is most operative during the
summer months.

2. Fiscal Department: Processes and prepares
payrolls, purchases all equipment and material, and
maintains monetary records of all financial matters
related to the Corporation.

3. Manpower Department: Operates the Tremont
Neighborhood Manpower Service Center, an arm of the
city-wide Manpower and Career Development Agency.
The Center, which screens and attempts to place job
applicants referred primarily by local Delegate
Agencies working in the field of manpower outreach,

came under official control of the Community Corporation on July 1, 1969 and shortly thereafter joined
the Corporation itself in its present location at
1924 Washington Avenue.[22]

4. Staff: Serves as the major communications
link between the Community Corporation Board of
Directors and the Community Development Agency, particularly with respect to the Corporation's Delegate
Agencies (see description below). The Staff is responsible for providing these agencies with technical assistance, primarily in the areas of housing,
education, and general information concerning program priorities and funding, as well as for prepar-
ing reports and evaluations of the Agency programs
for the Board of Directors.

DELEGATE AGENCIES IN TREMONT AREA

A brief word concerning the Delegate Agencies
themselves will complete the overview of the official structure and functioning of the community action program on the neighborhood level. Immediately
following the organization of the Planning Committee
or Community Corporation in each designated poverty
area, any local agency or group desiring to become
an official funded agency of the community action
program is required to form a Board of Directors of
at least 25 members. One-half of the Board must be
defined as poor, according to the CAP's figures for
"target population income," and two-thirds of the
members must be residents of the poverty area.[23]
A Chairman of the Board is then designated, along
with an Executive Director of the proposed Delegate
Agency, and the proposal for a particular program
is submitted to the Community Corporation. The proposal then must go through the entire cycle of the
funding process, which is described in detail below,
before the decision on its acceptance is made. If
the agency or group is finally accepted as a Delegate Agency, staff personnel for the Agency are
hired by the Director, with the approval of the Agency's Personnel Committee or Chairman of the Agency
Board. Similar to the setup of the Corporation

itself, the Director and the staff are responsible
for the daily administrative functions of the Agency,
while the Board of Directors is supposed to meet on
a monthly basis to make policy decisions concerning
the Agency's operations.

Outline of Funding Process

The relationship among the various functional
units comprising the total community action program,
including those on both the city-wide and neighborhood levels, is seen most clearly through an analysis of the complex decision-making process involved
in the funding of the Delegate Agencies within the
designated poverty areas. The following outline
summarizes the major steps involved in the total
funding process and identifies the various units responsible for carrying out each step.[24]

1. Federal Office of Economic Opportunity:
OEO drafts and sends general guidelines or instructions to the Community Development Agency.

2. Community Development Agency: CDA inter-
prets OEO's instructions for New York City and sends
its own guidelines, including priorities, to the
Council Against Poverty for the latter's approval,
modification, or rejection. The guidelines are then
distributed to the Community Corporations who, in
turn, distribute them to the interested local agencies or groups. This step is usually accomplished
around March of each program year.

3. Local Agencies or Sponsors: A local agency
or group sponsor in the poverty area requests funds
for a particular program by submitting a proposal to
the Community Corporation. The Corporation Staff
and the Community Development Agency's District
Staff are to lend technical assistance to these community groups in the preparation of such proposals.

4. Community Corporation Staff: The proposals
are examined by the staff and then submitted, with
its recommendations, to the Corporation's Proposal
Committee which, in turn, sends its own recommendations for program priorities and funding to the
Board of the Corporation.

5. Community Corporation Board of Directors: Using past program evaluations where available, the Board determines whether or not the program proposals submitted by the Proposal Committee meet with OEO and CDA guidelines, and decides which programs best meet an unserved community need and are thus deserving of funds. At this point, some proposals are accepted, while others may be rejected. Then a package of accepted and rejected proposals is assembled.

6. District Office, CDA: Generally by the middle of June, the proposal package is received by the District Office in charge of the particular Community Corporation. This office makes its recommendations on the package and then submits it to CDA staff evaluation.

7. Staff Evaluation, CDA: The staff reviews the package and adds their own written recommendations. Later, at a meeting held under the direction of the CDA Commissioner and top-level staff (Senior Staff), the final official recommendations of CDA are made on the package of proposals submitted by each Community Corporation.

8. Area Panel, CAP: The entire package with all the previous recommendations is then given to the appropriate Area Panel. At the Panel meeting, usually attended by six or seven Council members and two or three CDA staff members, the recommendation is formulated that the Council either approve, modify, or reject the package.* The Panel also interviews persons from the particular poverty area who may have filed an appeal.**

---

*Hockbaum concluded that the Area Panels normally recommend to the Council the decisions already reached by the CDA staff, especially its recommendations on budgetary items.

**Included in the entire funding cycle is an elaborate and complex system for appeals that exists for proposals that are rejected or modified anywhere along the funding process.

9.   New York City Council Against Poverty:
Council studies the recommendations of its Area
Panel and then approves, modifies, or rejects the
Community Corporation's package.*

10.   CDA Staff: The Council passes the package
back to CDA for the incorporation of any modifications made by the Council. The final package of
proposals is then sent to the Regional and New York
State Offices of Economic Opportunity.[25]

11.   Northeast Regional Office of OEO: OEO
staff examines the packages. If approved, the packages then move on to the next step.

12.   New York State Office of Economic Opportunity: Before funding can take place, the Gover-
nor's approval must be received. His is basically
a veto power that is seldom used.

13.   CDA Staff: Normally by early September
CDA informs the Corporation or the successful appli-
cant agency of OEO approval and prepares the final
budget and legal contracts.

14.   Delegate Agency: The local agency becomes
a Delegate Agency of the appropriate Corporation and
begins to operate its program.

Agencies Funded in Year "E"

For the program year 1969/70--Year "E" in the
terminology of CAP/CDA--with which this study is
concerned, the programs of 13 Delegate Agencies received final approval through the funding process.**

─────────────────

*Again, according to Hockbaum, Panel recommen-
dations are almost always ratified by the Council.

**The programs of an additional 14 local agen-
cies or groups were approved specifically for the
summer of 1969 and were funded for approximately
$182,400. These will not be reviewed in detail
since their operations lie outside of the time
period under consideration for the study. Also, it
should be noted that in deciding which agencies to
approve for the year-round programs, disagreements

Table 3.4 lists these 13 Delegate Agencies, their
stated program function, the specific Health Area
they were to serve, and the actual amount of money
received for program operation during the time period of this study.[26] The exact location of these
Agencies and the Tremont Community Corporation
within the Tremont poverty area can be seen in
Figure 2.

In summary, the total budget for Program Year E
(October 1, 1969 to September 30, 1970) was $679,210.
Approximately $527,493 was used to fund four manpower
outreach programs, three housing programs, two economic development programs, two education programs,
one recreation program, and finally, one senior citizens program. Between $140,012 to $151,717 was allotted for the operation of the Tremont Community
Corporation itself.*

Since it is through the funding process that
the key decisions are made that determine the actual
content of the community action program, the relationship between the neighborhood level units and

---

arose within the Tremont Community Corporation's
Board of Directors, which resulted in the resigna-
tion of the first Chairman of the Board. On September 22, 1969, the Board voted the Chairmanship to
one of the black members of the Corporation Board
of Directors.

*However, the Tremont Community Corporation ad-
ministers in actuality much more money than these
figures. The total amount administered for Program
Year E was approximately $994,317. Besides the
$679,210 mentioned above, the Corporation adminis-
tered the Manpower Center (budget: $199,210), the
Neighborhood Youth Corps (budget: $38,000), the
summer part of Program Account 59 (budget: $64,604),
and the Umbrella Project (budget: $72,726). More
will be said about each of these in later chapters.
Concerning the monies allocated, in general, different figures from different sources were found both
in CDA and Tremont Community Corporation files.
Thus, the above figures are reasonably correct.

TABLE 3.4

Delegate Agencies of the Tremont Community
Corporation, Program Year "E"

Delegate Agency	Program Function	Health Area	Budget
Tremont Community Council	Manpower outreach	17 and 19	$36,701
Federation of Puerto Rican Volunteers	Manpower outreach	10 and 17	41,279
Monterey Community Association	Manpower outreach	18 and 19	37,927
National Association of Puerto Rican Affairs	Manpower outreach	area wide	39,834
Tremont Housing Clinic	Tenant Information	18	43,734
Washington Avenue Neighborhood Association	Tenant Information	10 and 17	43,846
East Tremont Action Committee	Tenant Information	20 and 21.10	43,025
West Farms Villagers	Economic Development	20 and 21.10	36,615
Elsmere Tenants Council	Economic Development	20 and 21.10	43,321
East Tremont Neighborhood Association	Senior Citizens	20 and 21.10	41,634
Naval Cadets and Training Corps	Recreation	area wide	40,098
United Bronx Parents	Adult Education	18 and 19	41,065
Bronco Self-Improvement Association	Education Action	area wide	38,417

Source: From the files of the Tremont Community Corporation; and the Community Development Agency Memo of August 17, 1970.

the city-wide community action bureaucracy involved
in this process are most crucial ones. Viewing the
steps involved in this process, it is clear that
the city-wide bureaucracy, and particularly the Community Development Agency, possesses the greatest
measure of decision-making power over which programs
will be funded and put into actual operation in each
designated poverty area. Since it is at the neighborhood level that participation by the poor is the
most widespread and, at least potentially, the most
meaningful, the manner in which the bureaucracy ex-
ercises this power takes on crucial significance.
Thus, once again, it becomes most important to consider the goals toward which participation on the
part of the poor is aimed in the community action
program in New York City, and to question whether
or not there exists a discrepancy between official
descriptions and structure, and the actual functioning of this program, especially on the neighborhood
level. Against this background, we may now turn to
a description of the various methods employed in
the empirical investigation of this question in the
Tremont poverty area.

4

METHODS
AND
SAMPLING

This chapter describes the various methods of data collection used in the study, the subjects covered, and the sampling procedures employed. Four of the many methods available to social scientists were utilized: the techniques of observation, participant observation, content analysis, and interviewing.

TECHNIQUES OF OBSERVATION AND PARTICIPANT OBSERVATION

The research began with the basic technique of observation. Through the Executive Director of the Tremont Community Corporation, a personal acquaintance, access was gained into the various units of the community action program in the Tremont poverty area. As a means of gaining understanding into the nature of community action, our stated purpose in the Tremont community, an assignment was obtained through the Executive Director for one of the authors to work with the Corporation's Program Evaluation Specialist. For the most part, this involved accompanying him during the course of several months on visits to most of the Delegate Agencies in the area. This assignment served the very important function of securing a role in the Corporation Staff office, through which general acceptance by the Corporation employees was gained in a very

short time. At the same time, contact with the
various Delegate Agencies was afforded, as well as
the opportunity to meet the Agency Directors and
staff members, receipt of both verbal and written
information about their programs, and actual wit-
nessing of the evaluation procedures. Because of
the Evaluation Specialist's introductions, it was a
fairly easy matter to return and observe the work-
ings of the agencies in a more detailed manner at a
later time. Gradually, through contacts with several of the agencies, invitations were obtained to
attend the meetings of the Board of Directors.
Such contacts provided an additional way of becoming known and accepted in the community.

At the Corporation office itself, total access
to the files was gained within a matter of two to
three weeks, which included the minutes of the
Board of Directors' meetings, program evaluation
reports, monthly reports submitted to the Corporation from the Delegate Agencies, and a great deal
of information concerning funding and other key procedures of the community action program. Eventually
permission was granted to attend the Corporation's
Board meetings, and over a period of about seven
months these meetings were observed on a regular
basis.

In addition, working at the Corporation provided for frequent contact with officials from the
community action bureaucracy, in particular the Community Development Agency's District Office field
workers. Much significant information and insight
was gleaned from informal lunches and conversations
with these officials as well as many on the Corporation and Delegate Agency level, especially regarding the undercurrents of developments in the bureaucracy and local political maneuvers. At all stages
of the observation process, the great majority of
those connected with the community action program
were found to be exceedingly open and cooperative.

A participant observer role was created through
one of the authors' appointment by the Executive
Director as an advisor to the Proposal Committee of
the Corporation two months after initial contact
with the Tremont poverty area. This role provided

the opportunity to see at first hand how decisions
concerning program priorities and funding of the
Delegate Agencies are made at the Corporation level.
Likewise, the advisory position resulted in acquisi-
tion of permission from both the Council Against
Poverty and the Community Development Agency to fol-
low step by step the decisions made on the Tremont
Corporation package throughout the funding process.
(See Chapter 3.)

The methods of observation and participant observation yielded an extremely large number of written documents such as CAP and CDA guidelines and
other bureaucratic memos; minutes of meetings and
mandates issued by the Tremont Community Corporation; program proposals, evaluations, and actual
program descriptions from the Delegate Agencies.
A diary was kept of all meetings attended as well
as informal conversations. All this material was
analyzed in detail and yielded a great deal of information concerning stated goals and strategies,
program priorities, budgeting, and actual operation
of the various units, both on the city-wide and on
the neighborhood level, of the community action program. Much of this information was used in design-
ing the interview phase.

One difficulty encountered throughout the study
was that of an overwhelming amount of information.
Both the city-wide bureaucracy and neighborhood
level units expend a great deal of time and energy
on paperwork; thus, the volume of internal written
materials available on the community action pro-
gram--provided one has access--is enormous.

TECHNIQUE OF INTERVIEWING

The final technique employed in the study was
that of direct interviewing by means of a schedule
constructed on the basis of the theoretical framework and, in particular, the conceptual and operational definitions of the key variables, presented
in the preceding chapter. (See Appendix for a copy
of the interview schedule.) The primary function
of the interview procedure was to obtain information,

which when analyzed in conjunction with the observational data gathered through the methods described
above, made possible a process of cross-checking
for reliability of data, as well as the filling-in
gaps of information.

The time required for completion of the interview schedule varied considerably--from 45 minutes
to several hours--depending on the individual's
knowledge of and position in the community action
program and on his willingness to elaborate on de-
tails. Also, the schedule used for primary respondents, such as the Directors of the Delegate Agencies, contained more items and consequently took
longer to administer. The average time required
for all respondents, however, was about one hour
and 15 minutes.

The interviewing took place between mid-December
1970 and mid-February 1971. All interviews were
self-conducted in order to provide the maximum consistency, especially in those cases where Spanish
was needed. Most were conducted on the job although
some took place in respondents' homes. Because of
the several months of prior contact with the majority of respondents, there was a very high rate of
response (exact figures for response rates are included later in the chapter), and on the whole, ex-
cellent rapport was established.

The only difficulty of any significance encountered during the interviewing process was a result of the "New York Black Panther 13" trial in
progress at that time. A key prosecution witness
in this trial was a former Director of one of the
Delegate Agencies in the Tremont area who had been
exposed as an undercover police informer.[1] Publicity of this generated by the trial caused a certain amount of distrust and fear in sections of the
Tremont community, and resulted in some individuals'
reluctance to be interviewed. (Exact figures on
those so affected are included later in the chapter.)

DEVELOPMENT OF CATEGORIES FOR SAMPLE

The major decision involved prior to the interview stage of the research concerned the method to

be used in selecting a sample for study from among
the many persons who had, at that time, been in contact with the community action program in the Tremont area. Since the degree of participation--and
consequently the knowledge of and perspective taken
toward the program--varied widely among individuals
in the area, it was felt to be most important that
all such degrees of participation might be represented in the sample. A recent study by Peter Bachrach and Morton Baratz, Power and Poverty: Theory
and Practice, provided much insight in this endeavor.
Through their examination of various community action programs in the city of Baltimore, Bachrach and
Baratz identified three main groups of the poor, as
follows:

> 1. Those who have not partici-
> pated in any antipoverty programs,
> either as workers or receivers of
> benefits;
> 2. those who receive benefits
> and services from antipoverty pro-
> grams but do not participate in
> policy-making or administration of
> the programs; and
> 3. those who actively partici-
> pate in policy-making or administra-
> tion.[2]

They call the first group the "unexposed," the
second, the "nonparticipant beneficiaries," and the
third, the "participants." Thus, quite clearly,
these authors identified "participation" with
policy-making or program administration.

While Bachrach and Baratz's classification of
individuals found in a poverty program area was
felt to be extremely useful, certain adaptations
were made for the purposes of this study in order
to bring the classification in line with information about the Tremont area that had resulted from
the initial stages of the research. First of all,
it was felt that the "nonparticipant beneficiaries"
covered two quite distinct groups that should be
separated; one group consisting of those who receive

benefits from the community action program in the
form of jobs with either the Community Corporation
or the various Delegate Agencies, which do not involve policy-making or program administration; and
the other made up of those who receive only services
or participate in programs in a recipient capacity.
In this study, the term "nonparticipant beneficiaries" was applied to the latter group, while the
former was labeled the "participant beneficiaries."

The second change made in Bachrach and Baratz's
classification involved the addition of a group
whose potential significance, in the sense of having
been affected by the community action program, was
seen through the analysis of the funding process:
those who have tried to participate in policy-making
and/or administration, but who were refused. This
group, consisting of those sponsors of would-be
Delegate Agencies whose program proposals were rejected at one or another stage of the funding cycle,
was termed the "unsuccessfuls."

A final group was added shortly before the interviewing began, when according to a Council
Against Poverty mandate,[3] a Youth Advisory Committee
was set up within the Tremont Community Corporation.
Representatives of this group were included in the
sample to allow for the expression of more youthful
views on the Tremont community action program than
it was felt had been provided for in the sample of
the other groups.

Thus, the following classification of groups
with which the interview stage of the study was concerned emerged. It should be noted that Bachrach
and Baratz's first group, the "unexposed," was not
included in the study, since the major focus was on
examining the actual effects of the community action program in the Tremont area. Thus, those who
were not reached or who did not have direct contact
with the program were felt to be beyond the study's
scope. Also, the first three groups in this classification are those with which the study was primarily concerned.

Group I: The Participants consists of those
persons from the Tremont Community Corporation and
Delegate Agencies who actually participated in

policy-making or administration of the community action program during Program Year "E" (October 1,
1969-September 30, 1970). Included in this group
are: (a) the Tremont Community Corporation Staff,
including the Executive Office, as well as Administrative Staff Specialists; (b) the Tremont Community
Corporation Board of Directors; (c) the Directors of
the Delegate Agencies; and (d) the Delegate Agencies'
Boards of Directors.

Group II: The Participant Beneficiaries consists of those who participated in the community
action program as employees of the Tremont Community
Corporation or the Delegate Agencies during Program
Year "E," but who did not take part in policy-making
or program administration. Included here are:
(a) all Tremont Community Corporation personnel
other than those mentioned above in Group I, and
(b) the Delegate Agencies' personnel.

Group III: The Nonparticipant Beneficiaries
consists of those who received services from the
community action program or who participated in the
program in a recipient capacity during Program Year
"E." Included here are the clients of all the
Delegate Agencies in the Tremont area.

Group IV: The Unsuccessfuls consists of those
would-have-been Participants (policy-makers or program administrators) who submitted program proposals
to the Community Corporation for Program Year "E,"
and were rejected for initial funding.

Group V: The Youth consists of members of the
Youth Advisory Committee of the Tremont Community
Corporation.

THE SAMPLE

Having described the various groups with which
the interview stage of the study was concerned, we
may now turn to the specific question of the sample
itself as it was drawn from each of the five groups.

Group I: The Participants

The names and actual numbers of Participants
in each of the five categories described above were

determined from the Community Corporation files.
The distribution of these Participants, by their
unit of affiliation, actual position in the community action program, and ethnicity, is recorded
in Table 4.1.

The entire population of the Tremont Community
Corporation Staff and the Delegate Agency Directors
was included in the sample, since both categories
contained small numbers (10 and 13, respectively).
Of the Corporation Staff members, two had moved to
Puerto Rico and could not be reached at the time of
the interviewing, while two of the Delegate Agency
Directors also were not interviewed. One refused
to cooperate, while the other had been indicted on
charges alleging the theft of money from Agency payroll checks and could not be reached.[4]

A random sample of the members of the Boards
of Directors yielded 10 persons affiliated with the
Community Corporation Board and 16 individuals on
the Boards of the various Delegate Agencies. All
of these were interviewed.

Table 4.2 summarizes the relevant information
concerning the Participants interviewed for the
study, including the rate of response for each
category.

Group II: The Participant Beneficiaries

Lists of all personnel falling into this group
were obtained from both the Community Corporation
and the individual Delegate Agencies. Table 4.3
presents the distribution of Participant Beneficiaries, by unit of affiliation and ethnicity.

All eight of the Participant Beneficiaries affiliated with the Community Corporation were included in the sample, while a random sample of the
63 affiliated with the Delegate Agencies was taken,
yielding 16 persons in this latter group. All were
interviewed, as can be seen in Table 4.4.

Group III: The Nonparticipant Beneficiaries

In considering the issue of drawing a sample
of Nonparticipant Beneficiaries, or clients of the

TABLE 4.1

Distribution of Participants in Tremont Poverty Area, by Unit of Affiliation, Position, and Ethnicity, Program Year "E"

Unit of Affiliation and Position	Ethnic Group Affiliation			
	Puerto Rican	Black	Other	Total
Community Corporation				
Staff	6	3	1	10
Board of Directors	20	8	1	29
Delegate Agency				
Directors	5	4	4	13
Board of Directors	149	120	29	298
Total	180	135	35	350

Source: Compiled by the authors.

TABLE 4.2

Distribution of Participants Interviewed for the Study, by Unit of Affiliation, Position, and Ethnicity, with Rates of Response

Unit of Affiliation and Position	Ethnic Group Affiliation			Total Interviewed	Total in Sample	Response Rate (Percent)
	Puerto Rican	Black	Other			
Community Corporation						
Staff	4	3	1	8	10	80.0
Board of Directors	5	5	0	10	10	100.0
Delegate Agency:						
Directors	4	3	3	11	13	84.6
Board of Directors	9	6	1	16	16	100.0
Total	22	17	6	45	49	91.8

Distribution of Participant Beneficiaries in Tremont Poverty Area,
by Unit of Affiliation and Ethnicity, Program Year "E"

Unit of Affiliation	Ethnic Group Affiliation			
	Puerto Rican	Black	Other	Total
Community Corporation	3	5	0	8
Delegate Agencies	31	22	10	63
Total	34	27	10	71

Source: Compiled by the authors.

TABLE 4.4

Distribution of Participant Beneficiaries Interviewed for the Study,
by Unit of Affiliation and Ethnicity, with Rates of Response

Unit of Affiliation	Ethnic Group Affiliation			Total Interviewed	Total in Sample	Response Rate (Percent)
	Puerto Rican	Black	Other			
Community Corporation	3	5	0	8	8	100
Delegate Agencies	9	6	1	16	16	100
Total	12	11	1	24	24	100

Source: Compiled by the authors.

Delegate Agencies in the Tremont Area, attention
was first directed at the Delegate Agencies themselves. During Program Year "E," the time period
under study, 13 Delegate Agencies were funded for
operation in the area. One of these, Bronco Self-
Improvement Association, was dropped and funds cut
off midway through the program year when the Director was indicted on charges of stealing funds from
the Agency, as has been previously mentioned. Because of the fact that Bronco's Educational Action
program never actually functioned--and also because
all records of the Agency were destroyed in a somewhat mysterious fire (the third such fire during
Bronco's existence)--clients from this Agency, if
indeed such existed, were not included in the study.
This left a total of 12 programs--4 in the field of
Manpower Outreach, 3 in Tenant Information or Housing Action, 2 in Economic Development, 1 in Recreation, 1 in Adult Education, and 1 concerning Senior
Citizens.

   Through personal observation of program operation, as well as examination of program documents
and evaluation reports from the Trement Community
Corporation and the Community Development Agency,
the following information concerning these 12 programs was gathered:*

   1. The three programs in the field of Tenant
Information or Housing Action--Tremont Housing
Clinic, Washington Avenue Neighborhood Association,
and East Tremont Action Committee--appeared to offer
the best opportunities for both collective action
and the successful provision of relevant services
and thus for the exercising of influence; as it was
described in Chapter 2.

   2. The Naval Cadets and Training Corps' youth-
oriented Recreation program and East Tremont Neighborhood Association's Senior Citizens program were
both primarily recreational service programs, offering very few opportunities for the provision of
relevant services to the community at large.

---

*What follows is explained in much greater de-
tail in the next chapter.

3.   There appeared to be a very high degree of consistency between the two Economic Development programs--West Farms Villagers and Elsmere Tenants Council--and among the four Manpower Outreach programs--Tremont Community Council, Federation of Puerto Rican Volunteers, Monterey Community Association, and the National Association of Puerto Rican Affairs--in terms of actual program operation.

4.   The activities of the Adult Education program, sponsored by the United Bronx Parents, were practically nonexistent in the Tremont area.

On the basis of this information, and to allow for the testing of the study's major hypothesis under the most stringent conditions, clients from all three Housing Action programs, one Manpower Outreach, and one Economic Development program were included in a restricted population of Nonparticipant Beneficiaries. The five Agencies in this phase of the study were Tremont Housing Clinic, Washington Avenue Neighborhood Association, East Tremont Action Committee, West Farms Villagers, and Federation of Puerto Rican Volunteers.*

The files of these five Agencies were scrutinized for the time period of October 1, 1969 through September 30, 1970, and after spending several weeks in the attempt to make sense of the records, a list of the clients serviced during Program Year "E" was drawn up for each Agency. It should be noted that each Delegate Agency is required to maintain records of the numbers and characteristics of their clients, such as age, sex, ethnicity, race, income, and whether the individual is receiving welfare assistance. Such records are to be submitted in monthly reports to both the Community Corporation and the

---

*West Farms Villagers was chosen over Elsmere Tenants Council since, at the time of the interviewing, the latter's records had been subpoenaed for investigation by the City and were not available. Federation of Puerto Rican Volunteers was selected as representative of the four Manpower Outreach programs because of its median rating on Corporation evaluations.

Community Development Agency. However, investigation of the Agency records showed that in many cases
they were poorly set up, not kept up to date, or
even nonexistent. Furthermore, it seems likely that
the numbers submitted were often made up, blown up,
or roughly approximated. These facts should be kept
in mind in interpreting the data in Table 4.5, in
which is presented the numbers of clients serviced
by each of the five Agencies under consideration,
as determined from the only existing records.

TABLE 4.5

Distribution of Nonparticipant Beneficiaries
of Five Delegate Agencies in the Tremont
Poverty Area, by Agency, Program Year "E"

Delegate Agency	Total Number Serviced
Tremont Housing Clinic	190
Washington Avenue Neighborhood Association	102
East Tremont Action Committee	226
Federation of Puerto Rican Volunteers	246[a]
West Farms Villagers	122
Total	886[b]

[a]While this Agency's stated program function
was Manpower Outreach, it actually devoted much of
its efforts to welfare problems, as did the other
three Manpower programs. Of this figure, 144 were
clients with welfare problems, while 102 fall in
the manpower category.

[b]The total ethnic breakdown was approximately
60 percent Puerto Rican, 35 percent black, and 5
percent other.

Source: Compiled by the author.

A 2 percent random sample* was taken of the total 886 Nonparticipant Beneficiaries serviced by the 5 Delegate Agencies, yielding a total of 18 persons. Of the 18 in the original sample, 6 had to be replaced--5 because they had moved out of the area by the time of the interviewing and could not be traced, and 1 because she refused to allow herself to be interviewed. The breakdown, by Delegate Agency and ethnicity, of those actually interviewed is recorded in Table 4.6.

TABLE 4.6

Distribution of Nonparticipant Beneficiaries
Interviewed for the Study, by Delegate
Agency and Ethnicity

| Delegate Agency | Ethnic Group Affiliation | | |
	Puerto Rican	Black	Total
Tremont Housing Clinic	2	2	4
Washington Avenue Neighborhood Ass.	2	1	3
East Tremont Action Comm.	2	2	4
Federation of P.R. Volunteers	4	0	4
West Farms Villagers	2	1	3
Total	12	6	18

Source: Compiled by the authors.

_____

*Such a small sample was taken because this phase of the interviewing was seen as much less significant than that concerning the Participants and Participant Beneficiaries, particularly in light of the questionable accuracy of the information concerning the population from which the sample was drawn.

Group IV: The Unsuccessfuls

A total of 20 program proposals was originally submitted for Program Year "E," out of which 13 were ultimately funded, thus yielding 7 unsuccessful program sponsors. Out of this group of 7 Unsuccessfuls, 4 were nevertheless included in the community action program in the Tremont area in other capacities, and all 4 turned up in the sample of either the Participants or the Participant Beneficiaries.* The remaining 3 individuals constituted the sample of this fourth group, and all were interviewed accordingly.

Group V: The Youth

An accidental sample of six members of the Youth Advisory Committee, including the Vice-Chairman and Secretary, were interviewed in a group session. While this does not constitute any real sample of youth opinion in the area, it was judged to be not atypical on the basis of informal conversations with other youth and with the Adult Supervisor of the Youth Advisory Committee.

_____

*At this point it should be noted that throughout the sampling process, it was discovered that a significant number of individuals were involved in the Tremont community action program in more than one capacity. For example, it was not unusual to find that the same person was employed by one Delegate Agency, served on the Board of Directors of another, and unsuccessfully submitted a proposal for a Delegate Agency of his own. Such an individual thus was included in the populations of the Participant Beneficiaries, the Participants, and the Unsuccessfuls. Where such overlapping occurred in the actual samples drawn, the individual was included in his most significant position (ranging from Participant, Participant Beneficiary, Unsuccessful to Nonparticipant Beneficiary) and was replaced in the sample of all other groups of which he was a member.

In summary, then, a total of 96 persons were
interviewed: 45 Participants, 24 Participant Beneficiaries, 18 Nonparticipant Beneficiaries, 3 Unsuccessfuls, and 6 Youth.

EVALUATION OF THE METHODS UTILIZED

A few words evaluating the various methods
utilized in this study are in order. After critically surveying the many methods available to social
scientists, the techniques of observation, participant observation, content analysis, and interviewing
were chosen because these seemed to be most suited
to the particular types of data sought. More specifically, the initial methods employed in the study
were those of observation and participant observation since they allowed first-hand experience with
the operation of the community action program in the
Tremont area and also aided in correctly interpreting the type of discrepancies between verbal and behavioral patterns that plague much social scientific
research, especially evaluative research of the type
under consideration here.
The interviewing technique likewise was of
great importance since the data that it yielded provided a most necessary view against which the observational interpretations were able to be checked.
Most importantly, by providing the program participants with the opportunity to evaluate for themselves the consequences of the community action program, a researcher's own value bias may be controlled. It is worth noting, however, that no real
contradictions were found between the data yielded
through the observational and the interview phases
of the study.
Finally, utilization of a fairly tightly constructed interview schedule allowed for more precise analysis of the data around the key variables
posited as the operational indicators of influence
and social control outputs (separateness and separation, collaboration and containment, bargaining and
resocialization) than was possible through the
other methods employed.

Having reviewed the methods and sampling procedures used in the research, we may now turn to an analysis of the data that were obtained. Chapters 5 and 6 present a summary of findings of the first phase of the study that utilized the methods of observation, participant observation, and content analysis. The data presented in these chapters are termed observational in contrast with the interview data, which comprise the subject matter of Chapter 7.

5

OBSERVATIONAL
DATA I:
RESOURCES AND OPERATIONS
OF NEIGHBORHOOD LEVEL
UNITS

Our major purpose in this chapter, as well as in the one that follows, is to present a summary of the most relevant data that were obtained through the methods of observation, participant observation, and content analysis, as have been described in Chapter 4. The very large volume of information collected during this phase of the research necessitates that it be organized quite tightly around the primary aim for which it was gathered; that is, in relationship to the study's major hypothesis.

This research is aimed at determining whether or not the operation of the community action program in the Tremont poverty area can be best described as an influence output, with the community action bureaucracy serving as an advocate of the poor in their struggle against those authorities who control them; or, as a social control output, with the bureaucracy assuming the role of another authority with whom the poor on the neighborhood level must cope. To this end, two subhypotheses were developed that posited certain operational indicators of the key concepts of influence and social control outputs, and that were stated as follows:

1. To the extent that separateness, bargaining, and collaboration have taken place as a result of the community action program in the Tremont poverty area, this program can be described as an influence output.

2. To the extent that separation, containment, and resocialization have taken place as a result of the community action program in the Tremont poverty area, this program can be described as a social control output.

Certainly, then, the data presented here must focus on the provision of evidence for the occurrence, or lack of occurrence, of these six variables.*

With respect to the concept of influence, it has been seen in an earlier chapter that further insight may be gained through utilizing two approaches of measurement set down by William Gamson: the subjective probability approach and the influence attempts approach. While the first of these relies on informed observers, judgments as to whether or not a preferred outcome has a higher probability of occurrence, following some act of influence by potential partisans, and thus is beyond the scope of the observational data here under discussion, the second approach may be at least partially utilized in conjunction with the analysis of such data.** Here, influence is inferred if it can be shown through an examination of resources that a potential partisan group possesses the capability of influence, and that certain specific influence attempts have been made. These two concepts, then,

---

*While all six variables will be touched on in the presentation of the observational data, separation, separateness, and to a certain extent, resocialization have very important subjective dimensions, and thus will be covered to a fuller extent in Chapter 7, which presents the results of the interview phase of the research.

**The subjective probability approach is incorporated into the interview schedule, and will be discussed in detail in Chapter 7. Likewise, the concept of influence attempts is handled to a much fuller extent in the analysis of the responses to certain questions in the interview schedule that directly addressed this issue.

in addition to the six variables of influence and
social control, should be kept in mind in reviewing
the data presented here.

This chapter will focus on two very important
aspects of the operation of the neighborhood level
units of the community action program: their resources and functioning. In Chapter 6 attention is
turned to the examination of the most crucial relationships between the neighborhood level units and
the community action bureaucracy--those involved in
the cycle of the funding process. Thus, the observational data resulting from this research are organized around the two most significant questions
inherent in the major hypothesis: First of all,
how does the community action program actually operate on the neighborhood level?; and, second, what
is the role of the community action bureaucracy in
this endeavor?

THE RESOURCES OF NEIGHBORHOOD
LEVEL UNITS

In Chapter 3 a brief history of the community
action program in the Tremont area brought us to
the beginning of Program Year "E," October 1, 1969.
As of this date, the major decisions had been made
on the community action resources that would be coming into the area, and according to which the neighborhood level units--the Community Corporation, the
Neighborhood Manpower Service Center, and the 13
Delegate Agencies--would function for the program
year. These resources may best be analyzed under
the separate headings of funds received, as spelled
out in the operating budgets approved by and passed
down from the city-wide bureaucracy, especially the
Community Development Agency; the program personnel;
and technical assistance received for program operation.

Budgets of Corporation and Delegate Agencies

Since the budgets determine to such a significant extent what will be accomplished by each of

the neighborhood level units, as well as the quality
of the personnel, it is to that issue that our attention should first be directed. Table 5.1 presents the operational budget for the Tremont Community Corporation during Program Year "E." The most
salient feature of this budget is that $152,800 out
of a total amount of $175,268 was allocated for the
salaries, wages, and fringe benefits of the 18 regular employees during this year (see Items 1.1 and
1.2 in Table 5.1). Thus, the average salary of
those individuals whose duty it was to plan out,
administer, and technically assist the actual operation of the community action program in the Tremont
area was slightly less than $7,500. A relatively
small number of these employees--most notably the
Executive Director and his assistant and the Staff
Specialists--received salaries in excess of $10,000,
which brings this figure quite a bit lower for the
remaining number.

TABLE 5.1

Actual Operating Budget of the Tremont
Community Corporation, Program Year "E"

	Item	Budget Allocation
1.	PERSONNEL COSTS	$153,930
1.1	Salaries and wages	136,500
1.2	Fringe benefits	16,380
1.3	Consultants and contract services	1,050
2.	NONPERSONNEL COSTS	21,338
2.1	Travel	1,008
2.2	Space costs	5,496
2.3	Consumable supplies	1,675
2.4	Equipment	2,300
2.5	Other costs	10,869
Total costs		$175,268

Source: Information obtained from the Manning
Tables and Corporation Budget Submission Forms
found in the Tremont Community Corporation.

This pattern is seen, with even more significant results, on the level of the Delegate Agencies,
as shown in Table 5.2. As exemplified by the four
agencies whose budgets are recorded in this table,
between 85 percent and 90 percent of the total budgets of all Delegate Agencies were allocated to
personnel costs.*

Delegate Agency Directors received salaries in
the range of $7,800 to $10,000, with an average of
approximately $8,800; while staff personnel received
an average salary of $5,600 for full-time employment
(35 to 40 hours per week).[1]

By the time the costs of rent, travel, equipment, and supplies are added to those of personnel,
only about 2.5 percent of the total budget of each
Delegate Agency is left to cover the costs of actual
program implementation (see Item 2.5, Other costs,
in Table 5.2). Such a budgetary allocation, particularly in the case of those Agencies whose program implies the mobilization of large numbers of
community members into an effective unit for collective action (e.g., Housing Action, Education Action, and Economic Development), would appear to
very seriously limit, if not altogether exclude,
the operation of meaningful and influential action
programs.** Of course, those Agencies whose programs

---

*It may be noted that this is the normal allo-
cation for city agencies as well, giving rise to
their frequent complaints of being insufficiently
funded for effective program operation.

**Later in the chapter when the functioning of
specific Delegate Agencies is discussed, there was
widespread agreement among program participants that
any successful action program in Tremont needed to
be preceded by a massive campaign to educate the community to the desirability and/or tactics of group
confrontation. It was readily acknowledged, however,
that such a campaign would require hiring better
trained--and consequently more expensive--personnel
to make face-to-face contact with community members
to elicit their interest and support, in addition
to that of powerful third parties--something which

TABLE 5.2

Actual Operating Budgets of Four Delegate Agencies in the Tremont Poverty Area, Program Year "E"

Item	Tremont Community Council	Washington Avenue Neigh. Ass.	United Bronx Parents	West Farms Villagers
1. Personnel costs	$33,124	$39,940	$36,706	$31,650
1.1 Salaries and wages	29,840	36,036	31,960	28,500
1.2 Fringe benefits	2,984	3,604	3,196	2,850
1.3 Consultants and services	300	300	1,550	300
2. Nonpersonnel costs	3,577	3,906	4,359	4,965
2.1 Travel	480	384	96	--
2.2 Space costs	1,044	1,200	2,400	3,000
2.3 Consumables	715	870	940	1,120
2.4 Equipment	98	220	48	67
2.5 Other costs	1,240	1,232	875	778
Total costs	$36,701	$43,846	$41,065	$36,615

Source: Information obtained from copies of Delegate Agency Proposals and Budgets in files of the Tremont Community Corporation.

were primarily service (as opposed to group-action)
oriented--such as those in the areas of recreation,
senior citizens, and manpower outreach--fared quite
a bit better in this regard, since their programs
required no real outlay of funds other than for personnel to administer and distribute services and
for certain fixed operational costs.

The Tremont Neighborhood Manpower Service Center during Program Year "E" fit quite accurately
into this latter category. The Manpower Center received a total operating budget of $199,677, of
which $160,193 covered the salaries, wages, and
fringe benefits of 21 employees, while the remaining $38,884 was spent on fixed operating costs, in-
cluding rent, supplies, and equipment. The top two
employees, including the Director, received salaries
in excess of $10,000, leaving an average of about
$6,650 each for the remaining 19 employees.[2]

Program Personnel

Since the success of the operations of all
these neighborhood level units relied so heavily
upon personnel, the quality of those individuals employed during Program Year "E" should be briefly
considered.* As is to be expected, the observational

---

the present budgetary allocations for personnel would
not allow. Also, from the 2.5 percent of the budget
allocated to program implementation, would have to be
drawn funds to cover the costs of sustaining a mass
publicity program, including such things as the use
of mass media, sound trucks, printed leaflets, etc.

*More specific information of this type will be
found in Chapter 7, in the analysis of data on the
personal characteristics of interviewed respondents.
The judgments of personnel quality which follow here
were based primarily on their experience in community work or in the realm of one's particular job;
knowledge of the local area; and political "know-
how"; as were demonstrated in day-to-day activities.

phase of the research established the existence of
a generally high correlation between an individual's
overall competence and his or her salary. Most top-
level Community Corporation employees, receiving
salaries of between $10,000 and $13,500, had college
degrees and a fairly wide range of experience. Significantly, however, very few had direct experience
in community work, and in the case of the Staff
Specialists, in the area of their specialty. Also,
most did not come from the Tremont area, and were
not too knowledgeable about local affairs or problems. But even more importantly, most lacked the
necessary political skills to maneuver within the
established city bureaucracies or even within CDA
itself.

A similar picture emerges with respect to the
Manpower Center and Delegate Agency Directors.
While the majority of this group were from the Tremont area and were generally intelligent, very few
possessed either specific training or experience in
their Agency's program function, or for community
work in general. Likewise, because of their lack
of experience in dealing with bureaucratic structures or powerful individuals, most were unable to
provide meaningful assistance to their clients. As
for the other personnel of all the neighborhood
level units, the best that can be said is that salaries in the range of $5,000 to $7,000 cannot be
expected to attract qualified and experienced persons. Many in this group were former welfare recipients or relatives and friends of those higher
up in the program who, while contributing an important indigenous perspective, were not generally
equipped to handle the technical, operational, and
political aspects of the programs for which they
were employed.

Thus, on the basis of what was observed concerning the key resource of personnel, it appears
quite clearly that the community action program in
Tremont did not possess the necessary resources to
allow it to operate either meaningful service pro-
grams--distributing material rewards and aimed at
building up a strong political constituency of the
poor; or effective group action programs--aimed at

their direct political activation. Insofar as this situation prevented reasonable attempts at allevia- tion of the objects of discontent, the program clearly did not appear on this basis to be an in- fluence output.

Technical Assistance from Corporation and CDA

The third resource of the neighborhood level units that needs to be explored concerns technical assistance for program planning and operation, which, according to bureaucracy guidelines, is due the Delegate Agencies from both the CDA and the local Community Corporation itself.* CDA's role, particu- larly in relation to assistance provided in the preparation of program proposals and other matters related to the funding cycle, will be discussed fully in the following chapter. However, it should be noted here that direct observation on a frequent basis over a period of six months yielded very few examples of the provision of assistance by CDA for ongoing programs of Delegate Agencies.** As will be discussed later in this chapter, during Program Year "E" several Delegate Agency programs were floundering or, for all practical purposes, inopera- tive. Yet, visits to such Agencies by CDA District Office experts were very rarely witnessed. On the few occasions where such visits occurred, bureau- cracy personnel were extremely critical and pro- vided little positive assistance. As one knowl- edgeable Delegate Agency employee observed, "CDA doesn't give us any help. They come for an hour and look at the books and then leave before they even know what's going on."[3]

*Refer to Chapter 3 for a description of the specific units within CDA and the Corporation which are responsible for the rendering of technical as- sistance.

**This observation was supported by the inter- view data gathered from Delegate Agency Directors. See Chapter 7.

The Community Corporation Staff, due to their own lack of expertise and the overwhelming amount of paper work required from them, likewise were only slightly or not at all helpful in their roles as technical assistants.

One important aspect of the technical assistance to be provided by both CDA and the Community Corporation is program evaluation, through which a Delegate Agency should find out how its program is functioning in terms of the wider community and program weaknesses so that those areas may be improved. The fact that CDA did not during Program Year "E" conduct such program evaluations was attested to repeatedly at both Corporation and Delegate Agency Board meetings, especially those immediately prior to the time for submittal of program proposals for Year "F," when evaluations of present programs might have been particularly helpful. The minutes from these meetings contain numerous statements similar to one from a Director of a Delegate Agency in the field of Economic Development who also served on the Corporation Board: "Nobody on my staff knows anything about economic development. CDA doesn't have any right to cut out my program [for Program Year "F"]. They never even came and looked at what we're trying to do or told us anything was wrong with it."[4] A phone call to a top official in the Program Operations Division of CDA yielded the concession that in formulating decisions on future program funding, "we'll have to depend on Corporation Staff evaluations."[5]

However, the evaluations conducted by the Corporation Staff had little validity as a basis for CDA's decisions concerning the refunding of Delegate Agency programs. Neither were they of much use to the Delegate Agencies seeking to improve their programs. First-hand observation of the Corporation evaluation procedure revealed that the criteria according to which an Agency received a favorable rating stressed superficial conformity to formal standards, such as the possession of a file cabinet and some sort of filing system, the maintenance of books on expenditures, and the presentation of good physical appearance. In response to

those items on the Evaluation Forms that did directly address such questions as program effectiveness
or activities of the agency, such broadly worded ex-
pressions as "appears to be making strides toward
fulfilling its functional responsibilities," or
"appears to be rather active in the community" were
most often used, with little or no documentation.[6]

Furthermore, informal conversations with the
Evaluation Specialist revealed that the decisions
on which Agency programs would receive high or low
ratings were normally made before actual evaluation
took place. A description of what was found in the
visit to the Agency, as well as the scores received,
were adjusted to assure such preconceived outcomes.
Thus, the primary function of the Corporation evaluations may best be seen in terms of serving a political end--particularly insofar as "justification" for
decisions on refunding are concerned--and not at all
in relation to technical assistance.

With respect to this overall issue of technical
assistance--especially that coming from CDA--obser-
vation once again yielded the distinct impression
that the program in Tremont was not equipped with
the necessary resources to allow it to function as
a vehicle of influence in the community. Here it
should be noted that CDA's apparent indifference to
what was taking place at the neighborhood level in
one sense could be interpreted as neutrality or
"letting the local people run their own program."
However, since much of the program was operating
ineffectively--a fact obvious to CDA through even
minimal contact with the area--its failure to step
in and provide assistance in keeping with its own
statements of advocacy must lead us to suspect a
strategy of social control in its part.

In summary, then, our analysis of the resources
of the neighborhood level units of the community action program in the Tremont area suggests the following tentative conclusions with respect to the key
variables and major hypothesis of the study:

1. Because of the minimal amount of funds for
program implementation, the generally poor quality
of personnel employed by the program, and the lack
of meaningful technical assistance from CDA and the

Corporation itself, the Delegate Agency programs as
a whole appear to possess very little capability
for influence in the Tremont area.

2. Lacking the necessary resources, in the
form of funds, personnel, and technical assistance,
meaningful and effective service or action programs
would appear to be rendered impossible, pointing to
the existence of a policy of containment in the
area, as opposed to one of collaboration.

For further evidence in support of these conclusions and others we may turn to the analysis of
the actual functioning of the neighborhood level
units in the Tremont area.

ACTUAL FUNCTIONING OF NEIGHBORHOOD
LEVEL UNITS

In considering this entire question it would
be well to turn first to the Tremont Community Corporation since the operation of this unit bears
such a significant relationship to the total community action program in the Tremont area. Here we
must be concerned with the functioning of both the
Corporation Board of Directors and the Administrative Staff of the Corporation.

Board of Directors of Corporation

Perhaps the most striking feature of the Tremont Community Corporation Board of Directors during Program Year "E" was the struggle for control
of the position of Chairman that ensued throughout
a good part of the year. By late fall 1969 fairly
widespread dissatisfaction with the elected Chairman was voiced, particularly with respect to the
fact that meetings of the Board were being called
on the average of only once a month or less, rather
than bimonthly, as the bureaucracy guidelines and
Corporation by-laws specify. On December 19, a new
Acting Chairman, previously a member of the Corporation Board as well as Chairman of the Board of
Directors of one of the Delegate Agencies, was

voted in. However, the original Chairman challenged
this decision in an appeal to the city-wide bureaucracy and on March 17 was reinstated as Chairman in
a directive issued by the Council Against Poverty.[7]
On June 24, some two and one-half months later, he
was forced to resign as pressure against him increased and the previously elected Acting Chairman
took over for the remainder of the program year.

Certainly, this ongoing internal power struggle
had a significant bearing on what the Board was able
to accomplish in the way of policy review and
decision-making during the program year. Even without this additional factor, however, it seems unlikely that the Board, as constituted during 1969-70,
would have functioned as a very effective unit. Internal strife was rampant, with a very noticeable
ethnic split between the Puerto Ricans and the
blacks on the Board. Although the Chairman was
black, the Puerto Ricans maintained clear control,
and it was a generally known fact that they met as
a group before regular Board meetings to plan out
their strategy.[8] As a result, the blacks, who constituted less than one-third of the Board, were
constantly frustrated and bitter over what they
felt was an attempt by the Puerto Ricans to cut
them out of the total program.

Another factor that complicated relations
within the Board of Directors was that most Board
members had direct connections with the Delegate
Agencies. Some were employed by these Agencies
either as Directors or staff members; others had
relatives and close friends serving in such capacities; and a few even served on Delegate Agency
Boards of Directors or were actually Chairmen of
such Boards. The resulting conflicts of interest
came out clearly during those Board meetings at
which decisions and recommendations were formulated
on the program proposals submitted by both existing
and would-be Delegate Agencies. Such meetings were
characterized by general disorder and shouting
matches between individuals and factions, and,
throughout the year, were poorly attended by members of the Board. Some insight on this last
point, as well as others previously mentioned, was

gained in a conversation with one key community
leader and member of the Board following a Board
meeting at the time for submission of program proposals. Speaking of the Corporation Board members,
he stated:

> These people are building empires for
> their own prestige, not the community.
> . . . The program is buying off lead-
> ers and dividing the community. Blacks
> versus Puerto Ricans and Puerto Ricans
> versus Puerto Ricans. Most of the
> Board members don't really give a damn
> for the community. . . . People
> didn't show tonight [for the Board
> meeting] because they knew the money
> was divided already and don't really
> care about the Corporation budget.
> The whole thing is just formality.
> Even the [program] proposals are
> pretty much formalities.[9]

Executive Office and Staff

Largely because of the generally chaotic situation in which the Board of Directors regularly found
itself, real control of the Tremont Community Corporation fell to the Executive Office, and especially to the Executive Director. A former director of
the local office of the National Association of
Puerto Rican Affairs, the Executive Director was a
shrewd politician who, through his key position in
the total community action program's communication
network, maintained tight control over all operations of the Corporation. Because of his very articulate manner, and claiming "special information"
from the city-wide bureaucracy, he was generally
able to manipulate the operations of the Board of
Directors. Personal experience gained through serving on the Board's Proposal Committee provided overwhelming evidence of this.*

———————————

*For example, the Executive Director strongly
desired to acquire control of the existing East

This same type of control was applied to the
Administrative Staff, as well as to the black Assistant Director who was generally relegated to the
most insignificant tasks of the Corporation.
Through many hours of conversation the impression
was firmly established that the Executive Director
evoked strong feelings in almost everyone connected
with the community action program in the Tremont
area. While the older Puerto Rican leaders, in particular, viewed him as a primary means of maintaining Puerto Rican control in the community, many
others, especially the blacks, strongly resented
his centralized control and interpreted his actions
as "not wanting people around who are intelligent
or a threat to his position."[10] Another widely expressed criticism of the Executive Director was his
failure to follow through on recommendations made to
him or even on his own stated plans.

The administrative staff itself was also the
subject of a fair amount of criticism by those familiar with the operation of the Tremont Community
Corporation. The Housing Specialist, from all appearances, was almost totally nonfunctional in his
assigned role, and was a source of great frustration
to the three Delegate Agencies in the field of Housing Action who looked to this office for program assistance. The Information, Program, and Evaluation
Specialist was generally suspect in the eyes of the
Delegate Agencies because of his role in program
evaluation. On the other hand the Education Specialist was enthusiastic and seemingly well-regarded
but received little support from either the Board of
Directors or the Executive Director. He finally

Tremont YMHA building. He claimed that the Corporation Staff made this the top priority for Program
Year "E." However, conversations with the Staff
proved that they were not even consulted. The rest
of the meeting was devoted to dividing the money
among the various agencies and no one was encouraged or allowed to question the decision on the "Y."
The Executive Director knew that the Board normally
rubber stamps the recommendations of the Proposal
Committee (his decisions), which was exactly what
happened.

resigned in frustration when it became evident that
neither the Executive Director nor Chairlady would
call a meeting of the Board's Education Committee
to deal with problems regarded as pressing by the
Specialist.[11]

The lower staff most often appeared to be pre-
occupied with paperwork concerning fairly minute de-
tails of program operation. In conversations they
revealed surprisingly little knowledge about what
was occurring at the level of the Delegate Agencies
or the community action bureaucracy and the accusation was voiced more than once that the Executive
Director worked to maintain his control by keeping
the Corporation Staff, the Board of Directors, and
the Delegate Agencies isolated from one another and
from the community action bureaucracy. Regardless
of the truth of this accusation it was apparent
that the Tremont Community Corporation as a whole
did little during Program Year "E" to remove their
isolation from the community at large, as reflected
in the extremely small numbers who participated in
the Corporation elections of January 1969.* No
real attempts by the Corporation to go out into the
community to encourage participation by residents
or to make known the presence of the community action program in the Tremont area were witnessed during this time. It was not until early 1971 that a
sign, indicating its existence, was put up on the
outside of the building housing the Corporation.[12]

One further significant aspect of the overall
functioning of the Tremont Community Corporation
concerns the area's official representative to the
Council Against Poverty whose role it was to serve
as the major communications link between the bureaucracy and the Corporation. Even though this individual maintained formal and informal contacts with
the Tremont area--in addition to his role as representative to CAP, he served during Program Year "E"
as a member of the Corporation Board of Directors,
the Chairman of one Delegate Agency Board, and a
member of the Boards of two other Delegate Agencies--

---

*These elections were described in Chapter 3.

he was the target of constant criticism for his
failure to relay information on bureaucratic decisions or mandates to the area. From all appearances
then, the CAP representative served to keep Tremont
isolated from the bureaucracy, rather than to encourage the latter's assistance or advocacy in the
area. The fact that the bureaucracy was aware of
this problem of communication is reflected in the
following statement by one member of the CDA District Office staff: "The community here in Tremont
looks upon us as the enemy, the Man, the investiga-
tor. They don't trust us and seem to think CAP and
CDA want to control them."[13] Nevertheless, no meaningful efforts by the bureaucracy to change this
image were witnessed in the Tremont area during Program Year "E."

What has been seen then, regarding the functioning of the Community Corporation in the Tremont
poverty area, appears to lend support to the tentative conclusions formulated earlier, which described
the operation of the community action program in
this area primarily in terms of social control. We
have noted that neither the Corporation itself,
through its administrative staff, nor the city-wide
bureaucracy, through the area's representative to
CAP, rendered meaningful program assistance to the
Delegate Agencies, again suggesting that the program has not resulted in increasing the capability
for influence of the poor in Tremont. In addition,
the actual operation of the Corporation Board of
Directors and Staff points to the occurrence of
separation, rather than separateness, in the sense
of increased isolation of various groups and units
in the area from one another. That the community
action program in Tremont has resulted in heightening the antagonistic ethnic identity (type-two isolation) of individuals in the area is suggested by
the functioning of the Board of Directors, as well
as the Executive Director. Likewise, some evidence
was seen that the establishment of the various
units of the program as a solid interest group in
the area (type-four separateness) was also dis-
couraged through actions of the Executive Director.

Neighborhood Manpower Service Center

Before turning to look at the functioning of the 13 Delegate Agencies for a further testing of these conclusions, a brief word should be included about the activities of the Tremont Neighborhood Manpower Service Center, operated by the Community Corporation during Program Year "E." The major functions of the Manpower Center in relationship to the community action program are to screen, test, and attempt to place in training programs or permanent employment those clients referred to the Center by the Delegate Agencies, in particular, those working in the area of Manpower Outreach. The specific activities and accomplishments of the Center during Program Year "E" are summarized in Tables 5.3 and 5.4.

TABLE 5.3

Summary Report of the Tremont Neighborhood Manpower Service Center, Program Year "E"

No. of Clients	Male	Female	Total
Interviewed	3,407	4,304	7,711
Not referred	1,684	2,441	4,125
Referred	1,723	1,863	3,586
Referred to other agencies	955	982	1,937
Referred to jobs or training programs	768	881	1,649

Source: Information gathered from a Report of the Acting Director of the Tremont Neighborhood Manpower Service Center to the Corporation Board of Directors, October 24, 1970, pp. 1-3.

As can be seen from Table 5.3, of the total
number of clients interviewed (7,711), slightly
fewer than half (3,586) were referred anywhere at
all, and only 1,649 were referred to either jobs or
training programs. All others were either considered not referable because of a lack of qualifications, placed on a waiting list, or sent to other
agencies including State and private employment
offices. Table 5.4 presents a more detailed breakdown of those who were referred to jobs or training
programs by the Center. Here it can be noted that
614 clients were placed in jobs, while 890 were
placed in training programs.

TABLE 5.4

Breakdown of Those Referred to Jobs or Training
Programs by the Tremont Neighborhood Manpower
Service Center, Program Year "E"

No. of Clients	Male	Female	Total
Failing to report for job placement	23	19	42
Refusing job	21	16	37
Referred but not accepted at job	36	30	66
Actually placed in job	272	342	614
Placed in training programs	416	474	890
Total	768	881	1,649

Source: Information gathered from a Report of
the Acting Director of the Tremont Neighborhood
Manpower Service Center to the Corporation Board
of Directors, October 24, 1970, pp. 1-3.

However, a Manpower Center follow-up study conducted during the program year revealed that after
90 days approximately 40 percent of those placed in
jobs were no longer working, usually because of dissatisfaction with the job. It was also discovered
that about 50 percent of those placed in training
programs dropped out within a similar time period.[14]
Applying these figures to what has been seen above,
it may be concluded that during Program Year "E" the
Manpower Center in Tremont succeeded in placing only
1,504 clients, or about 19 percent of the total number interviewed, in jobs or training programs, and
that 690 of these or about 9 percent of the total,
were still to be found in their jobs or training 90
days after placement.[15]

This statistical summary of the functioning of
the Manpower Center can be well understood in the
context of the concept of creaming or the process
by which mainly the least poor are included in poverty programs. With respect to this process it has
been recently noted that:

> Efforts to improve the condition of
> the poor, when effective, generally
> result in improving the conditions of
> those at the top of the bottom, leav-
> ing the bottommost untouched. Those
> left behind may be worse off then be-
> fore. Their relative deprivation may
> grow, or their feelings about them-
> selves may become negative. The se-
> lective mobility of some may mean the
> selective debasement of many others.[16]

Delegate Agencies

Manpower Outreach Programs

That such a process was operative in the Manpower Center was widely recognized by those familiar with its activities, especially the four Delegate Agencies in the Tremont area with the specific
program function of Manpower Outreach: Tremont

Community Council, Federation of Puerto Rican Volunteers, Monterey Community Association, and National
Association of Puerto Rican Affairs. While none of
these Agencies maintained reliable, up-to-date statistics on the actual number of persons serviced,
or the specific services rendered, it was learned
through observation of their activities and through
informal conversations with personnel of the Agencies that, in most cases, attempts were made to
place clients directly in jobs through personal contacts rather than by working through the Manpower
Center. Frequent complaints were voiced concerning
the testing system, long waiting periods, and general lack of success of the Center in aiding the
unemployed. However, it did not appear that the
Delegate Agencies were significantly more successful in this regard, with the possible exception of
the National Association of Puerto Rican Affairs,
which, because of its city-wide affiliation, had a
fairly wide range of contacts.

All of the Delegate Agencies in this program
category were engaged, at least part-time, in the
administering of assistance to clients with welfare,
housing, educational or other personal problems.*
Such assistance most commonly took the form of making telephone calls to an individual's welfare case
worker, landlord, or other official within the problem area. In brief, these activities, like those
in the area of manpower, were, in the case of all
four Agencies, almost totally service-oriented and
no attempts at group bargaining with established
powerful institutions in the area were evidenced.

---

*It should be noted that for Program Year "E,"
Federation and Monterey actually submitted proposals for programs in the area of Welfare Action,
while Tremont Community Council requested funds for
an Educational Action program. However, because of
a number of factors that came into the funding process, as will be seen in Chapter 6, and because
Welfare Action was dropped by the bureaucracy as a
program category in 1969, all these agencies were
switched to Manpower Outreach.

In general, however, these Agencies were ineffective regarding both their primary manpower goal and their related activities.

One additional point worth noting is that despite the very close similarity of program activities the four Agencies displayed no indication of substantial cooperation among themselves, each attempting to enhance their own prestige in the eyes of those seeking help.*

Senior Citizens and
Recreation Programs

Two other Delegate Agencies that may be very briefly discussed are East Tremont Neighborhood Association (ETNA) and Naval Cadets and Training Corps, which during Program Year "E" sponsored programs in the areas of Senior Citizens and Recreation, respectively. Both of these programs provided services of a predominantly recreational nature-- ETNA serving primarily older Jewish residents of the Tremont area (as well as many outside the area), while the Naval Cadets' activities were aimed especially at black and Puerto Rican adolescents. The highlights of ETNA's program included serving inexpensive hot lunches, sponsoring cultural events and providing a place for cardplaying, sewing, and informal conversation for its clients. In addition, some individual assistance in the areas of welfare, housing, and medicare was available through a part-time social worker employed by the agency. ETNA was almost totally isolated from the other Delegate Agencies in Tremont, which tended to view this program extremely critically because of its lack of

---

*The only exception to this that was seen was that Federation occasionally referred its clients to NAPRA because of the latter's good reputation for getting jobs for the unemployed. It is suspected that the evaluation policy that stresses numbers of persons helped, as opposed to the quality of that help, contributes to the lack of cooperation mentioned here.

commitment to servicing older blacks and Puerto
Ricans. The suggestion was widely voiced that such
a program continued to exist only because ETNA's
Board Chairman was a fairly powerful, established
community leader and the Corporation did not wish
to engage him in a struggle.* Generally, then, the
activities of this program clearly appeared to be
nonrelevant to the large majority of the Tremont
community, and consequently ETNA possessed little
opportunity for increasing the influence of sizable
numbers of the poor in the area.

The program activities of the Naval Cadets included sports and games; classes in mathematics,
English, leadership, and band; arts and crafts, and
group counseling. This Agency's primary function,
in the eyes of both the personnel and the parents
of the young clients, appeared to be keeping the
boys off the streets and occupied in constructive
activities. While apparently successful in terms
of the various activities undertaken, Naval Cadets
was rendered quite ineffectual by the announcement
from the city-wide bureaucracy early in Program
Year "E" that in the upcoming year the Recreation
program function was to be eliminated from the community action program. Thus, throughout the year
under study, the personnel of this Agency appeared
to be primarily concerned with finding new jobs for
themselves, rather than building up the Cadets'
constituency and program.

Economic Development Programs

The two programs in the area of Economic Development, Elsmere Tenants Council and West Farms
Villagers, like ETNA and Naval Cadets, were primarily involved in the distribution of services. Actually neither of these groups had requested funds
for programs in this area, and were clearly not prepared in terms of skills or personnel to operate

---

*Support for this contention was found in the
examination of the actual operation of the funding
process, which is discussed in Chapter 6.

effective Economic Development activities. Elsmere,
while essentially continuing its most ineffectual
1968/69 program in the area of Welfare Action, did
make an attempt to establish a Consumer Buying Club
for milk and dairy products, which eventually showed
a profit of $24 a month.[17] The Agency Director and
others in the office often talked about starting a
larger cooperative in a building across the street,
but nothing came of this discussion. In general,
Elsmere appeared afraid to take any significant action, perhaps because their former Director had
turned out to be a police undercover agent. As a
result, most of the personnel of this agency seemed
to be making a conscious effort not to appear militant.

West Farms Villagers, on the other hand, did
not even attempt to undertake any activities in Economic Development--although the Director was involved with the Corporation's Economic Development
Committee in attempting to set up an Economic Development Corporation[18]--maintaining their previous
year's program in Adult Education exactly as before.
This consisted basically of day and evening sessions
in which English as a second language and other subjects leading up to the high school equivalency examination were taught. While the Director claimed
that some 250 persons were reached by the program
annually, there were never more than seven to eight
students to be seen at West Farms at any one time.
In talking with several of these individuals it was
learned that many people in the community were
afraid to come out at night and had no place to
leave their children during the day. When this
point was mentioned to the Agency Director, he replied, "Sure, we can identify and discuss the problems in the area and maybe some solutions, but we
can do very little about them."[19] Thus, the services offered by West Farms Villagers seemed to be
of value only to a very small portion of those in
the Tremont area.

Education Programs

Those Agencies that, during Program Year "E,"
were officially approved for programs in the area

of Education were United Bronx Parents and Bronx
Community Self-Improvement Association (Bronco-SIA).
Little can be said about the activities of UBP,
since repeated observation confirmed that this program was, for any practical purpose, totally inoperative in the Tremont area during the year under consideration. While the Director of the Agency was a
woman with fair educational qualifications, the
Agency was really under the control of a different
woman who was extremely active in both educational
and community action politics on a city-wide level,
but who had no real contacts with the Tremont community itself. Thus, the resources of the Agency
were never applied toward improving the condition
of local residents. The following remarks from the
Corporation's evaluations appear to provide an accurate description of United Bronx Parents:

> This agency remains no more than a
> controlled satellite, dependent upon
> the "director-in-absentia," Mrs. A.
> It is difficult to identify United
> Bronx Parents as our own community
> agency, geared to the needs and spe-
> cific desires of this community. The
> numbers of participants serviced, ser-
> vices rendered, and materials and sup-
> plies utilized do not justify the
> amount of budget expenditures.[20]

Concerning the second Agency in this program
category, Bronco-SIA, once again little can be said.
During the program year the budget for this program
was suspended by the Community Development Agency
when it was discovered that payroll funds were being appropriated by the Director for her personal
activities, rather than for those of the agency.
From what information was available, primarily
through the Evaluation Specialist, it appears as
though even prior to the suspension nothing in the
way of community activities was undertaken by this
group, and that the Agency office was used primarily as a social club. While it was rumored in the
community that Bronco was a "tough group" with "black
radicals" in it,[21] this could not be confirmed since

at the time of this study the program was no longer
in operation.

Housing Programs

The final program category that needs to be examined is that of Tenant Information or Housing Action in which programs were sponsored by three Agencies: Washington Avenue Neighborhood Association
(WANA), East Tremont Action Committee (ETAC), and
Tremont Housing Clinic (THC). It was in this category that the only significant attempts at organization of group action were observed, and thus
these three agencies should be looked at in greater
detail.

The first of these, WANA, appeared to be the
weakest in terms of actual results obtained. Nevertheless, from their rather well-kept records, a
fairly detailed listing of the services and activities undertaken during Program Year "E" can be obtained. These included contacting officials to remove abandoned cars in the area; obtaining information for tenants regarding rents and rent increases;
contacting landlords about tenant complaints concerning painting, plumbing, garbage, lighting, etc.;
and lastly, attempting to organize tenant strikes in
certain buildings in the area. In the eyes of the
Agency personnel, the first three activities yielded
better results than the last one,* and then only after much harassing of officials, landlords, and
housing administrators. They seemed to be depressed
because there was so little they could accomplish in
view of the strict limitations their budget placed
on their activities, and saw themselves as merely
providing a helping hand to a few individuals. The
idea was totally discounted that, through their activities, they were helping to make housing institutions such as the Rent Control Office, Department of
Buildings, or Housing and Development Administration

---

*While not expressed, the reason for this ap-
peared to be that none of WANA's personnel were
trained or experienced in community organization or
group action.

more responsive to the poor. In their monthly reports to the Corporation the idea was frequently expressed that without a much larger-scale program such established institutions could not really be affected.[22]

ETAC, while in agreement with these sentiments, appeared to have a much more experienced staff, and consequently, a generally higher rate of success in undertaking activities similar to those of WANA. The Director was a former Building Inspector for the City and was able to get around quite well in the massive housing bureaucracy. Both he and his staff attempted to shun administering of individual services in favor of organizing rent strikes and tenant associations to take over abandoned buildings in the area; planning and staging demonstrations by area residents at City Hall and other agencies to protest unsafe buildings; and attempting to organize certain buildings into cooperative apartments. Some of these activities appeared to have been successful. For example, agency records indicated that in April of 1970, ETAC sponsored a series of demonstrations at the Neighborhood City Hall Office on Arthur Avenue, which eventually resulted in the City's declaring an abandoned building a fire hazard and having it demolished.[23] However, others suffered because of a lack of funds to keep them going, most notably the cooperative apartment movement, which was grounded when neither the Agency nor the tenants themselves were able to put up even minimal funds for the down payment on buildings.

The personnel, while enthusiastic about their activities, seemed to feel a definite lack of responsiveness on the part of the housing bureaucracy. For example, many complaints were heard that the Buildings Department and Rent Control Offices often would not send out building inspectors at the Agency's request, "so we frequently lose before we get started."[24] It was felt that a massive campaign needed to be undertaken to educate the community to the tactics of group confrontation so that the Agency's program would have more impact in the Tremont area. As one community organizer employed by ETAC noted during an informal conversation, "In the last few years about 28 of our 70 rent strikes were

partially or totally successful but then nothing
much happened. The people come for help, get
strikes and help, and then forget us, 'till the
next time. They seem to be afraid to really stand
up and get organized and think they'll be taken to
court or thrown out of their apartment."[25]

Despite such difficulties, ETAC was unquestion-
ably the best organized, the most action-oriented,
and consequently the most successful in attempting
to bring about influence for area residents, of any
of the Delegate Agency programs observed in the Tremont area. Nevertheless, it should be noted that
the degree of success that they experienced could
undoubtedly have been enhanced had they united and
pooled resources with the other agencies also working in the housing area. Interagency competition
and rivalry for clients and success stories, as was
seen in the case of the four Manpower Outreach programs, appeared to prevent this.[26]

The third agency in this program category, Tremont Housing Clinic,* from all appearances stood
somewhere between WANA and ETAC in results obtained
from the same kind of activities as those undertaken
by the other two Housing Action agencies. The Director of THC was an extremely competent and active
young woman who was eager to get the community organized and involved in group-action activities.
However, the Agency staff was totally untrained in
this regard, and apparently unable to act without
specific instructions from the Director. As a result, the Agency's quite detailed records showed
numerous examples of totally unsuccessful attempts
at meaningful action.[27] Some evidence of success
in the area of providing services to individuals
with housing problems was available, but even here,
it appeared that such success was almost always a
result of the energy and determination of the Director herself and came only after time-consuming strug-
gles with various offices in the housing bureaucracy.

---

*The Board of Directors of the Tremont Housing
Clinic was called the Tremont Little League, which
caused many people unfamiliar with the program to
believe baseball to be its main activity.

The following rather lengthy account of one such
struggle is included in its entirety because it
captures so well the frustrations and the costs of
even minor victories in the area of Housing Action.[28]
In addition, it points out clearly the serious limitations of all the Delegate Agencies in bringing
about meaningful change for the poor, no matter how
sincere or dedicated the employees.

This particular incident began with the attempt
by Tremont Housing Clinic to restore heat, hot water,
gas, and electricity to a building in the immediate
vicinity. In this quest the Director's report indicated that she had called the following persons:

1. Mr. B., Assistant Chief Inspector of Buildings, Bronx, 1932 Arthur Avenue; "He said that there
was nothing he could do";

2. Emergency Repairs-Project Rescue; "There
was nothing they could do because of the vacate order on the building";

3. Mr. W., Public Relations, Department of
Buildings; "He said that he would see what he could
do";

4. Mr. S., Bronx Borough President's Office;
"He said that he would see what he could do";

5. Mr. K., Bronx Little City Hall; "He didn't
think that there was anything he could do";

6. Mayor's Task Force; "They said that they
would get in touch with the Assistant Commissioner
who may be able to do something."

Subsequently, the report noted that "Late Mon-
day afternoon [two weeks later] the electricity and
some gas service was restored but I am not sure who
was responsible for this success."

One of the families in this building, a welfare mother with ten children, had to be relocated
because of the recurring problem with essential
services. It was decided to move the family into
a hotel, and the following steps were taken:

1. Mr. G. of the Department of
Relocation got space for her family
in the Concourse Plaza Hotel in the
Bronx.

2. No provision is made to help
the family move so once again myself

and co-workers helped this family to
move with all the belongings which
could be used in a hotel.

3. The primary problem was that
there would be no place to put the
furniture which this family owns. At
one time it was the Welfare Department
who was responsible to get furniture
in storage but they no longer handle
it, as I was to find out.

4. I called Mrs. R's caseworker
to see if some arrangements could be
made for the furniture. I spoke to
about three persons all of whom had
no idea what I was talking about. I
then called the Director of the Crotona Branch. His secretary said that
she would bring up the problem and
would call me back.

5. I was called by a Mr. K., the
Assistant Director, who at the time
informed me that everything was all
set and that I should call private
storage companies to make arrangements for the furniture. He informed
me that the Department of Social Services would pay for the storage when
Mrs. R. went to pick up her possessions.

6. I was a bit confused that I was
asked to do this rather than her caseworker but to insure that it got done
I began calling storage companies. I
called over five before I got one company to agree to pick up the furniture.
It became obvious that most storage
companies will have nothing to do with
a welfare client's furniture. Kinder-
man Storage located at 2165 Jerome
Avenue agreed to take the furniture
as long as they got a letter from the
caseworker stating that the Department
of Social Services would be responsible
for the bill.

7. I called Mr. K. informing him
that a letter was necessary and he

said that he would call or write a
letter. I reiterated that a letter
was requested and our conversation
ended.

   8. The next day, I called Kinder-
man Storage to confirm the transaction
and to confirm the pick-up date which
was the following day. (During these
two days Mrs. R. and her oldest boy
slept in the apartment to protect
their belongings.) Mr. B., the one
with whom I had been making these arrangements, said he had been called
and the arrangements had not gone
through. A Mr. Y. had called him and
when Mr. B. asked for the letter, Mr.
Y. said that he had no authority to
send one and that in fact, no one had
the authority to send one. I asked
Mr. B. to please not stop the pick-up
order, at least until closing that
evening. He agreed.

   9. I went to the Department of
Social Services to speak to Mr. K.
Mr. Y. joined us. I could not take
notes of that meeting so the following is from memory. Mr. Y. confirmed
that he had spoken to Mr. B. and that
he had asked for a letter. Mr. Y. then
told me that a letter could not be
written because it would constitute a
contract without the Department knowing what the final bill would be.
Mr. B. could not give him an estimate
because he had not seen the amount of
furniture involved. That morning Mr.
Y. wrote a memo to someone downtown
(he could not divulge to whom) which
would arrive there sometime that afternoon. The memo was detailed in ex-
plaining the problem but Mr. Y. informed me, unofficially, that it was
extremely doubtful that approval
would come through for the furniture
to be stored. I was then unofficially

told that it would be beneficial to
pull any strings possible. The situation was difficult because they could
not tell me who would make the final
decision. Divulging that kind of information is against Department policy.
As a side note it is interesting to
add that the memo had references to
the Bureau of Encumbrances stating
that when furniture is stored by them
it is often never seen again. Also
the Bureau can only store for 30 days
and then furniture is put up for auc-
tion. Thirty days in the case of Mrs.
R. was not nearly enough time.

10. I called the Bronx Borough
President's Office to find out if they
had any contacts powerful enough to
help get that memo approved. They
said they would see what they could do.

11. I called the Washington office
of Congressman Gilbert as 1915 Daly
[the building] is located in his district. The secretary who answered
took all the information and said that
they would do what they could.

12. At 4:30 that afternoon I received a call from Mr. B. saying that
he had been given the go-ahead and
that the furniture would be picked up.
I also received a call from the Borough President's office confirming
this.

As in the case of getting the
lights and gas turned back on, I am
not sure who was finally responsible
for this success.

At this point there are still
families living in 1915 Daly Avenue
who have not been relocated into
apartments and will not go to hotels
because of the problems involved with
the furniture. I have since found
out that there is another serious

problem involved here. Once a family
moves to a hotel, which can be necessary in terms of safety to lives,
they are no longer eligible for the
priority lists in the projects. In
other words, their only way out is to
stay where they are or to lie to the
Public Housing Interviewer and state
that they still live in a vacate order building. In the case of Mrs. R.
this problem has become a reality.
If Mrs. R. does get into a project it
would be in the strictest sense of the
word, a miracle--it just doesn't happen for large families. In several
days she will have another burden to
face. The Concourse Plaza Hotel will
not allow her family to stay there
for longer than 30 days. This is the
time when the Department of Relocation
closes her case and no longer pays the
bill. It will then be up to the Department of Social Services to relo-
cate her and to pay the hotel bills.
Because they have been negligent in
the past the hotel cannot afford to
let her stay there. Her family will
be moved again into a more inferior
and run down place--often places of
ill repute in terms of drugs and pros-
titution. She may be forced to live
in these conditions for many months.
The case of 1915 Daly Avenue is not
closed but in a sense it is, because
the system in which we work has made
it a hopeless case and that can be
very much the same as a closed case.

Frustrated by such lengthy and relatively insignificant activities, through which the Housing
Action program's potential for serving as a vehicle
for influence were "reduced to zero," the Director
of THC finally went outside the community action
structure and joined with the Bronx Housing Crisis

Coalition, an angry ad hoc coalition of militant
community and church groups. Previous to one of
the Coalition's demonstration activities, a widely
publicized parade down 149th Street from the Grand
Concourse in the Bronx,[29] the Director related that
she received several phone calls from the Community
Development Agency threatening her with loss of her
Directorship if any violence issued from the parade
or if she utilized THC in any way in this regard.
This, together with her year-long experiences with
the community action program in Tremont, led her,
in a private conversation, to make the following
observations:

> If one tries to get the community or-
> ganized and make waves, then CDA low-
> ers the boom, takes away your job,
> and finds more agreeable replacements.
> Let's face it, rather than confronta-
> tion, CDA's strategy seems to be to by-
> pass the established agencies who have
> power and encourage the Corporation to
> get control of their own service agen-
> cies. And I guess that's okay as long
> as local people are responsive to their
> own kind--which I doubt, since it's
> usually the "poor" with middle-class
> mentalities who get the top jobs and
> run the show.[30]

From what has been seen concerning the functioning of the 13 Delegate Agencies in the Tremont
poverty area, this statement appears to serve as a
most accurate conclusion.

CONCLUSIONS: SUMMARY IN TERMS
OF INDICATORS

The most significant data resulting from the
observation of the operation of the Delegate Agencies and the Tremont Community Corporation itself,
as well as from the analysis of program resources
undertaken, may now be summarized in terms of the

major variables that have been posited as indicators
of influence and social control outputs for the purpose of this study. Before presenting the data that
provide evidence for the occurrence or its lack, of
the study's six most significant variables (separateness and separation, collaboration and containment, bargaining and resocialization), it may be
noted that the observational phase of the research
yielded very little data that would allow us to
conclude that the community action program in Tremont resulted in establishing to any significant
degree the participants' "capability of influence"
as the term has been defined by William Gamson.
Rather, from the examination of program resources
and the functioning of the Community Corporation,
it was concluded that very little technical assistance was available to the Delegate Agencies from
either the Corporation or the city-wide bureaucracy.
Likewise, the minimal funds received for program
implementation and the generally poor quality of
personnel appeared to further undermine their potential for undertaking successful "influence attempts." Thus, on the basis of the data resulting
from this partial utilization of Gamson's "influence attempts" approach to the measurement of this
key concept, we may state that the overall program
in the Tremont area could not be accurately described as an "influence output."

Turning now to our six major variables, we
draw the following conclusions: (Because of the
closely parallel operational definitions that have
been constructed for the study, the variables of
separateness and separation, and those of collaboration and containment are here considered together.)

1. Separateness and separation: Examination
of the resources and actual functioning of the program's neighborhood level units failed to uncover
any evidence of the growth of feelings of separate-
ness--in the sense of poor identity, ethnic identity,
coalitional ethnic identity, or interest group iden-
tity--as a result of the program. While this may
well have been because the observational methods
employed in this phase of the research were not
well suited to the measurement of the important

psychological dimensions inherent in this variable, evidence was, however, uncovered for the occurrence of separation. Specifically, through the examination of the functioning of the Corporation's Board of Directors, Executive Director, Staff, and representative to the Council Against Poverty, it was discovered that both antagonistic ethnic identity and fragmented interest group identity were being fostered through the Tremont program. With regard to the latter concept, it is particularly significant that the various neighborhood level units of the community action program were not functioning as a coherent whole, either among themselves or with the city-wide bureaucracy. Additional evidence of this was provided in the observation of the almost total lack of cooperation among Delegate Agencies with similar program functions (in particular, among the four Manpower Outreach agencies and the three agencies in the category of Housing Action). Thus, such data as were obtained through this phase of the research pointed in the direction of the social control variable, separation, as opposed to the influence variable of separateness.

2. Collaboration and containment: The data that provided the most precise evidence of these two variables were obtained through the observation and examination of the individual Delegate Agency programs. Here it was seen that the majority of such programs could not be characterized as relevant, successful, and effective, either in terms of the provision of social services or through the organization of group action. Specifically, two of the 13 agencies, United Bronx Parents (UBP) and Bronco-SIA, were almost totally inoperative in the Tremont area during Program Year "E"; while a third, Elsmere Tenants Council, appeared to be functioning only minimally. Naval Cadets, an Agency whose youth program had apparently enjoyed a fair measure of success in the past, was in the process of being phased out and was thus rendered quite ineffectual; while ETNA's Senior Citizens program serviced a very limited group of area residents and was generally regarded as nonrelevant and isolated in terms of the community at large.

Finally, three of the Agencies in the category
of Manpower Outreach--TCC, Federation of Puerto
Rican Volunteers, and Monterey Community Associa-
tion--experienced very little success in obtaining
employment or any other meaningful assistance for
its clients. The operations of these eight Delegate Agencies, then, point quite clearly to a policy
of containment within the area's community action
program insofar as such nonrelevant, unsuccessful,
and ineffective programs were sanctioned and for
the most part allowed to continue operating unas-
sisted by the city-wide community action bureaucracy.
Significantly, these eight Agencies provided very
little threat to existing controlling institutions,
and no indication whatsoever that the stated goals
of advocacy planning and action, forcing the institutions that service poor people to be more responsive to their needs, or instilling a sense of power
to those who once were powerless were being achieved.
Neither did they appear to be setting up the type
of social service programs that could be expected
to result in the development of a strong constituency among the poor and thus in their increased influence at a later time.

Three other Delegate Agencies--WFV, which operated primarily in the area of Education; and WANA
and THC in the category of Housing Action--appeared
to possess the potential for building up meaningful
and effective service programs--and thus for the
occurrence of collaboration--even though at the
time of the study their services were reaching only
a relatively small proportion of area residents.
All of these Agencies were hindered in their activities by a lack of resources, particularly skilled
and experienced personnel; but nevertheless, were
attempting to offer the type of services that would
seem to have broad appeal in the Tremont area.

Only two Agencies--the National Association of
Puerto Rican Affairs (NAPRA), operating in the area
of Manpower Outreach; and ETAC in the field of Housing Action--could be said to have indicated some
meaningful degree of collaboration during Program
Year "E," since the programs sanctioned by the community action bureaucracy and operated by these

Agencies appeared to have experienced a rather high
degree of success--NAPRA, in the provision of needed
manpower services; and ETAC in organizing group or
collective action activities at correcting housing
problems in the area. In the case of NAPRA, in particular, however, it appeared that such success was
a function of its affiliation with its own city-wide
structure of agencies rather than an affiliation
with the community action program itself.

On the basis of the observational data obtained
with respect to the variables of collaboration and
containment, the social control variable once again
appeared to be significantly more operative in the
Tremont program during the period under consideration.

3. Bargaining: In reviewing the data obtained
from examining the functioning of the 13 Delegate
Agencies, it was seen that only one, ETAC, had, to
any significant extent, utilized collective action
to engage a dominant target system (landlords and
housing institutions), bringing about outcomes
favorable to the poor, and thus fulfilling the operational definition constituted for this influence
variable. The other two Agencies in the area of
Housing Action, WANA and THC, evidenced some few
bargaining attempts, but without any real measure
of success. Finally, the bargaining that did take
place during Program Year "E" was totally one-step
bargaining, involving no cooperation among Delegate
Agencies. On the basis of this variable, the observational phase of the study yielded very little
data in support of the occurrence of influence as a
result of the Tremont community action program.

4. Resocialization: While the methods employed in this phase of the research were unable
to uncover program participants' value and behavioral orientations--and thus whether or not a process of resocialization was at work within the Tremont program--some evidence was obtained regarding
the community action bureaucracy's enforcement of
acceptable values and behavior on the part of program personnel, most notably in the case of the
Tremont Housing Clinic's action-minded Director.
The process of creaming or exemption, which was

seen to be operative within the Manpower Center, provides some soft evidence of the importance for program clients, as well, to present acceptable images
in order to qualify for certain services.

The resources and actual functioning of the
various units of the community action program in
Tremont indicate that such a program can be best
described as a social control output, rather than
one of influence.

The role of the community action bureaucracy
in structuring, assisting, and guiding the program
in Tremont needs to be more closely examined in order to determine whether the bureaucracy is an advocate of the poor on the neighborhood level, as it
claims to be, or whether its real interest lies
with controlling, buying off, and keeping the poor
quiet. It may be noted that the Council Against
Poverty and particularly the Community Development
Agency provided no meaningful assistance to those
programs which were attempting confrontation with
established, controlling institutions. Neither did
they work to correct program malfunctioning. Despite their stated intentions, our examination of
the operation of the community action program on
the neighborhood level suggests that the bureaucratic agencies did not actually fulfill the advocacy role assumed in their own guidelines and program mandates--in the sense of encouraging and assisting either the operation of relevant and potentially powerful social service programs by the poor
themselves, or the organization of large-scale collective actions.

For further insight we turn to the remaining
data gathered during the first phase of the study,
which resulted from a detailed examination of the
operation of the funding process, a process through
which the crucial relationships between the bureaucracy and the program's neighborhood level units
may be much more clearly seen.

CHAPTER

6

OBSERVATIONAL
DATA II:
THE FUNDING PROCESS
IN OPERATION

The data presented in Chapter 5 concerned the
operation of the units of the community action program in the Tremont poverty area during Program Year
"E" (October 1, 1969-September 30, 1970), and were
obtained primarily through observation of the program during much of that year. Our concern in the
present chapter is to view in detail the decision-
making process through which the neighborhood level
program is structured, prior to actual operation,
by the local Community Corporation and especially
the community action bureaucracy. The data that
are presented here were gathered primarily through
participating in this process as an advisor to the
Tremont Community Corporation Proposal Committee,
which was active from early April of 1970 to late
June of 1970. From July through mid-September, all
additional stages of the funding cycle were observed
by special permission of the Council Against Poverty
and the Community Development Agency. Consequently,
the major decisions that will be discussed are those
concerning the structuring of the community action
program in Tremont for Program Year "F," October 1,
1970-September 30, 1971. Since this program year
falls outside the time period with which this study
is concerned, our focus in reviewing the funding
process in operation should not be so much on the
content of the decisions that were made as on the
procedures in reaching those decisions, procedures
which are applicable to each neighborhood level

118

program for any program year. Specifically, our aim
here is to examine the role of the community action
bureaucracy vis-à-vis the Tremont community so as
to decide whether the bureaucracy is functioning
primarily as an advocate of the poor, or as an agent
of social control.

YOUTH DEVELOPMENT PROGRAMS: ACCOUNT 59

The operations of the Tremont Community Corporation Proposal Committee got off to a rather late
start in undertaking its major work in 1970 because
of a chaotic situation brought about by OEO's announcement in early February of new and much strict-
er guidelines for the involvement of youth in the
summer programs operated by Community Corporations.[1]
Up to this point little mention has been made of the
summer programs, mainly because such short-term,
three-month activities generally had little impact
on the community, and because they did not receive
much attention from either the community action
bureaucracy or the Corporation itself.* However,
this situation changed abruptly with the announcement of the new guidelines for Youth Development
Programs. In brief, these mandated the elimination
of the summer-only programs funded by community action monies, in favor of a small number of year-
round programs aimed specifically at the youth of
the poverty area. Since during the summer of 1969
14 summer programs had been funded in Tremont, and
an even larger number of sponsors had already submitted proposals for the summer of 1970, the new
policy met with an angry reaction in this area, as
well as in poverty areas throughout the City. As a
result, the New York City community action bureaucracy set up an Umbrella Project through which the
Community Corporations could "alleviate the community

---

*"Impact" is here used in the sense of result-
ing in meaningful and relevant programs. Many
critics of these programs contend that the main impact is one of cooling off the community.

tension created by the new approach for Youth Services Programs."[2]   As explained in a report to the
Tremont Community Corporation Board of Directors
prepared by the Chairlady of the Proposal Committee,

> This project is designed to ease the
> transition from a short-term program
> with many sponsors to a more stable on-
> going program with fewer sponsors.
> This Corporation Umbrella Program will
> allow the sponsors, who are not chosen
> to operate youth programs, to receive
> some assistance and carry out a few
> selected activities.[3]

In late March the Community Development Agency
announced that the Tremont Corporation would receive
an operating budget of $72,726 to fund summer pro-
grams--for a final time--under the Umbrella Project,
and a total of $209,797 under Program Account 59 to
cover three year-round youth programs ($64,604 to be
used during the summer months of 1970, and $145,193
for operations during Program Year "F").[4]
During the next two months there was much confusion and bickering within the Corporation and the
Tremont community itself, as a large number of sponsors (most of whom were already operating Delegate
Agency programs) hurriedly prepared program proposals
and jockeyed for part of these funds. At the end, a
total of 21 proposals had been submitted for the
three new youth programs alone. The actual procedures used by both the Corporation and the community
action bureaucracy in deciding how the Umbrella
Project funds would be allocated were obscured in
the rush and chaos of the entire process. The Program Account No. 59 proposals, on the other hand,
followed the regular--although somewhat abbrevi-
ated--cycle of decision-making, involving the Corporation Staff, Proposal Committee, and Board of
Directors as well as both agencies of the city-wide
bureaucracy, as was outlined in ideal form in Chapter 3.* Concern with these proposals took up most

---

*For our purposes the content of these deci-
sions have little significance since those programs

of the Proposal Committee's time during April and
May, and thus it was not until mid-June that the
Committee turned its attention to the regular pro-
gram proposals for Program Year "F."

YEAR-ROUND PROGRAMS

The proposals taken up for consideration by the
Committee at its first year-round meeting on June
18th were themselves the result of some measure of
confusion and chaos in the Tremont community, which
should be briefly reviewed so that the complete
cycle of the funding process may be seen. As with
each program year, this cycle began with the Federal
Office of Economic Opportunity. For Program Year
"F" no major changes were initiated by OEO, so the
general community action guidelines remained the
same as in the previous year. However, the specific
guidelines for the New York City program did undergo
some fairly significant reformulations at the hands
of the CDA and the CAP.

Perhaps most importantly, to the 1969/70 goals
that established CAP as an advocate of the poor, and
called for neighborhood level programs aimed at
bringing about increased institutional responsiveness to the needs of the poor, was added the goal of
"moving minority group members to employment placement in established city agencies."[5]

---

funded under the Umbrella Project generally continued the summer program tradition of low community impact, while none of the three Account No. 59
programs were really operative by the end of Program Year "E." However, without going into detail,
it should be noted that the decision-making procedures utilized and observed with respect to the Account No. 59 proposals were almost identical to
those later observed in conjunction with the regular year-round proposals for Program Year "F."
Most importantly, the results of this first observation provide additional support to the conclusions
concerning the role of the bureaucracy in the total
community action program, as will be formulated at
the end of this chapter.

This specifically involved increased coordination of the community action program with previously existing social service institutions in the various poverty areas in order to "better service low-income communities."[6]   Thus, somewhat of a shift may be noted from Program Year "E"'s stated confrontation goals of changing established institutions to employment goals in established agencies for Program Year "F."

One further policy change emanating from the city-wide bureaucracy involved setting up a stipend of $25 per month for expense allowances for each member of the Board of Directors of the 26 Community Corporations. The stated purpose of this new policy was to attempt to stimulate wider participation of the Board members in activities undertaken by the Corporations, but undoubtedly aimed at correcting the widespread problem of nonattendance at Board meetings.[7]

By mid-May these new guidelines, together with the bureaucracy's priorities for Delegate Agency programs, were sent out to the various Community Corporations throughout the City. Twenty-seven program categories were spelled out and grouped into four divisions: mandated, recommended, acceptable, and disallowable programs. Included in the guidelines were detailed descriptions of the objectives and recommended activities for each of the mandated and recommended program categories, all of which represented very little change from Program Year "E."[8]

COMMUNITY MEETINGS ON PROGRAM GUIDELINES

Upon receiving the guidelines from CAP-CDA, the Chairman of the Tremont Corporation Board of Directors called a meeting to discuss the new policies and decide how these should be made known to the Tremont community. Neither this meeting, nor two others, ever took place, since a quorum of Board members failed to show up. However, several informal meetings of the Executive Director, the Chairman of the Board, and the area representative to the Council Against Poverty were held, at which

decisions were made to run the Corporation through
the Executive Committee until the Board could as-
semble a sufficient number of members, and to hold
three public meetings throughout the poverty area
for the purpose of informing the community about
the guidelines for Delegate Agency programs for
year "F." These meetings were scheduled for the
end of May and the first week of June; however,
none of the three ever materialized as a total of
only eight or nine persons attended. Although the
Executive Director and other Corporation officials
blamed the extremely low participation on community
apathy, it seems much more reasonable to conclude
that such a turnout was due to an almost complete
lack of publicity about the meetings. Notices were
sent out to the existing Delegate Agencies, which
apparently kept the meetings secret to ward off new
competition for funds.

Finally, on June 9, a last-attempt meeting was
held at Public School 59 that was attended by about
30 people, almost all of whom were familiar faces
in the Tremont program. The Executive Director of
the Corporation chaired the meeting, explained the
program priorities issued by the city-wide bureaucracy and announced that the deadline for submitting
program proposals would be June 15. Many complaints
were raised that such a deadline did not allow
enough time to work up a good proposal, particularly
for those programs not currently in operation. In
response, the Director of the CDA District Office
who attended the meeting agreed to make available
to the community some model programs drawn up by
the bureaucracy, and stated that "If you don't have
time to write up your own proposal, use the model
programs and just sign the forms."[9]

Two days later, on June 11, the Corporation
acquired a few copies of these model programs, all
of which were in the mandated categories. From
then until June 15 utter confusion reigned in the
Corporation Office as the various program sponsors
fought over the use of the few copies available and
demanded information that no one seemed prepared to
give out. Both the Corporation and CDA District
Office Staffs were on hand, ostensibly to lend

technical assistance in the preparation of program
proposals, but mainly they contributed to the confusion by giving contradictory answers to questions
raised by the sponsors. This chaotic situation was
further aggravated because, according to bureaucracy
mandates, each program sponsor was required to submit 20 copies of his proposal and the duplicating
facilities of the Corporation were not operating
during that week. The impression emerged during
these several days that the procedures of drawing
up program proposals set down by the bureaucracy
were hardly designed to encourage widespread community participation as all but the most determined
sponsors gave up in disgust. Certainly the overwhelming amount of paperwork required served only
to further compound the obstacles and confusion,
and little if any attention was able to be directed
to the actual content of the proposed program itself. But perhaps the most depressing aspect of
the situation was the widespread assumption that
the very act of submitting proposals was a mere for-
mality since they would never really be considered.
One Corporation official stated quite openly that
"L. and N. (the two top officials of the CDA District Office) and everybody else at CDA already
knows who will get the money--we're just going
through the formalities."[10] And as one depressed
and tired Delegate Agency Director put it, "We have
no say in the priorities, in the program content,
or in who gets funded here in Tremont. Big community participation!"[11]

CORPORATION'S PROPOSAL COMMITTEE MEETINGS

Between June 15 and 18, the proposals that had
been submitted were in the hands of the Executive
Office, and from all indications no one on the Corporation Staff was given the opportunity or time to
review and evaluate them to any sufficient degree.
Nevertheless, on the evening of June 18 the Director appeared at the meeting of the Proposal Committee to present the recommendations of the Corporation Staff.

The first order of business at the Committee
meeting was a detailed explanation by a CDA District
Office official of the estimated total budget for
the Tremont poverty area in Program Year "F," and
the CAP-CDA priorities for budgetary allocations.
These priorities called for 20 percent of the area's
total budget to be allocated for Education programs,
15 percent for Housing programs, 15 percent for Manpower Outreach, and 10 percent for Economic Development, with the remaining 40 percent going to the
operation of the Community Corporation itself. It
is interesting to note that all four program categories mentioned fall within the mandated division,
thus raising the question of exactly how those programs labeled as merely recommended or acceptable
could ever be included in an area's overall program.
However, no one on the Proposal Committee questioned
this matter, the general feeling seeming to be that
it was safer to stay with mandated programs anyway.

A summary of the program proposals submitted
to the Corporation was then presented by the Executive Director who focused the greatest amount of attention on a proposal that he himself was sponsoring. This proposal called for setting up, in a recently vacated YMHA building, a multiservice Center,
offering a wide range of services to children of all
ages. While the central administration of the East
Tremont Childhood and Youth Development Center would,
according to the proposal, fall under the Tremont
Community Corporation, the plan was for the facility
to attract a number of established agencies in the
fields of health, day care, youth recreation, etc.,
into the area, each of which would then provide
their special service through the Center. The potential for the Center to attract funds from a number of sources outside the community action program
was especially stressed.[12] However, it was estimated that approximately $80,000 in community ac-
tion funds would be needed initially to activate it.
And since this type of multiservice center fell outside the four priority program categories, the Executive Director clearly saw the need to juggle these
around in some fashion so as to free some funds for
the Center. He recommended that the allocation for

Education programs be cut back "on behalf of the
Staff" since the Board's "Education Committee can
assume much of this work anyway."[13] He also suggested that the Corporation's allocation be cut
back from 40 percent to 25 percent of the total budget, and that these funds be applied to the Center.
Others at the meeting countered that if such a cut
were made the freed funds should be applied to Manpower Outreach programs since there were already
four manpower agencies among which only 15 percent
of the total budget would have to be divided. To
this the CDA District Office official replied that
a stronger justification should be used in arguing
the case, and suggested that increased unemployment
in the area be stressed in seeking to raise the Manpower Outreach allocation.

    After much debate, which continued over two
subsequent meetings of the Proposal Committee, the
recommendations of the Executive Director were endorsed by the Committee, that 11 Delegate Agencies
and the multiservice center be funded. The overall
decisions of the Proposal Committee may be seen in
Columns 5-8 of Table 6.1. In evaluating these decisions several significant points should be mentioned. First of all, at no time during the delib-
eration of the Proposal Committee did Committee members actually read the submitted proposals. There
was apparently total agreement with the Executive
Director when he stated that, "There's no need to
read them since they're the same as the models and
few of them are innovative."[14] Secondly, throughout
the discussions that occurred at the Proposal Committee meetings, vague and often directly contradictory reasoning was used in arguing for either acceptance or rejection of a specific proposal. In one
case (UBP), a bad evaluation was used as a rationale
for cutting a program; in another (ETNA), where an
even worse evaluation rating had been recorded, the
agency was kept in. In rejecting one newly proposed
program (Fordham-Tremont), it was noted that "it has
no previous record"; yet another new program (NEED)
was recommended for funding.

    Thirdly, as can be seen from comparing Columns
2 and 7 of Table 6.1, the Tremont Community Council

was changed from a Manpower Outreach program to an Education program, since the manpower funds were tight and yet many obviously wanted this agency to remain in the overall program. This gives a fairly good indication of the insignificant nature of the program proposals from the viewpoint of actual content. Finally, a vast discrepancy often existed between the budget request for a particular program and that recommended by the Committee (see Table 6.1, Columns 4 and 8). Assuming that a sponsor's program proposal and estimated expenses had been well thought out, it is reasonable to conclude that a budget cut of $20,000, $30,000, or, as was the case with Naval Cadets, $70,000, would render the program altogether inoperative. This matter, though, like so many others, was never raised by the Committee members or others in attendance at these meetings.

CORPORATION'S BOARD OF DIRECTORS' MEETINGS

The Committee-approved package of proposals was then passed on to the Tremont Community Corporation Board of Directors for consideration at its June 24 meeting. After a great deal of heated discussion, the recommendations of the Proposal Committee concerning the Delegate Agencies for Program Year "F" were accepted, with the one change that Beck Memorial, a new program, be accepted in place of WFV. The reason given for this substitution was that WFV had not shown during Program Year "E" "any significant signs of meaningful action or success in the area funded, Economic Development."[15] However, since this was the case with so many of the Delegate Agencies, any number of which were recommended for refunding, the Board's action should be interpreted more as a matter of personal antagonisms and community politics than as a decision backed by accurate and impartial evaluation.

The issue of whether the East Tremont Childhood and Youth Development Center should be recommended for funding was held over to another meeting, called for early July. Again, a quorum of Board members failed to show up since, as the

TABLE 6.1

Summary of Key Decisions Made Throughout Funding Cycle on Tremont Area's
Program Proposals for Program Year "F"

		Original Data			Decisions of Tremont Community Corporation Staff and Proposal Committee		
Column 1	Column 2	Column 3	Column 4	Column 5	Column 6	Column 7	Column 8
Sponsor of Proposed Program	Category of Proposed Program	Operating Budget, 1969-70	Requested Budget, 1970-71	Program Accepted	Program Rejected	Category of Program	Approved Budget, 1970-71
1	SC	$ 41,634	$ 65,371	x		no change	$ 40,000
2	MO	41,279	59,683	x		" "	40,000
3	MO	37,927	48,308	x		" "	40,000
4	MO	39,834	70,298	x		" "	40,000
5	HA	43,734	50,896	x		" "	40,000
6	HA	43,025	67,909	x		" "	40,000
7	HA	43,846	56,442	x		" "	40,000
8	ED	36,615	41,780	x		" "	40,000
9	ED	40,098	106,464	x		" "	40,000
10	MO	36,701	44,018	x		EA	40,000
11	EA	41,065	49,047		x		--
12	ED	43,321	58,745		x		--
13	ED	--	65,000	x		no change	40,000
14	AE	--	69,336		x		--
15	ED	--	45,000		x		--
16	Ms	--	80,000	x		no change	80,000
17		151,717	177,210	x		--	177,210
	Total	$679,210[a]					$697,210

[a]Included in this figure was $38,417 used
by Bronco-SIA, which did not submit a proposal
for 1970/71.

[b]These were the final decisions of the Board.
On the first vote taken, WFV was rejected, and
Beck Memorial accepted in its place.

[c]Columns 11-14 represent the final decisions
agreed upon by these three units. Some minor
differences existed originally between the recommendations of the District Office and those of the
CDA Staff. Also, the budgets were prepared almost
totally by the District Office.

[d]NEED was accepted at this stage in place of
WANA, and took over WANA's budget of $46,059.

Decisions of Tremont Community Corporation Board of Directors		Decisions of the Community Development Agency District Office, Staff, and Senior Staff[c]				Decisions of the Council Against Poverty, Tremont Area Panel and CAP		
Column 9	Column 10	Column 11	Column 12	Column 13	Column 14	Column 15	Column 16	Column 17
Program Accepted	Program Rejected	Program Accepted	Program Rejected	Category of Program	Approved Budget	Program Accepted	Program Rejected	Category of Program
x		x		no change	$ 42,625	x		no change
x		x		" "	44,969	x		" "
x		x		" "	42,022	x		" "
x		x		" "	40,237	x		" "
x		x		" "	45,674	x		" "
x		x		" "	45,857	x		" "
x		x		" "	46,059		x[d]	
x[b]		x		" "	44,318	x		no change
x			x̲	" "	--		x	
x		x		ED̲	44,538	x		no change
	x		x̲	no change	42,136	x		" "
	x		x		--		x	
x			x̲		--	x̲[d]		Housing
	x[b]		x		--		x	
	x		x		--		x	
x		x		no change	88,264	x		no change
x		x			170,459	x		" "
					$697,210			

Key for Column 1

1. ETNA
2. Federation
3. Monterey
4. NAPRA
5. THC
6. ETAC
7. WANA
8. WFV
9. Naval Cadets
10. TC Council
11. UBP
12. Elsmere
13. NEED
14. Beck Memorial
15. Ford.-Tremont
16. ETCYD Center
17. Community Corp.

Key for Columns 2, 7, and 13

AE - Adult Education
ED - Economic Development
EA - Education Action
HA - Housing Action
MO - Manpower Outreach
Ms - Multi-service
SC - Senior Citizens

Chairman of the Board expressed it, "These people
are only interested in how the money is distributed.
Once most of that is done, you never see them
again."[16] On July 10, another meeting of the Board
was called to allow for appeals by sponsors whose
program proposals had not been accepted; once again,
this had to be postponed for lack of a quorum. Besides, as it turned out, many of the rejectees were
never notified of the appeals date, which seems to
be the normal pattern in such cases. Finally, on
July 13, the Board of Directors did manage to as-
semble and rather hastily approved the funding of
the Center and the Program Year "F" Corporation budget of $177,210. At the close of the meeting, with
very little explanation, the Board, on the recommendation of the Executive Director, voted to reverse
its decision of June 24 on the matter of WFV and
Beck Memorial. Through private conversations with
key members of the Board it was later learned that
the major factor resulting in WFV's ultimate inclusion was that the area's representative to the CAP
was Chairman of the Board of WFV, and had used his
considerable influence in the community to bring
pressure on the Corporation Board. Some expressed
surprise with the original vote and acknowledged
that it must have been due to a "slip-up" somewhere
along the lines of communication.[17] In any case,
by mid-July, the entire package of proposals and
recommendations had been sent to the CDA District
Office. For the next several weeks, this office
and the city-wide CDA Staff reviewed the package,
developed their own recommendations, and finalized
the budgets for those Delegate Agencies that were
approved for funding, as well as for the Tremont
Community Corporation itself. Meanwhile, on July
18 a lengthy appeals meeting was held at CDA at
which the program sponsors rejected by the Tremont
Corporation Board of Directors, Staff, and Proposal
Committee were invited to voice their complaints.
Following this meeting, one CDA official conceded
privately that, "It really doesn't matter much which
programs get in and which don't--they're all horri-
ble. The goals of the programs aren't realistic at
all and the people who are running them don't know
what they're talking about."[18]

CDA, SENIOR STAFF MEETINGS

On August 12 officials from the District Office and Staff met with the CDA Senior Staff, including the Commissioner and his Assistants, for the purpose of making final the recommendations on the Tremont package that would then be sent to the CAP's appropriate Area Panel. The meeting began with a lengthy discussion of the ETCYD Center, during which the majority opinion appeared quite clearly to be against this project because this outlay of monies would seriously endanger other Delegate Agency programs already minimally funded. However, after allowing this discussion to proceed for a while, the CDA Commissioner spoke out very strongly in favor of the Center, stressing the idea of using the facility to attract additional funds from other sources that would bolster the community action program in the Tremont area. Noting the importance of the Community Corporation's retaining control of the administration of the Center, he added, "It's good to spend one dollar to get ten, just so long as you don't lose control of the dollar."[19] Following the Commissioner's remarks, debate on the Center was cut short, as the other participants in the meeting apparently began operating on the assumption that this matter had been decided, and started making the necessary rearrangements in their own preferences.

Discussion then turned to the matter of individual Delegate Agency programs, over which there was relatively little disagreement. The most significant final decisions that were made, and that can be seen from Columns 11-14 in Table 6.1 were as follows:

1. That 10 Delegate Agency programs be funded for Program Year "F" rather than the 11 recommended by the Tremont neighborhood level units;

2. that Naval Cadets and NEED be dropped in order to secure approximately $88,000 for the ETCYD Center. The reason given for dismissing Naval Cadets was that it did not seem likely that they would be able to function effectively in the category of Economic Development, for which they had applied, since their staff was essentially a

hold-over from their 1969/70 Recreation program.
NEED was apparently recommended for rejection simply
because it was a new program, and was thus easier to
dismiss than any other. (At this point only ongoing
Agencies from Program Year "E" had been accepted for
funding in Year "F.") The decision on NEED, however,
was not unanimous, as the District Office officials
argued unsuccessfully that its proposed Economic Development program seemed much stronger than that of
WFV, which had never achieved anything in this area.
In any case, the decisions on both Naval Cadets and
NEED reversed the recommendations of the Proposal
Committee and Board of Directors in the Tremont
area;

3. that UBP be included in the program. This
decision, too, was contrary to the recommendation
of the neighborhood level units; and the fairly obvious, although unexpressed reason for it was that
the UBP's real Director was a powerful figure in
community action politics;

4. that Tremont Community Council's program,
which had started out in the category of Manpower
Outreach and been changed by the Tremont Proposal
Committee to Education, be switched into the category of Economic Development in order to provide
further strength to this last program category.
This decision seemed to be an admission of the fact
that although WFV's program was quite weak, it
really couldn't be eliminated.

The necessary adjustments were made on the budgets of the approved Delegate Agencies, and confirmed as presented in Column 14 of Table 6.1.

On the day following the Senior Staff meeting,
CDA officials met with the Corporation Executive
Director, Chairman of the Board, and CAP representative from Tremont to explain the changes which the
package had undergone at the hands of the CDA. Although some objections were brought up by the Tremont program officials, this meeting ended with
their acceptance of the CDA recommendations on behalf of the Tremont area.

CAP, TREMONT AREA PANEL MEETINGS

The Tremont Area Panel took up consideration
of the package at its meeting of August 20. The
primary purpose of the meeting was to hear appeals
from sponsors whose programs had been rejected anywhere along the line and in this regard complaints
were first heard from representatives of Elsmere
Tenants Council. However, as had been the case
with at least two prior appeals by this group, the
panel took no action on their complaints. Some discussion then ensued concerning UBP and criticisms
were voiced on its ineffectiveness in the Tremont
community during Program Year "E." However, the
"Director-in-absentia" of UBP was a member of the
Area Panel by virtue of the fact that she also
served as CAP representative from Hunts Point Poverty Area, and thus was on hand to defend her own
program. She countered that UBP functioned much
more effectively than the Tremont Community Corporation itself, and launched into a lengthy attack
on the Executive Director's reputation in the area.
This argument was finally ended when the Area Panel
Chairman succeeded in obtaining the panel's endorse-
ment of a recommendation that had come out of CDA,
that UBP assume the duties of the Corporation Education Specialist and that the latter office be dis-
solved. Those at the meeting appeared satisfied
that this action would guarantee UBP's functioning
as part of the Tremont program during Program Year
"F."

The Chairman of the Tremont Community Corporation Board then spoke at some length concerning the
serious problems that had arisen over the fact that
too many black programs had been cut and warned of
disturbances in the Tremont area if this situation
was not rectified.[20] He strongly recommended that
NEED, a black program, be included in the overall
plan for the coming year, sparking some measure of
discussion on which program would be cut in order
to free funds for NEED's inclusion. Finally, the

Tremont representative to CAP suggested that WANA
was a weak, nonblack program, which had suffered
from "poor administration," and which could be eliminated to make room for NEED. Even though such a
substitution required that NEED's program function
be changed from Economic Development to Housing Action (since NEED would in effect simply assume
WANA's budget), a vote on this was hastily taken
and NEED was in. This represented the only change
from the recommendations of CDA made by the panel
(Columns 15, 16, and 17 in Table 6.1). From the
Area Panel the Tremont package was sent to the full
CAP, and on August 27, this body "rubber-stamped"
the panel's recommendations. Even though the decisions that came out of the Tremont Area Panel were
the final ones on program funding for Program Year
"F," a postscript should be added concerning the appeals process that followed the emergence of the
Tremont package from the Council Against Poverty.
Actually, only one agency, WANA, filed an appeal
during this final stage; however, this case provides
considerable insight into the meaning of the entire
appeals procedures as set up by CAP-CDA.

CAP, APPEALS MEETINGS

Following the August 27 meeting, CAP announced
an appeals meeting that was held on September 24,
at which WANA presented a well-documented statement countering the criticism of their program at
the Area Panel meeting. Some days later, on September 28, having heard of no change in CAP's decision, the Director of WANA sent a desperate letter
to the OEO Regional Director accompanied by a 40-
page detailed report. The bulk of this letter is
reprinted here since it describes so well many aspects of the entire funding process.

> Gentlemen:
>   During the first week of Septem-
> ber, 1970, persistent rumors concern-
> ing our Program and its upcoming Con-
> tract and subsequent funding for

program Y. F., were spread throughout
the Tremont area. The rumors were as
follows: that Washington Ave. Neighborhood Ass. was rejected for funding
and that **NEED**, another Program, a new
one, was recommended as its replace-
ment. These rumors triggered our organization to investigate the matter.
We subsequently found out that the
rumors were not rumors, but in fact,
a reality. We didn't know the reason
for our being rejected and we have
not as yet received any official noti-
fication concerning this matter from
the Tremont Community Corporation,
the CDA or the Council Against Poverty.

We recently learned that our Program was recommended by the Tremont
Community Corporation Board, and by
the CDA for funding, but at a CAP Tremont Panel meeting held on August 20,
1970, we were rejected for some obscure and inadequate reason, "poor
administration," even though we have
a CDA evaluation rating of "A" and a
Tremont Community Corporation rating
of "B."

NEED, the Program used as our re-
placement was denied funds by the CDA
and the Corporation Board while trying to acquire an Economic Development
Program and they have no background of
housing experience.

Without any official communication whatsoever, we managed to present our appeal in the CAP meeting
held on the 24th of September 1970.
Having no possibility of finding out
the outcome, two days before the end
of our Contract, we make this emergency appeal: On the ground that:

1. Obscure, capricious and inadequate reasons for being rejected.

2. We were not officially notified by HRA, CDA, CAP, and the Tremont
Community Corporation in due time
about this decision and were subsequently denied the right of appeal.

3. The legality of the panel decision to reject our Program after the
Tremont Community Board had recommended
it.

4. The invalidity of the alleged
charge of "poor administration": it
is based in an incomplete report concerning administrative irregularities:
(see annexed copies and testimony of
its clearance). It has to be assessed
that the initiative was taken by the
present Director, at the time just
commencing his incumbency.

5. The irregularity of the Panel
decision: in the same Panel WANA was
rejected and NEED was funded: it
shows the intention of sentencing
WANA beforehand, denying the normal
procedure of five days for appeal and
the right to be heard in a special
panel. All of this added to the lack
of any communication. Neither Tremont
Corporation, neither CAP, have re-
ceipts of Telegrams or certified letters.

6. The whole sneaky underhand
way in which this matter was conducted by Mr. S., TCC panel representative: Is an evident connection between NEED and Mr. S; jobs were offered to members of our staff ten days
before the Tremont CAP panel was held
on August 20.[21]

After several follow-up letters, on December
3, WANA finally received a reply from the OEO Regional Director, stating that CAP had been in-
structed to provide the Agency with another appeals
hearing to be held no later than January 3, 1971.

The hearing was arranged but had to be postponed
when only four of the necessary five Council members showed up. At WANA's insistence another meeting was convened, but this time no one in attendance
knew anything about the Tremont program or WANA's
specific case and referred the matter back to the
Area Panel. Some three months later, on April 12,
1971, the panel informed the Agency that their appeal had been upheld by both CAP and CDA and that
they should indeed have been funded for Program
Year "F." However, this concession was accompanied
by an expression of regret that the funds had already been distributed and that there was no money
left with which to reinstate WANA's program. Thus,
after a seven and a half month struggle, the Director and staff of WANA wound up with the bureaucracy's agreement that they were clearly justified
in their appeal, but with no money and no program.[22]

SUMMARY OF FUNDING PROCESS
AND CONCLUSIONS

Having reconstructed the entire process of the
funding cycle through which the Tremont area's program proposals for Program Year "F" passed, we may
now turn to a summary of the most significant aspects of the procedures utilized within this process:
1. With regard to Delegate Agency program content, the city-wide bureaucracy bears almost total
responsibility since local sponsors have no opportunity to determine program priorities, are required
to work from a strict set of CDA program options,
and are subtly pressured into accepting mandated
programs. Thus, the nonrelevant or ineffectual nature of so many of the Delegate Agency programs
(e.g., those in such categories as Senior Citizens
and Economic Development), which was seen in Chapter 5, may be clearly interpreted as the desired
policy of CAP-CDA, in direct contrast to their
stated goals of bringing into poverty areas the
type of social service and group action programs
that would result in a powerful poor.

2. The power of the city-wide bureaucracy to
determine the content, focus, and structure of the
neighborhood level community action program is re-
inforced by the crisis management nature of the entire process of drawing up and submitting program
proposals. Unrealistic deadlines; poor communications among the bureaucracy, the Community Corporation and the program sponsors; and an almost total
lack of technical assistance from either CDA or the
Corporation Staff create a situation where most
sponsors are forced to submit proposals for the
bureaucracy's model programs. Through such a process, creative programs aimed at alleviating the
objects of discontent as perceived by local citizens are made almost impossible.*

3. The proposals themselves, with respect to
both budget and content, are mere formalities. Sponsors are assigned to various program categories on
an indiscriminate basis and budgets are drawn up
without consideration of a sponsor's proposed activities. Examination of the funding process likewise substantiates the fact that program evaluations are simply mechanisms to be used, or disre-
garded, in justification of decisions made on altogether different criteria.

4. Such a situation encourages destructive
competition among the sponsors and allows certain
powerful individuals, on either the neighborhood or
city-wide level, to establish control over significant aspects of the overall program. This was especially clear in the case of the Executive Director

---

*During the time for the submittal of program
proposals at the neighborhood level, the Corporation Staff received a number of inquiries from area
residents concerning the possibility of obtaining
community action funds for Drug Control and Reha-
bilitation programs. However, since this was not
one of the bureaucracy's mandated or recommended
program categories, these persons were told that
such activities would not be funded, except as a
component part of a program in an approved category.

of the Tremont Community Corporation who was able
to push through the ETCYD Center at all levels of
the funding process, at the expense of certain Delegate Agency programs. The great importance of connections is reflected in the fact that only very
rarely are new programs accepted into the overall
program.

5. Analysis of the funding process provides
additional support for the contention that CDA
holds the major power position in the entire bureaucratic structure of the community action program.
Three key decisions regarding the acceptance or rejection of certain Delegate Agency programs, made
by the neighborhood level units, were overturned by
CDA. The CAP Area Panel and the full CAP in turn
rubber-stamped CDA's decisions on the most crucial
issues of budgets, assignment of program categories
and the ETCYD Center, making only one significant
change regarding the specific Delegate Agencies,
and then only in order to insure racial quiet.

6. The appeals process built into the total
funding cycle appears to operate more as a safety-
valve technique and a procedure to discourage challenges to Corporation and especially bureaucratic
decisions, than as a meaningful structure through
which a rejected sponsor may be protected. In almost no case did an appeal at any stage of the
cycle directly bring about a reversal of decisions
with respect to funding.

Thus, from an examination of the funding process, the general policy of containment that was
established as operative in the Tremont community
from the operation of the neighborhood level units
may be clearly attributed to the city-wide bureaucracy. Likewise, the bureaucracy seems to bear responsibility for much of the isolation and lack of
cooperation among Agencies on the neighborhood
level and the resulting lack of two-step bargaining
that has been previously established.

We must conclude that it is apparently not in
the interests of the bureaucracy to move the poor
into a position of real influence within the poverty area but to keep the pressure off the political system, while allowing the guise of participation.

Finally, the authoritative role that CAP and CDA play with respect to the neighborhood level units, especially the would-be Delegate Agencies themselves, as is demonstrated at almost every step of the funding process, provides further evidence that the bureaucracy is, in essence, an agent of control over the participants in the community action program.

The data gathered through examination of the resources and functioning of the neighborhood level units in Tremont, and through observation and reconstruction of the funding process, have yielded much evidence in support of the two key ideas of this study's major hypothesis:

1.   That, despite the stated goals of the community action program in New York City that imply that the neighborhood level program should be an influence output, the operation of the program in the Tremont poverty area may best be described as a social control output; and,

2.   that although the community action bureaucracy describes itself as an advocate of the potential partisans, the poor, in actuality it functions primarily as a social control agent and as another authority with whom the poor must cope.

7

INTERVIEW DATA:
RESPONDENTS' VIEWS
OF THE PROGRAM
IN THE
TREMONT POVERTY AREA

Through summarizing the large amount of data that was obtained in the first and primarily observational phase of this study, we have presented a certain objective picture of the structuring and operation of the community action program on the neighborhood level. Our concern now is with the presentation of a more subjective perspective on that program, which emerges through an analysis of the views expressed by the individuals who, in a very real sense, know it best--those who directed, administered, worked in and received the services of the Tremont area program during Program Year "E."

Before turning to the analysis of these data, it may be well briefly to review the major categories of respondents who were included in the sample of persons interviewed. In the first group, that of the Participants (hereafter abbreviated as "P's"), were included 45 program policy-makers or administrators representing the Tremont Community Corporation Staff and Board of Directors, the Directors of the various Delegate Agencies, and the Delegate Agency Boards of Directors. The second group, the Participant Beneficiaries (PB's), consisted of 24 non-policy-making employees of the Tremont Community Corporation and the Delegate Agencies. The third group, that of the Nonparticipant Beneficiaries (NPB's), was made up of 18 clients of five selected Delegate Agencies in the Tremont poverty area. These three groups of respondents are, for

the purposes of the study, the most significant,
since the individuals included here are those who
had the most direct and sustained contact with the
community action program during the program year
under consideration. Thus, the major focus of this
chapter is on the views of the P's, the PB's, and
the NPB's. However, the views of two additional
categories were included in the study in a supple-
mentary manner, and are summarized briefly at the
end of the chapter. These two groups were the Unsuccessfuls (U's), consisting of three rejected
sponsors of Delegate Agency programs proposed for
Program Year "E"; and the Youth, made up of six
members of the Tremont Community Corporation Youth
Advisory Committee.

PERTINENT CHARACTERISTICS OF RESPONDENTS

Certain pertinent characteristics of the first
three categories of respondents, including sex, education, age, ethnicity, area of residence, and economic position, have been recorded in Tables 7.1-
7.10. This information serves as a background according to which the data presented in the remainder of the chapter may be interpreted. Looking
briefly at the first of these tables, it can be
clearly seen that, on each of the three levels of
participation spelled out for this study (P's,
PB's, and NPB's), women were more involved in the
Tremont area community action program than were men.
This fact is most striking in the case of the PB's
and the NPB's, while among the P's the distribution
according to sex is about even. Deeper analysis of
data obtained on the P's showed that of all the
neighborhood level units, only the Community Corporation Staff had a preponderance of men.
As one would expect, the data in Table 7.2
confirm the fact that the P's were the best edu-
cated of those involved in the program, while the
NPB's had completed the least amount of education.
Perhaps the most striking point to be noted here is
that 8 of the 45 P's had college degrees and 6 of
these had gone on to graduate school, while only

TABLE 7.1

Distribution of Participants, Participant
Beneficiaries, and Nonparticipant
Beneficiaries, by Sex

Sex	P's	PB's	NPB's	Total	Percentage
Male	22	5	4	31	35.6
Female	23	19	14	56	64.4
Total	45	24	18	87	100.0

Source: Compiled by the authors.

TABLE 7.2

Distribution of Participants, Participant
Beneficiaries, and Nonparticipant
Beneficiaries, by Education Completed

Education Completed	P's	PB's	NPB's	Total	Percentage
Less than grade school	2	0	2	4	4.6
Grade, with some high school	6	3	15	24	27.6
High school	16	15	1	32	36.8
Some college	13	5	0	18	20.6
College	2	0	0	2	2.4
Some graduate school	6	1	0	7	8.0
Total	45	24	18	87	100.0

Source: Compiled by the authors.

one of the 18 NPB's had completed high school. In
Table 7.3 the fact that the very large majority
(82.9 percent) of all those involved in the Tremont
community action program were between the ages of
22 and 44 can be seen; while only 2.4 percent were
21 years or younger, and 14.8 percent over 45. Although the PB's as a group were somewhat younger
than the P's, these data attest at least partially
to the accuracy of the fairly widespread complaint
of the youth in the area that the program was run
by the middle-aged, and thus reflected a somewhat
conservative position.

The ethnic breakdown of the P's, the PB's, and
the NPB's, as recorded in Table 7.4, shows that of
all three groups, the Puerto Ricans comprised roughly 50 percent. Overall, the blacks made up about
40 percent of those involved in the program, while
the percentage of other participants varied from
about 15 percent (7 out of 45), in the case of the
P's, to 0 percent among the NPB's. According to
the 1965 figures, the ethnic breakdown in the entire Tremont poverty area was approximately 23.3
percent Puerto Rican, 19.5 percent black, and 57.0
percent other white; thus both the blacks and
Puerto Ricans appear to have been overrepresented
in the community action program while the other
groups were significantly underrepresented. The
generally higher economic position of non-Puerto
Rican whites in the area, as well as a lack of organization relative to other ethnic groups in the
area; a lack of desire to participate, as seen particularly in the case of the Italians; and the fact
that most whites were significantly older; most
likely were the reasons for this situation.

The data in Table 7.5 show that the great
majority of P's, PB's, and NPB's had, at least at
one time, lived in the Tremont area. However,
closer analysis of the P's and PB's revealed that
five of the eight Tremont Community Corporation
Staff members, and four of the eight Corporation
employees had never lived in the area. Thus, nine
out of a total of eleven outsiders involved in the
total community action program in Tremont were
found in the Corporation itself, giving this unit

TABLE 7.3

Distribution of Participants, Participant
Beneficiaries, and Nonparticipant
Beneficiaries, by Age

Age Group	P's	PB's	NPB's	Total	Percentage
16-21	0	2	0	2	2.4
22-29	8	13	4	25	28.7
30-44	28	7	12	47	54.1
45-64	9	2	2	13	14.8
Total	45	24	18	87	100.0

Source: Compiled by the authors.

TABLE 7.4

Distribution of Participants, Participant
Beneficiaries, and Nonparticipant
Beneficiaries, by Ethnicity

Ethnicity	P's	PB's	NPB's	Total	Percentage
Puerto Rican	21	12	11	44	50.6
Black	17	11	7	35	40.2
Other	7	1	0	8	9.2
Total	45	24	18	87	100.0

Source: Compiled by the authors.

TABLE 7.5

Distribution of Participants, Participant
Beneficiaries, and Nonparticipant
Beneficiaries, According to Whether
or Not They Had Ever Lived in
Tremont Poverty Area

Ever Lived in Area	P's	PB's	NPB's	Total	Percentage
Yes	39	19	18	76	87.4
No	6	5	0	11	12.6
Total	45	24	18	87	100.0

Source: Compiled by the authors.

TABLE 7.6

Distribution of Participants, Participant
Beneficiaries, and Nonparticipant
Beneficiaries, by Length of Time
Lived in Tremont Poverty Area

Length of Time in Area	P's	PB's	NPB's	Total	Percentage
6 months-1 year	0	3	1	4	5.6
1-2 years	5	1	3	9	11.8
2-3 years	7	3	2	12	15.8
3-4 years	6	3	2	11	14.4
4-5 years	6	0	5	11	14.4
5-6 years	2	1	2	5	6.5
7 or more years	13	8	3	24	31.5
Total	39	19	18	76	100.0

Source: Compiled by the authors.

a rather nonindigenous outlook. The remaining 76
individuals who had lived or were still living in
the Tremont area at the time of the study are distributed in Table 7.6 according to length of time
lived in Tremont.* From the data recorded here, it
may be concluded that this did not appear to significantly affect participation in the community
action program for any of the three groups. However, about one-third of the P's (13 of 39), who
had lived for at least some time in Tremont, and
slightly less than one-half of the PB's (8 of 19),
had spent seven or more years there, suggesting
that there was a slight tendency for those with
longer residence to become actively involved in the
program.

Tables 7.7 and 7.8 present data on how the P's,
the PB's, and the NPB's viewed their own economic
position, relative to that of other people in the
area, before and after becoming involved in the
Tremont community action program. Before the program, the majority of P's saw themselves as above
average or higher; most of the PB's placed themselves around the average in the community; while
most of the NPB's considered themselves below average or lower. After contact with the community action program, none of the NPB's--the most poor of
the poor--felt that their economic position had
changed, while among the P's and PB's some perceived
movement may be noted.

From the data in Table 7.9 it is possible to
get some idea of what subjective economic position
means in objective terms. On the whole, the data
on annual income lend support to the subjective
placement made by the three groups of respondents.
The data in Table 7.10 are somewhat more revealing
with respect to the Tremont community action program's economic effect on the P's and PB's. Most
significantly, among both categories of P's here
considered--the Tremont Corporation Staff and the

---

*Only five of this group, including four P's
and one PB, were not living in the area at the time
of the study.

TABLE 7.7

Distribution of Participants, Participant
Beneficiaries, and Nonparticipant
Beneficiaries, by Subjective
Economic Position Before
Tremont Community Action Program

Economic Position	P's	PB's	NPB's	Total	Percentage
Near bottom	3	4	6	13	14.8
Below average	8	8	7	23	26.4
Average	8	7	4	19	21.9
Above average	20	3	1	24	27.6
Near the top	6	2	0	8	9.3
Total	45	24	18	87	100.0

Source: Compiled by the authors.

TABLE 7.8

Distribution of Participants, Participant
Beneficiaries, and Nonparticipant
Beneficiaries, by Subjective
Economic Position at Time
of Study, 1969/70

Economic Position	P's	PB's	NPB's	Total	Percentage
Near bottom	2	1	6	9	10.5
Below average	6	3	7	16	18.3
Average	13	12	4	29	33.3
Above average	15	7	1	23	26.4
Near the top	9	1	0	10	11.5
Total	45	24	18	87	100.0

Source: Compiled by the authors.

TABLE 7.9

Distribution of Participants, Participant Beneficiaries, and
Nonparticipant Beneficiaries, by Annual Income, 1969/70

Annual Income	P's	PB's	NPB's	Total	Percentage
Don't know	1	0	0	1	1.1
$ 3,000-3,999	2	3	8	13	14.8
4,000-4,999	2	1	2	5	5.5
5,000-5,999	6	12	0	18	19.7
6,000-6,999	5	6	3	14	16.1
7,000-7,999	9	2	4	15	17.2
8,000-8,999	5	0	1	6	6.9
9,000-9,999	6	0	0	6	6.9
10,000 or over	9	0	0	9	11.8
Total	45	24	18	87	100.0

Source: Compiled by the authors.

TABLE 7.10

Distribution of Participants and Participant Beneficiaries, by Position
and Annual Income, Before and After Affiliation with the
Community Action Program in the Tremont Area

Annual Income	Participants				Participant Beneficiaries			
	TCC Staff		DA Director		TCC Employee		DA Employee	
	Before	After	Before	After	Before	After	Before	After
Don't know	0	0	2	0	1	0	1	0
$3,000-4,999	0	0	0	0	2	0	3	4
5,000-6,999	3	0	5	0	4	6	8	12
7,000-8,999	5	0	4	9	1	2	4	0
9,000 and over	0	8	0	2	0	0	0	0
Total	8	8	11	11	8	8	16	16

Source: Compiled by the authors.

Delegate Agency Directors--definite increases in income may be noted following affiliation with the
program. In the case of the PB's, a somewhat small-
er yet still noticeable proportion of those employed
by both the Corporation and the Delegate Agencies
showed economic advancement. Taken as a whole, then,
the data presented in Tables 7.7-7.10 provide additional evidence for the fact that the community action program in Tremont served as a vehicle for
creaming, or improving the lot of the least poor of
the poor.

     With this background material in mind, we may
now turn to an analysis of the respondents' views
concerning the extent to which the community action
program in the Tremont poverty area during Program
Year "E" constituted primarily an influence or social control output. The data gathered through the
application of Gamson's two approaches to measuring
influence will be considered first, followed by the
analysis of those data pertaining to each of the
six operational indicators of influence and social
control.

                SUBJECTIVE PROBABILITY APPROACH

     It will be recalled that the subjective proba-
bility approach essentially involves inferring the
occurrence of influence on the part of a group of
potential partisans, if, in the eyes of certain informed observers, an outcome preferred by the partisan group is a better bet, following some action or
event. Applying this approach to our study, the
partisan group was defined as those in the Tremont
poverty area, and their preferred outcome that of
influencing existing institutions that service the
poor.* The informed observers were taken to be the
P's and PB's in the community action program, while
the action or event under consideration was the program itself. Two key questions were put to the informed observers:

----

     *For further clarification of the subjective
probability approach see pp. 25-26.

1.   Before the community action program came
into Tremont, what chance of influencing existing
institutions did the people in Tremont have?--and--
2.   What chance of influencing existing institutions do the people in Tremont now have because
of the community action program?

The responses to these two questions by both
the P's and PB's are recorded in Tables 7.11 and
7.12.

TABLE 7.11

Responses of Informed Observers on Chances of
the Tremont People Influencing Institutions
Before Community Action Program

Response	P's	PB's	Total	Percentage
Don't know	6	3	9	13.1
No chance	28	14	42	60.9
A slight chance	11	7	18	26.0
A good chance	0	0	0	0.0
Total	45	24	69	100.0

Source: Compiled by the authors.

TABLE 7.12

Responses of Informed Observers on Chances of
the Tremont People Influencing Institutions
as a Result of Community Action Program

Response	P's	PB's	Total	Percentage
Don't know	2	1	3	4.3
A much worse chance	1	1	2	3.0
A slightly worse chance	4	2	6	8.7
Same as before	7	3	10	14.5
A slightly better chance	26	12	38	55.0
A much better chance	5	5	10	14.5
Total	45	24	69	100.0

Source: Compiled by the authors.

It may be noted that a large majority of informed observers (60.9 percent) felt that the people
in the Tremont poverty area had no chance of influencing institutions before the community action program, while 26.0 percent responded that they had a
slight chance. As a result of the community action
program, however, 69.5 percent indicated that the
people had a slightly better or much better chance
of exercising influence over these institutions,
whereas only 11.7 percent felt that the chances
were worse. In support of the latter position, the
following comments were voiced during the interview
with two program participants: "The leadership is
in a self-interest bag. This whole set-up means we
have a conflict of interest organization and the
leaders end up using their energies fighting each
other instead of the institutions." "Before getting
funds from the people downtown (bureaucracy) the
people here in Tremont did much for themselves and
the community. Now we've sold our souls for a few
cents and the 'Man' has us in his pocket."

On the other hand, those who felt that the program had improved the people's chances for influence
tended to stress the potential of the program,
rather than what it had accomplished to date, noting such factors as "The Corporation isn't recognized by anybody yet since it hasn't built a power
base--but just you wait." Thus, it appeared that
the influence that many said that the people in Tremont gained was potential rather than actual.

INFLUENCE ATTEMPTS APPROACH

Further clarification on this point comes from
an analysis of the responses obtained through application of the influence attempts approach. This
approach rests on the assumption that influence may
be implied if a partisan group can be shown to possess resources that provide the capability of influence, and if the group has undertaken certain
influence attempts (see Chapter 2). Key resources
that would have to be possessed by the partisan
group under study in order that the capability of

influence might be inferred as noted earlier, would
be sufficient funds to undertake programs of influence; skilled personnel to direct, administer, and
operate such programs; and technical assistance for
program planning and operation from both the Tremont
Community Corporation and the CDA. Since it was
felt that the existence, or lack thereof, of the
first two types of resources could best be documented through an analysis of objective data, questions were included in the interview schedule only
on the issue of technical assistance. Specifically,
the following two questions were asked of the 11
Delegate Agency Directors in the sample with respect
to both the Corporation and CDA:

1. How often did you get technical assistance
from the Tremont Community Corporation? (or CDA)--
and--

2. How would you describe the quality of the
technical assistance from the Corporation? (or CDA).

Eight of the Directors said that they had never
received assistance from either unit. The remaining
three indicated that they had "only a few times,"
and in reference to the Corporation, responded that
the quality of technical assistance was "very poor."
Two of the three also characterized the assistance
from CDA as "very poor," while one described it as
"poor." These data clearly confirm the tentative
conclusion reached from the analysis of the observational data early in Chapter 5, that the Tremont
community action program has not provided the residents of the area with the necessary capability of
influence.

With respect to measuring the influence attempts undertaken by the partisan group, Gamson
notes that both the persons who have made such attempts and those for whom they were made must be
questioned concerning their quality and extent of
use. For the purposes of the study, the decision
was made to question the Delegate Agency Directors
and the NPB's in this regard.

Since by influence is meant the ability of potential partisans to alleviate the stress coming
from the objects of discontent, it was felt that
any questions concerning influence attempts had to

be based on the way in which the individual Delegate
Agency was attempting to alleviate such stress.
This necessitated asking each Delegate Agency Director what exactly his or her agency was doing, to
which all 11 Directors responded that--either by design or because of no other choice--they were, for
the most part, "helping people with their problems,"
on either a group or individual basis, as opposed
to undertaking group action with the aim of forcing
institutional responsiveness. The following series
of questions were designed to get at the influence
attempts undertaken by the Delegate Agencies and
were asked of the Agency Directors:
       1. Specifically, whom do you contact directly
in order to help people with their problems?
       The responses to this question varied widely
according to the Agency's specific program function,
but included such groups and individuals as landlords, the Buildings Department, Rent Control Office, Pest Control, Sanitation Department, teachers
or principals of schools, District Superintendent
of District 12, caseworkers and welfare supervisors
in the local Welfare Centers, employers, the Manpower Center, and Legal Services Bureau. This question was followed by two others:
       2. Of the various individuals or groups you
just mentioned, which one helped you the most?
Which next? Finally, which next?--and--
       3. How satisfied were you with each of these
top three?
       Here the responses of the Directors indicated
that they ranged from feeling "slightly satisfied"
to "slightly dissatisfied" with their three "most
helpful" contacts. Next, a question was asked with
respect to all of the contacts mentioned:
       4. Overall, how successful do you feel you
are in getting the help you seek for the people who
need it?
       Of the 11 Directors questioned, 2 indicated
that they were "very unsuccessful"; 3 were "slightly unsuccessful"; 5 were "slightly successful";
while only 2 felt "very successful." It is prob-
ably interesting to note the examples of success
mentioned by the 7 Directors in the last two

categories: "I personally went to the welfare center and spent hours getting a person's welfare check
straightened out." "We got some apartments painted
and pipes fixed." "We supplied people with information about how much rent they have to pay." "I got
a housekeeper for a rich lady." Finally, one last
question was asked of those Directors who indicated
that their influence attempts were generally unsuccessful:

    5. Why do you think your efforts don't meet
with greater success?

The reasons that were most often given in response to this question were "too much bureaucracy
to fight," "we don't have the right personnel," "we
don't have enough money to really do anything," and
"the poor don't want to fight."

To complete the inquiry into the issue of influence attempts, the perspective of the NPB's was
sought. After asking the 18 members of this group
which Delegate Agency they contacted, how often,
and why, they were then asked the following two
questions:

    1. What did you actually get from _____
(name of Delegate Agency) on this occasion?--and--

    2. Overall, how satisfied were you with what
you got?

To the first question, 5 of the NPB's responded
that they had gotten nothing at all, while 10 replied that they had gotten some specific individual
help, and only 3 mentioned that the Agency contacted
had provided opportunities for some sort of group
action. Concerning the question on satisfaction, 5
of the 13 who received assistance indicated that
they were either slightly satisfied or very satisfied with the specific Delegate Agency; 5 were
slightly dissatisfied and 3 were very dissatisfied.
(It is interesting to note that these last 2 were
among the 3 brought into group action.) Thus, the
NPB's as a group supported the contention of the
Delegate Agency Directors that the community action
program was providing some individuals with specific assistance in certain service categories.
However, because of the low capability of influence
possessed by the Delegate Agencies, as well as the

widespread lack of success of the influence attempts
undertaken, it may be inferred through this approach
that the community action program in the Tremont
area did not result in significantly increasing the
influence of the area residents.

EMPIRICAL INDICATORS APPROACH:
INFLUENCE VS. SOCIAL CONTROL

We must now consider the respondents' views
concerning each of the six variables used here as
the operational indicators of influence and social
control so that these two key concepts be measured
in a more concrete fashion.

Separateness and Separation

The first two variables which must be analyzed
are separateness, or the establishment by any group
of its identity as a separate grouping within a society; and separation, or an individual's or group's
isolation from other individuals or groups with whom
they share certain objective but latent interests.
With respect to separateness, it should be kept in
mind that the concept implies in part a subjective
feeling on the part of the partisan group, which in
itself does not comprise influence, but rather is a
preliminary condition for the occurrence of influence. In Chapter 2, four types of separateness
were outlined, and operational definitions constructed for each of these, which, in turn, were
measured through certain specific questions in the
interview schedule. First, however, a question
aimed at getting at the general identity of all respondents was asked. Specifically, each of the P's,
the PB's, and the NPB's was asked to name the three
most important groups with which he identified.
The responses to this question are recorded in
Table 7.13.

For the purpose of measuring the four specific
types of separateness, each individual was placed
in a category according to the first group with

TABLE 7.13

Groups with Which Respondents Identified, Ranked by Importance

Group of Identification	P's			PB's			NPB's			Total		
	1st	2nd	3rd	1st	2nd	3rd	1st	2nd	3rd	1st	2nd	3rd
No response	0	2	20	0	2	14	0	11	15	0	15	49
No one	0	0	0	2	0	0	8	0	0	10	0	0
Poor	34	6	1	16	2	0	2	3	0	52	11	1
Delegate Agency	2	12	5	0	11	2	0	2	2	2	25	9
Corporation	2	4	7	3	0	2	0	0	0	5	4	9
Blacks	4	8	2	1	4	2	2	1	0	7	13	4
Puerto Ricans	3	6	8	1	3	4	4	1	1	8	10	13
Coalition of ethnics	0	3	0	0	2	0	0	0	0	0	5	0
Com. leaders	0	4	1	1	0	0	0	0	0	3	4	1
Church	0	0	1	1	0	0	2	0	0	3	0	1
Total	45	45	45	24	24	24	18	18	18	87	87	87

Source: Compiled by the authors.

which he identified. Of the 87 persons interviewed,
the data in the table show that 10, or 10.4 percent,
indicated that they identified with no one or no
group; 52, or 59.8 percent, indicated identification with the poor;* 15, or 17.0 percent with an
ethnic group; and 7, or 8.0 percent with a neighborhood level unit of the community action program.
Each of these categories was then examined in greater detail, with respect to the operational definition constructed for each type of separateness.
The data that resulted are here analyzed under the
headings of the four specific types of separateness,
followed by the formulation of conclusions based on
the variable as a whole.

Type-one Separateness:
Poor Identity

In order to measure the extent to which individuals in Tremont had established their identity
as a separate status group of the poor, opposed to
the dominant groups who exploit and insulate them,
the 52 respondents who indicated general identity
with the poor--including 34 P's, 16 PB's, and 2
NPB's--were asked the following four questions:
1. Do you feel that the poor in Tremont have
to unite as a group to bring about changes in their
conditions?
To this question, all 52 responded affirmatively
2. Against whom do you think the poor have to
unite as a group to bring about change?
While each respondent was encouraged to name
his top three target systems, only the data regarding the one considered most important have been recorded in Table 7.14, for the purpose of simplifi-
cation. The most significant feature of this table

------

*It is interesting to note that many of this
group, in particular a large proportion of the 34
P's included here, were not themselves poor. It
seems likely that their identification with the
poor was based primarily on the fact that helping
the poor was the stated rationale behind the entire
community action program.

is that the large majority of both the P's and PB's
who identified with the poor saw local, state, and national political structures as the primary target
system against whom the poor have to unite. As a
second choice, these two groups overwhelmingly
named such established bureaucracies as welfare,
housing, and employment agencies.

TABLE 7.14

First-Choice Target Systems
Identified by Respondents
with General Poor Identity

Target System	P's	PB's	NPB's	Total
Middle or upper class	1	0	0	1
Corporation or Delegate Agencies	1	1	0	2
CAP-CDA	0	0	0	0
Political structures (local, state, and national)	21	11	1	33
Established bureaucracies	4	1	0	5
School systems and policies	6	1	0	7
Landlords	1	2	1	4
Total	34	16	2	52

Source: Compiled by the authors.

3. Did you feel this way before getting involved with the Tremont community action program,
i.e., that the poor have to unite as a group
against _____?

Thirty-six of the 52 respondents in this category, or 69.2 percent, said that they had felt this
way before their involvement with the Tremont program, while 16 or 30.8 percent stated that they had
not.

4. Did you come to feel this way because of
the Tremont community action program?

To this question all 16 who had not felt this
way before, indicated that the program was responsible for their change in feeling.

Thus, while 52 out of a total of 87 P's, PB's,
and NPB's, showed evidence of type-one separateness,
only 16 of these 52 had acquired such feelings of
separateness as a result of the Tremont community
action program.

Type-two Separateness:
Ethnic Identity

What needed to be measured here was the extent
to which persons in the Tremont area had established
their identity as separate ethnic groups, opposed to
perceived dominant, exploitative groups. To do this,
the 15 respondents--7 P's, 2 PB's, and 6 NPB's--who
had indicated identification with either the blacks
or Puerto Ricans were asked the same four basic
questions as were used to tap type-one separateness,
substituting the name of the particular ethnic group
in place of the poor.

All 15 responded that their specific ethnic
group had to unite as a group to bring about changes
in their living conditions. The target systems
identified most frequently were, once again, political structures and established bureaucracies; and in
the case of 3 of the 7 blacks in this category, the
police. Six of the 7 blacks indicated that they had
felt this way prior to involvement with the community action program, while the remaining member of
this group said that he had come to feel this way
as a result of the program. Of the 8 Puerto Ricans

questioned with respect to ethnic identity, 4 felt
this way before the program, while 4 came to feel
this way because of it. Thus, only 5 of the 15 respondents indicating type-two separateness, acquired such feelings through the community action
program in Tremont; 4 of them Puerto Ricans.*

In addition to the 15 respondents indicating
first-choice identification with an ethnic group
(see Table 7.13), a fairly large number identified
with such a group on a second- or third-choice
basis--17 with the blacks, and 23 with the Puerto
Ricans, for a total of 40. Because of the significant size of this group, these 40 individuals were
likewise questioned regarding ethnic separateness
in order to provide additional insight into the extent of occurrence of this phenomenon in the Tremont community. Of greatest interest here was the
fact that only 4 of the 17 blacks with secondary or
tertiary feelings of ethnic separateness had these
feelings because of their involvement with the community action program; while the respective figures
for the Puerto Ricans were 10 out of 23. This analysis resulted in a similar conclusion: that the
program brought about roughly one-third of the ethnic separateness evidenced in Tremont at the time
of this study, and then primarily in the case of
the Puerto Ricans.

Type-three Separateness:
Coalitional Ethnic Identity

This type of separateness, involving the extent to which individuals in Tremont had established their identity as ethnic groupings united
into a broader coalition of ethnic groups in the

-----

*The fact that more Puerto Ricans than blacks
acquired ethnic identity through the program is no
doubt due to the fairly high degree of organization
of this group in the Tremont area. Because of the
resulting heavily Puerto Rican control of the program, more members of this group were able to be
brought in.

area, was not actually measured in detailed fashion,
since none of the 87 P's, PB's, and NPB's indicated
general identity with such a coalition on a first-
choice basis, and only 5 did so on a secondary
basis. On the basis of these figures, it was concluded that no meaningful type-three separateness
resulted from the community action program in Tremont during Program Year "E." Additional support
for this conclusion was found through the analysis
of type-two isolation, or antagonistic ethnic identity, as will be seen later in this chapter.

Type-four Separateness:
Interest Group Identity

In order to measure the extent to which individuals in Tremont had established their identity
as a solid interest group composed of the various
neighborhood level units of the community action
program, the 7 respondents indicating general identity with either the Tremont Community Corporation
or a Delegate Agency--4 P's and 3 PB's--were questioned in a manner similar to that used in the case
of type-one and type-two separateness.

As expected, all of the 7 responded that the
various neighborhood level units of the community
action program had to unite as a group in order to
bring about meaningful changes in the Tremont community. However, when questioned about the target
systems for such an interest group, 2 of the 5 individuals identifying with the Corporation named
the Corporation Board as the major target, 1 named
CAP-CDA, and only 2 looked to outside political
structures. Of the 2 respondents identifying with
a Delegate Agency, 1 said the primary target should
be the Corporation Board, while the other named
CAP-CDA. Also of note was the fact that, out of
the 7 individuals in this category, 5 naming other
primary targets agreed that the community action
bureaucracy was the second most important target.

An analysis of the responses to these questions of the large number of persons (29) who identified, on a secondary basis with either the Corporation or a Delegate Agency, yielded a similar

picture. Four of the 29 indicated that the Corporation Board was the primary target for the community
action interest group, 7 chose the community action
bureaucracy, while the rest looked to other bureaucratic and political structures. As the second
most important target system, 12 named the community
action bureaucracy.*

Thus, while a rather significant number of respondents identified with a neighborhood level unit
of the community action program on either a first
or second choice basis two factors prevent us from
concluding that meaningful type-four separateness
has taken place: First, the fact that none of these
individuals gave evidence of identifying with a coalition of such units, but rather only with a particular unit; and second, the fact that the target
systems most frequently mentioned were internal to
the community action program itself, rather than
the dominant groups that controlled the interests
of the people in the Tremont area before the program came about, and at which the program purported
to aim.

With regard to the entire question of separateness, then, the following conclusions may be formulated on the basis of the respondents' primary iden-
tifications:

1. While poor identity was indicated by 52 of
the 87 respondents, the community action program in
Tremont was responsible for bringing about such
feelings for only 16, or about one-third, of the 52.
Of these 16, 8 were P's and 8 were PB's.

2. Ethnic group identity was evidenced by 15
of the 87 respondents, but again only one-third of
this number, or 5 respondents, indicated that their
feelings were a result of the community action

---

*These figures suggest that perhaps one major
result of the community action program has been the
creation of a "paper tiger" enemy, which is the program itself, i.e., that the program may be functioning as a means of diverting the opposition of the
poor away from external target systems, insofar as
opposition is being focused on the program's own
units.

program. Three of this group were P's, 1 was a PB,
and 1 an NPB; and significantly, 4 of the 5 were
Puerto Ricans.

3. None of the 87 respondents indicated coalitional ethnic identity, either as a result of the
program or otherwise.

4. While the community action program appeared
to have brought about identification with one of the
program's neighborhood level units for 7 of the 87
respondents--4 P's and 3 PB's--no solid interest
group identity was evidenced.

5. Overall, regardless of its origin, 67 of
the 87 respondents indicated a type of separateness--
either poor identity or ethnic identity--while 7
others had achieved what perhaps may be interpreted
as a first step toward interest group identity.
From this we may conclude that a significant number
of those questioned possessed feelings that may be
interpreted as at least a preliminary condition for
the occurrence of influence by those groups with
which they identified.

Before turning to a consideration of whether
or not such potential influence became actual
through the community action program in the Tremont
area, we should first look at the other side of the
concept of separateness--that of separation--since
the responses to the questions asked with regard to
this latter concept provide additional insight into
the various types of separateness as well.

In Chapter 2 three types of separation--or iso-
lation--were outlined and defined operationally.
The way in which each of these was measured through
the interview schedule is described below. It
should be kept in mind that, if separateness serves
as a preliminary condition for the occurrence of
influence by potential partisans, then separation
may be seen as a primary condition for the exercising of social control by authorities.

Type-one Isolation:
Nonidentification

To measure this concept of personal isolation,
or the extent to which those affected by the community action program in Tremont had not established

their identity in relation to any group in the area,
reference was first made to the responses or the
general identity question, which have been recorded
in Table 7.13. The ten individuals--2 PB's and 8
NPB's--who indicated identification with no one in
the area were singled out, and asked to respond to
the 9 items in Dean's Social Isolation Subscale
(see Appendix). The reasoning here was that, even
though these respondents did not voice any type of
group identification, a more substantive measure
needed to be employed in order to infer that such
individuals were, in fact, personally isolated. As
can be seen from Table 7.15, 6 of the 10 respondents
were according to this scale either somewhat or very
isolated, in spite of their involvement with the
community action program in Tremont. It should be
noted that one of this isolated group was a PB,
while the remaining 5 were NPB's.

TABLE 7.15

Frequency Distribution of Ten Respondents
with No Group Identification, According to
Score Received on Dean's Social
Isolation Subscale

Scale Scores	Interpretation	Frequency
1	Very integrated	0
2	Very integrated	1
3	Integrated	0
4	Integrated	0
5	Neutral	3
6	Isolated	2
7	Isolated	2
8	Very Isolated	2
9	Very Isolated	0

Source: Compiled by the authors.

Type-two Isolation: Antagonistic
Ethnic Identity

What was involved here was the measurement of
the extent to which the ethnic group members affected by the community action program exhibited
antagonism toward other ethnic groups in the area,
and did not see an ethnic coalition as possible.
Once again, the term ethnic group members was defined with reference to the general identity data
since it was felt that self-identification--on a
first, second, or third choice basis--with an ethnic group provided the most meaningful criterion by
which to judge such group membership. The relevant
parts of Table 7.13 have been reproduced in Table
7.16 with the first, second, and third identification choices of all respondents combined, and from
these data can be seen those who were included in
the group questioned concerning antagonistic ethnic
identity.

TABLE 7.16

Ethnic Group Identification of Participants,
Participant Beneficiaries, and
Nonparticipant Beneficiaries

Ethnic Group Identified with	P's	PB's	NPB's	Total
Blacks	14	7	3	24
Puerto Ricans	17	8	6	31
Total	31	15	9	55

Source: Compiled by the authors.

These 55 respondents--including 31 P's, 15
PB's, and 9 NPB's--were then asked the following
three questions:
1. Do you feel that the blacks and Puerto
Ricans in Tremont are able to work together toward

common goals, or that there's conflict and antagonism between the two groups?

The responses to this question are recorded in
Table 7.17. Forty-two, or 76.4 percent, of the 55
ethnic group members indicated the existence of ethnic group antagonism in the community.

TABLE 7.17

Responses of Ethnic Group Members on
Relationship Between Blacks and
Puerto Ricans in Tremont

Relationship	P's	PB's	NPB's	Total	Percentage
Marked by con- flict and antagonism	24	10	8	42	76.4
Able to work together	7	5	1	13	23.6
Total	31	15	9	55	100.0

Source: Compiled by the authors.

2. Would you say that you have come to feel
this way through your involvement with the Tremont
community action program?

To this question 35 of the 42 who felt there
was ethnic antagonism responded affirmatively, indicating that about 83 percent of this antagonism
had been a result of the community action program
while the remaining 17 percent had merely continued
despite the program.

3. Do you see a united coalition of blacks
and Puerto Ricans in Tremont as possible at this
time?

Here, 46 of the 55 ethnic group members, or
83.6 percent, responded that such a coalition was
not possible.

Thus, through this series of questions, we were provided with fairly overwhelming evidence that type-two isolation was occurring as a result of the Tremont community action program or that it was continuing.

Type-three Isolation: Fragmented Interest Group Identity

Here we were concerned with measuring the extent to which those associated with the various Delegate Agencies in the Tremont area saw themselves in competition with other Delegate Agencies, particularly for funds and other resources, and did not view the formation of all units of the area's community action program into a strong interest group as possible. The group selected for questioning on this issue was made up of those associated with the various Delegate Agencies, and consisted specifically of 11 Delegate Agency Directors, 16 members of the agency Boards of Directors, and 16 agency personnel--for a total of 27 P's and 16 PB's.

Two questions were asked of each of these 43 respondents:

1. Do you feel that the community action program in Tremont has resulted in the various Delegate Agencies uniting together and cooperating with each other, or that the Delegate Agencies are too much in competition with one another for such things as funds and clients?

For the respondents' views see Table 7.18. Most striking was the fact that of the 43 persons associated on a close basis with the Delegate Agencies in Tremont, 37, or 86.1 percent, felt that the relationship among the agencies was marked by competition rather than cooperation, evidencing a very high degree of fragmented interest group identity.

2. Do you see a united coalition of all the Delegate Agencies in the area as possible at this time?

This question yielded responses identical in distribution to the previous question, with 37 or 86.1 percent of the respondents indicating that such a coalition was not possible, while only 6, or 13.9 percent, saw it as a possibility.

TABLE 7.18

Responses of Those Associated with Delegate
Agencies on Relationship Among Delegate
Agencies in the Tremont Area

| Relationship | Delegate Agency | | | | |
	Directors (P's)	Board of Directors (P's)	PB's	Total	Percentage
Marked by competition	10	13	14	37	86.1
Marked by unification and cooperation	1	3	2	6	13.9
Total	11	16	16	43	100.0

Source: Compiled by the authors.

In summary, regarding the variable of separation, or isolation, we note the following:
1. There was very little evidence of personal isolation among the respondents in the sample, with only 6 individuals--1 PB and 5 NPB's--indicating such nonidentification.
2. There was, however, fairly conclusive evidence of antagonistic ethnic identity in the Tremont community, with 42, or 76.4 percent, of the 55 ethnic group members questioned indicating conflict and antagonism between the blacks and Puerto Ricans. The bulk of this antagonism, 83.3 percent, was attributed to the community action program. As additional evidence of this type of isolation, 46 ethnic group members, or 83.6 percent, did not see an ethnic coalition as possible in Tremont. It should be noted that this finding totally supports the conclusion reached earlier regarding the absence of

type-three separateness or coalition ethnic identity in the area.*

3. Our findings concerning fragmented interest
group identity clearly support the conclusion that
the community action program in Tremont had not resulted in bringing about a solid interest group consisting of the program's neighborhood level units.
Thirty-seven, or 86.1 percent, of the 43 respondents
associated with the Delegate Agencies indicated that
the relationship among the agencies was one of competition and did not see a community action coalition as possible.

4. It was previously found that a rather significant number of the 87 persons interviewed possessed the preliminary condition for the occurrence
of influence through their feelings of either type-
one or type-two separateness (poor identity or ethnic identity). However, on the basis of the very
high degree of antagonistic ethnic identity and
fragmented interest group identity evidenced through
our analysis of separation--most of it a direct result of the community action program--it seems reasonable to conclude that such potential influence
was not developed by the program. It appears most
likely that the program capitalized on the prior existence of ethnic identity in particular and created
a situation that turned this into antagonistic ethnic identity. Through direct policies of the community action bureaucracy, particularly with regard
to the funding process as it has been previously
reconstructed, as well as the very structure of the
program itself on the neighborhood level, a similar
situation was brought about through which the occurrence of fragmented interest group identity was
fostered.

On the basis of our analysis of the variables
of separateness and separation we may conclude that

---

*That much conflict and antagonism exists
among the various ethnic groups in Tremont is well
known to observers of the area. The perception of
this by active participants in the program and
their feelings that it will continue is regarded as
most significant.

the latter, the social control variable, was much
more significantly operative in the Tremont community action program during Program Year "E."

Collaboration and Containment

Collaboration and containment were defined in
Chapter 2 in terms of the positive and negative aspects of the process of cooptation of the poor by
the community action bureaucracy; collaboration said
to be occurring if the cooptation process favors the
poor in the sense that the bureaucracy makes significant outcome modifications favorable to them, and
containment occurring if the process favors the bureaucracy in the sense that its outcomes are protective of the interests of the dominant groups that
control it (including political institutions and officials and the established social welfare agencies).
Since the goal for a program characterized by a
policy of collaboration would be alleviating the
objects of discontent--through relevant and effective service or action programs controlled by the
poor--while that for a program governed by a policy
of containment would be alleviating the sources of
pressure--manifested through the existence of service or action programs rendered nonrelevant and ineffective due to a lack of necessary resources--the
following operational definitions of the two variables were developed: To the extent that relevant
and meaningful service programs, controlled and administered by legitimate representatives of the poor,
or effective neighborhood level action programs have
been sanctioned by the community action bureaucracy
and accepted by those in the Tremont poverty area,
the poor have been positively coopted, and collaboration has occurred. And, to the extent that nonrelevant, unsuccessful, and ineffective service or
action programs have been so sanctioned and accepted, the poor have been negatively coopted and
containment has occurred.
Measurement of these variables first required
determining the extent to which action programs or
service programs under the control of the poor were

perceived to be operative in the Tremont area during
Program Year "E." To this end, definitions of various types of programs were developed through reference to Kenneth Clark and Jeannette Hopkins' outline of the four major goals of community action
programs in general:

> 1. The goal of provision of help
> through services (especially educational
> and social) from the community of afflu-
> ence to the community of need.
> 2. The goal of opening up oppor-
> tunities by the community of affluence
> for the community of need so that the
> poor can enter the more fortunate com-
> munity.
> 3. The goal of provision of help
> through the participation of the poor
> to help themselves, participation in
> the extension and provision of ser-
> vices through individual effort or
> through organization . . . [This goal
> rests on the assumption that] condi-
> tions of poverty are not inevitable,
> but that the poor bear some responsi-
> bility for alleviating their own con-
> dition at the same time as the afflu-
> ent bear responsibility for helping
> through services. Such self-help can
> be (a) individual, as in the case of
> teenagers seeking job training, or
> (b) group-oriented, as in the case of
> block organizations working for neigh-
> borhood rehabilitation.
> 4. The goal of providing the op-
> portunity for the poor to take the
> leadership themselves through indepen-
> dent action, primarily political, to
> secure power as a countervailing force
> in the larger community to deal with
> the basic cause of poverty itself to-
> ward the end of the elimination of
> poverty. The primary assumptions on
> which this action-oriented goal rests

are: (a) that the predicament of the
poor is due <u>not</u> to a lack of service
and "opportunity" but primarily to
their condition of <u>powerlessness</u>;
(b) that poverty will never be abol-
ished until the poor themselves gain
power to reverse their condition;
[and] (c) that the victims of long-
standing injustices must be organized
to identify their problems, determine
methods to alleviate the perceived
problems, develop and sustain the type
of organization for collective action
which can survive when confronted with
internal and external conflicts.[1]

It may be noted that the first two goals actually relate to a community action program that may
be best characterized as elitist, involving no meaningful participation by the poor, and thus placing
such a program outside the context of either containment or collaboration as defined in this study.
The last two, on the other hand, would characterize
a participatory program, both providing at least
the potential for collaboration, and consequently
increased influence, on the part of the poor--goal
#3, through setting up a structure that could poten-
tially be used for building up a viable political
constituency of the poor themselves; and goal #4,
through the more direct--but not necessarily more
successful--strategy of large-scale group or collective action.

Each of the four goals was paraphrased in more
basic language as appears below, and all respondents
were asked to indicate which of the four they felt
best described what was happening through the program in the Tremont area.

1. Middle-class people are setting up programs in Tremont and are trying to help the poor
with the problems they're having with such things
as jobs, landlords, and not enough education.

2. Middle-class people are giving some of the
poor people in Tremont the chance to step up into
the middle class through things like getting them

into training programs and good jobs and helping
them to go back to school.

3. Some of the poor people in Tremont are getting money to set up programs that try to help the
rest of the people in the community with the problems they're having with things like jobs, landlords, and not enough education.

4. Some of the poor people in Tremont are getting the chance to set up programs that are trying
to get the people in the community organized into
real power groups so they can stand up against
those who are controlling them and trying to keep
them poor.

The responses yielded through asking this question of all 87 individuals in the sample are recorded in Table 7.19.

TABLE 7.19

Respondents' Views on "What Is Really Happening
Through the Tremont Community Action Program,"
According to Four Descriptive Statements

Statement Number	Type of Program Described	P's	PB's	NPB's	Total	Percentage
1	Elitist-services	8	3	10	21	24.1
2	Elitist-opportunities	12	8	2	22	25.3
3	Participatory-implying service strategy	22	12	6	40	45.9
4	Participatory-implying action strategy	3	1	0	4	4.7
Total		45	24	18	87	100.0

Source: Compiled by the authors.

Forty respondents, or 45.9 percent of the total 87, indicated the existence of a participatory program, primarily utilizing a strategy of services; whereas only 4 respondents, or 4.7 percent, felt that the Tremont program was best characterized as participatory, but primarily utilizing a strategy of group action. The remaining 49.4 percent did not see the program as participatory in either respect. Most striking here is the fact that 10 of the 18 NPB's in the sample characterized the community action program as one through which the middle class was administering services to the poor, indicating that they looked upon most of the P's and PB's as the nonpoor and perhaps as outsiders. Eight of the 45 P's and 3 of the 24 PB's concurred in this view. A significantly larger proportion of both groups, however, indicated their agreement with the statement that described the program as one through which the poor were being given the opportunity to step into the middle class. Here, it seems likely, particularly in view of the data presented earlier in this chapter concerning the program's economic effect on the respondents, that many of the P's and PB's who agreed with statement #2 did so with reference to their own experiences with the Tremont program, rather than what the program was accomplishing in the community at large.

Having obtained the above information, a second step was undertaken in order to establish the existence of a policy of either collaboration or containment in the area. What remained to be determined was whether or not the respondents viewed as relevant or effective the participatory structure that they perceived as resulting from the community action program in Tremont, and that implied the potential for the occurrence of collaboration. Specifically, those 44 individuals--25 P's, 13 PB's, and 6 NPB's--who characterized the Tremont program as participatory in either respect were asked the following question: Overall, do you feel that the community action program in Tremont has enough resources--enough funds, trained personnel, and technical assistance from the community action bureaucracy--to allow it to operate in an effective manner and in a way that the poor are actually helped?

The responses to this question are recorded in
Table 7.20.

TABLE 7.20

Respondents' Answers to Question on Whether
Program Has Enough Resources to be
Effective, According to Type
of Program Perceived

Type of Program Perceived	P's		PB's		NPB's		Total		Percentage	
	Yes	No	Yes	No	Yes	No	Yes	No	Yes	No
Participatory-service strategy	4	18	3	9	1	5	8	32	20.0	80.0
Participatory-action strategy	0	3	0	1	0	0	0	4	0.0	100.0
Total	4	21	3	10	1	5	8	36	18.2	81.8

Source: Compiled by the authors.

The overwhelming majority of respondents--those
who perceived a strategy of services as well as
those who saw a strategy of action--did not feel
that the program possessed the necessary resources
to allow it to operate in an effective manner or in
a way that the poor were actually helped, despite
the perceived participatory structure. All of the
4 respondents who characterized the program's primary strategy as one of group action indicated this
negative view; while 32 persons, or 80 percent, of
the respondents who perceived a strategy of services
voiced the same feeling. Thus, 36 individuals out
of the 44 questioned, or 81.8 percent, gave evidence
that despite the community action program's potential for the occurrence of collaboration, the actual
operation of the program in Tremont was containment.

Only 8 persons--4 P's, 3 PB's, and 1 NPB--consti-
tuting 18.2 percent of the 44, saw collaboration as
actually occurring through the program. These figures are presented in summary fashion in Table 7.21.

TABLE 7.21

Summary of Respondents' Views on Whether
Actual Outcome of Program Was
Collaboration or Containment

Outcome of Program	P's	PB's	NPB's	Total	Percentage
Collaboration	4	3	1	8	18.2
Containment	21	10	5	36	81.8
Total	25	13	6	44	100.0

Source: Compiled by the authors.

     Summarizing what has been seen regarding the
variables of collaboration and containment, the
first significant point is that almost half (43, or
49.4 percent) of the 87 persons interviewed, in describing the community action program in Tremont in
clearly elitist terms, involving no cooptation of
the poor by the authorities, did not see even the
potential for collaboration by the poor in the area.
Secondly, on the basis of the data in Tables 7.20
and 7.21, we may conclude that collaboration occurred on only a very slight scale during Program
Year "E," whereas containment was indicated by the
responses of slightly fewer than half (36, or 41.4
percent) of respondents interviewed. Thus, once
again, we are presented with strong evidence that
the social control variable was predominantly operative in the program during the year under consideration.
     Having looked at the extent of occurrence of
the preliminary conditions for influence and social

control, as well as the extent to which a policy of
influence or social control characterized the community action program's operation in the Tremont
community, we may now turn to a closer examination
of exactly what, in the eyes of the respondents,
the program accomplished in this area during Program Year "E." Of first concern here will be the
influence variable of bargaining.

Bargaining

For the purposes of the study two kinds of bargaining were defined: one-step and two-step bargaining (see Chapter 2). One-step bargaining may be
said to have occurred to the extent that an individual Delegate Agency has, through the use of collective action, engaged a dominant target system
over a specific issue, and has brought about a
change in power and/or resources in favor of the
poor. In order to measure this variable, Delegate
Agency Directors, personnel, and clients were selected for questioning, since these individuals
were the ones most closely connected with the specific activities of the agencies and in the best
position to provide information regarding bargaining attempts. The decision was made to exclude
members of the Delegate Agency Board of Directors
from this group because initial research had revealed the fact that so many Board members were out
of touch with exactly what the Agencies were doing.
The group questioned thus consisted of 11 P's (the
Directors), 16 PB's (the personnel), and 18 NPB's
(the clients). Each of these respondents was asked
the following questions preceded by the general introduction:

> Now I'd like to ask you some questions
> about collective action. By collec-
> tive action I mean people getting or-
> ganized and doing something as a group
> in order to try and get power for them-
> selves and take power away from the
> groups who are controlling them. [Ex-
> amples of collective actions, such as

labor strikes, sit-ins, demonstrations, etc., were given in addition
to this explanation.]

1. Have you ever heard about any collective
action sponsored by _____(Delegate Agency of
respondent)?

The responses to this question, in Table 7.22,
were predominantly negative, with 29, or 64.5 percent of the 45 respondents indicating that they had
never heard of any collective action sponsored by
their Delegate Agency.

TABLE 7.22

Responses of Delegate Agency Directors,
Personnel, and Clients on Whether or Not
They Had Heard of Collective Action
Sponsored by Their Delegate Agency

Have heard of collective action	Directors (P's)	Personnel (PB's)	Clients (NPB's)	Total	Percentage
Yes	5	7	4	16	35.5
No	6	9	14	29	64.5
Total	11	16	18	45	100.0

Source: Compiled by the authors.

The significance of the responses of the P's
and PB's in this regard is no doubt greater than
that of the NPB's responses, since the first two
categories were in daily contact with the Agencies
throughout the program year. In any case, the 16
persons--5 P's, 7 PB's, and 4 NPB's--who had heard
of at least one collective action by their agency

were asked to think of the one action which they
thought had the best results (if there was more
than one), and to answer the next two questions in
reference to that action:

2. Who was this collective action aimed
against; what was the specific issue involved?

All 16 respondents described one of five specific instances of collective action undertaken by
five different Delegate Agencies. While the de-
tails of these actions varied widely, they may be
briefly and generally summarized as follows:

Action #1, undertaken by the Federation of
Puerto Rican Volunteers, involved a demonstration
at the local Neighborhood City Hall that aimed at
getting two stop signs placed at busy intersections
in Tremont. One P, one PB, and one NPB described
this action.

Action #2, mentioned by five respondents--one
P, two PB's, and two NPB's--concerned a rent strike
organized by ETAC against a landlord who owned a
great deal of residential property in the area, and
who was accused of overcharging rents and not keeping up with repairs on his buildings.

Action #3 was an attempt by Tremont Housing
Clinic to organize a tenants' association in one
particular building for the purpose of attracting
someone sympathetic to the housing needs of the
poor to purchase the building after the former, and
highly unpopular, landlord, had abandoned it. Four
respondents--one P, two PB's, and one NPB--recalled
this particular collective action.

Action #4, sponsored by Elsmere Tenants Council and described by one P and one PB, concerned an
attempt to organize a boycott of a local supermarket
accused of charging exceptionally high prices for
poor quality merchandise.

Action #5 involved picketing a neighborhood
theater that showed "dirty movies." This action,
sponsored by Tremont Community Council, whose Director was the Pastor of St. Joseph's Catholic Church,
was mentioned by one P and one PB.

The 16 persons were then asked about the degree of success obtained through this action, as
follows:

3. How successful would you say this collective action was concerning getting some power for the poor in Tremont?

The responses to this question appear in Table 7.23. Ten persons--3 P's, 5 PB's, and 2 NPB's described the collective action taken by their Delegate Agency as very successful.

TABLE 7.23

Respondents' Views on Degree of Success Obtained by the Collective Action with the Best Results, Sponsored by Their Delegate Agency

Degree of Success	P's	PB's	NPB's	Total	Percentage
Very successful	3	5	2	10	62.5
Slightly successful	1	1	0	2	12.5
No success at all	1	1	0	2	12.5
Total	5	7	4*	10*	100.0*

*Includes two NPB's who responded with "don't know."

Source: Compiled by the authors.

To get an idea of how frequent such collective actions were and whether or not such success was typical, the 16 respondents were asked two additional questions:

4. Besides the collective action that you have just described, how many other collective actions would you say _____ (Delegate Agency of respondent) sponsored?--and--

5. On the whole, how successful do you feel these other collective actions were?

Eleven of the 16 respondents, including 4 P's, 6 PB's, and 1 NPB, recalled between one and three additional collective actions undertaken by their Delegate Agency during Program Year "E." Three NPB's did not know of any such actions other than the one originally mentioned, while the remaining 2 respondents--1 P and 1 PB--indicated that their Agencies had sponsored more than 6 additional collective action attempts during the program year. The 13 respondents' views on the general degree of success obtained by the additional actions undertaken by their Delegate Agency are recorded in Table 7.24.

TABLE 7.24

Respondents' Views on Degree of Success
Obtained by All Additional Collective
Actions Sponsored by Their Delegate Agency

Degree of Success	P's	PB's	NPB's	Total
Very successful	0	0	0	0
Slightly successful	2	3	1	6
No success at all	3	4	0	7
Total	5	7	1	13

Source: Compiled by the authors.

Significantly, none of the 13 felt that the additional collective actions had been very successful, and less than half indicated that they had been even slightly successful. In view of what has been seen, then, it appears that during Program Year "E" meaningful one-step bargaining occurred only on a very limited basis. Only 16, or slightly more than one-third, of the 45 respondents closely associated with the Delegate Agencies in Tremont

knew of even one collective action attempt sponsored
by their particular Agency. Referring to the action
with the "best results," 10 of these 16 termed it
"very successful." However, the high degree of
agreement among the 16 in identifying and describing the very successful collective actions, as well
as the fact that all additional collective actions
undertaken by the Delegate Agencies were characterized as "not successful at all" or only "slightly
successful," leads one to conclude that a few clas-
sic "success stories" in the area of one-step bargaining were produced during the year by a small
number of Delegate Agencies. This conclusion re-
ceives additional support from the data yielded
through asking the original Delegate Agency group
of 45 respondents about which of the Delegate Agencies, other than their own, sponsored collective
action, and how successful they felt such action
had been. Thirty of the 45 were not able to answer
these questions; while 15 mentioned either the Tremont Housing Clinic, or the East Tremont Action Committee in this regard, and only 5 felt that the collective actions sponsored by these two agencies had
been very successful.

The picture was even more clear with respect
to two-step bargaining, which was defined as several Delegate Agencies uniting and, through the use
of collective action, engaging a dominant target
system over a specific issue, bringing about a
change in power and/or resources in favor of the
poor.

To measure the extent to which two-step bargaining had occurred in the Tremont area, similar
questions were included in the interview schedule;
substituting the term "joint collective action" in
place of a collective action sponsored by one particular Delegate Agency. To summarize the most significant information yielded through these questions: of the 45 respondents in close association
with the Delegate Agencies, only 11, or 24.4 percent, had ever heard of any joint collective actions by Agencies in Tremont. Significantly, the
11 included no Delegate Agency clients or NPB's, 6
Directors (P's), and 5 personnel (PB's).

Further questioning revealed that all 11 knew of only one such action and that all were referring to a bus trip to Washington which had been organized by the community action bureaucracy in September of 1970 for the purpose of protesting the proposed cuts in antipoverty funds to the State, and especially New York City--an action which did not really fall within the operational definition of two-step bargaining since the issue was an internal one to the community action program itself, and the action resulted from no initiative on the part of the Delegate Agencies in Tremont. It was concluded that no real two-step bargaining had occurred in the area during Program Year "E."

Our analysis of the variable of bargaining has provided little evidence that the community action program in the Tremont poverty area accomplished on a widespread level the type of activities through which we could conclude influence on the part of the partisan group, the poor. Certainly, our findings with regard to bargaining are totally consistent with earlier conclusions regarding the high degree of antagonistic ethnic identity and fragmented interest group identity present in the area, as well as the policy of containment which characterized such a significant part of the total operation of the community action program in Tremont.

Resocialization

With regard to the variable of resocialization, we are concerned with four possible outcomes of the community action program concerning the value orientations and behavior of the individuals affected by that program:

1. continued acceptable socialization--whereby a previously acceptable individual continues to be acceptable;

2. deviant resocialization--whereby a previously acceptable individual becomes deviant;

3. continued deviant socialization--whereby a previously deviant individual continues to be deviant; and,

4. acceptable resocialization--whereby a previously deviant individual becomes acceptable.

For the purpose of the study, an "acceptable"
value orientation and behavior was defined in terms
of the pattern of particularistic politics, implied
in the traditional ideology of representative democracy; while a "deviant" value orientation and behavior was defined with reference to the patterns
of either pluralistic politics, typically involving
a multisided conflict among groups, or status group
politics, characterized by large groups engaged in
bipolar confrontation. These three patterns were
taken to represent three different strategies for
helping the poor rise out of poverty. The extent
to which social control was operative in this regard is to be seen primarily in terms of the occurrence of the process of "acceptable resocialization," marked by an individual's shift from either
a pluralistic or status group value orientation and
behavior to a particularistic value orientation and
behavior. In light of the important concepts of
exemption or creaming, the process of continued acceptable socialization, or that by which an individual continues to maintain a particularistic
value orientation and behavior as a result of the
community action program, may well be equally significant insofar as the social control of potential
partisans by authorities is concerned (see Chapter 2).

To measure the extent of the occurrence of these
processes, two major steps were involved: first, the
past and present value orientations of the 87 P's,
PB's, and NPB's in the sample were measured; and
secondly, past and present behavior patterns, in
terms of organizational membership, were determined
as a check on their expressed values.

The first step began by asking all 87 respondents this question:

1. I'm going to show you three statements
that describe three different ways to help the poor
get out of poverty. Which of these do you feel is
the best way?

        A. Each poor person should vote
    for the candidate that will best

represent him and leave it up to that
official to find ways of getting the
poor the help that they need. (Particularistic strategy.)

B. Each poor person should join
groups formed around some problem
that the poor face--such as poor housing or lack of jobs. The leaders of
these groups would then represent the
members in trying to solve these problems and in fighting against those in
power. (Pluralistic strategy.)

C. Each poor person should join
with large groups of other poor people
to develop leadership among the poor
themselves. The members of these
groups themselves, under their leaders, would then openly confront the
people in power. (Status group
strategy.)

After indicating their preferred strategy, the
respondents were asked this question:

2. Before you got involved with the Tremont
community action program, which of these three ways
did you feel was the best way to help the poor get
out of poverty? When there was a change indicated
between questions 1 and 2, the respondent was asked
if this change was due to his involvement with the
community action program. All respondents who indicated a change replied that this factor had been
at least partially responsible.

On the basis of the responses to questions 1
and 2, Table 7.25 was constructed, in which the
past and present value orientations of the respondents have been classified according to the appropriate type of socialization-resocialization process at work. Perhaps the most striking feature
of this table is the very significant number of respondents, 59, or 67.8 percent of the 87 questioned,
who indicated continued deviant socialization.
Fifty-two individuals (see Rows 3a and b)--29 P's,
13 PB's, and 10 NPB's--or 59.8 percent continued
unchanged in their deviance, while 6--3 P's and

TABLE 7.25

Respondents' Value Orientations Before and After
Involvement with the Tremont Community Action
Program, by Type of Socialization-
Resocialization Occurring

Type of Socialization-Resocialization	P's	PB's	NPB's	Total	Percentage
1. Continued Acceptable Socialization:					
(a) particularistic to particularistic strategy	0	0	4	4	4.6
2. Deviant Resocialization:					
(a) particularistic to pluralistic strategy	3	2	0	5	5.7
(b) particularistic to status group strategy	8	6	4	18	20.7
3. Continued Deviant Socialization:					
(a) pluralistic to pluralistic strategy	2	5	3	10	11.5
(b) status group to status group strategy	27	8	7	42	48.3
(c) pluralistic to status group strategy	3	3	0	6	6.9
(d) status group to pluralistic strategy	1	0	0	1	1.1
4. Acceptable Resocialization:					
(a) pluralistic to particularistic strategy	0	0	0	0	0.0
(b) status group to particularistic strategy	1	0	0	1	1.1
Total	45	24	18	87	100.0

Source: Compiled by the authors.

3 PB's--shifted to an even greater degree of deviance (Row 3c), and only one P became slightly less deviant in his value orientation (Row 3d).

An additional 23 respondents, or 26.4 percent of the sample, gave evidence of having become deviant through their involvement with the program. From Row 2b we can see that most of these changed from viewing a particularistic strategy as best to preferring a status group strategy. Thus, at the time of the study, some 94.2 percent of the respondents indicated that they were still, or had become, deviant in their value orientations. Only 4 individuals, or 4.6 percent of the sample, maintained an acceptable value orientation, and significantly, all of these were NPB's. Only one person, a P--comprising 1.1 percent of those questioned--indicated acceptable resocialization, from a preferred strategy of status group politics to one of particularistic politics.

We might have concluded on the basis of the respondent's stated value orientations that the major impact of the Tremont community action program was in the direction of increasing deviance, rather than increasing acceptability, with an emphasis on a strategy of status group politics. However, through the second step of the measurement process a much different picture emerged.

Here, the emphasis was on determining whether or not the individuals' past and present value orientations were reflected or expressed through a type of behavior. Since our concern was primarily focused on political values, involving different strategies of helping the poor get out of poverty, it was decided to view behavior in terms of membership in organizations working in the general area of helping the poor.

Of first concern was the examination of past organizational membership. The respondents were asked the two following questions:

1. Before the community action program came into Tremont, did you work with any group or organizations who were trying in some way to help the poor get out of poverty?--and--(if the first question was answered affirmatively),

2.   Could you describe the type of activities
with which each of these groups or organizations
was involved?   (Prodding was used here in order to
determine whether the group had a particularistic,
pluralistic, or status group orientation.)

Any type of organization that involved neither
"multisided conflict among groups" nor engagement
by large status groups in "bipolar confrontation,"
was characterized as reflective of a particularistic orientation. Most frequently mentioned groups
in this category were church-related organizations,
which occasionally took up collections of food and
clothing for the poor; the Police Athletic League
and other groups concerned with sponsoring recreational activities for the poor; National Association of Puerto Rican Affairs, whose office in Tremont prior to its affiliation with the community
action program was primarily concerned with helping
newly arrived Puerto Ricans find jobs, housing and
other necessities; traditional political clubs; and
various social service groups such as those working
in the area of day care. Organizations with a
pluralistic orientation mentioned by respondents
were primarily those groups concerned with organizing tenants' associations and other interest groups
related to the issue of housing, which later became
Delegate Agencies. Finally, groups such as the
Black Panthers, Young Lords, National Welfare Rights
Organization, and Puerto Rican Community Development
Project, were interpreted as reflective of a status
group orientation.[2]

Having determined and classified the past behavioral orientation of the 87 respondents, each
person was then asked the same two questions with
respect to his current organizational membership.
Respondents were asked to include here, in addition
to any other organizations, their affiliation with
the specific unit or units of the community action
program.*

_____

*In classifying these units according to par-
ticularistic, pluralistic, and status group orientations, the following guidelines were used, based

Thus present and past organizational membership was able to be characterized as particularistic, pluralistic, or status group oriented; through
comparing present behavioral orientation with past,
each individual was able to be classified according
to the exact socialization-resocialization process
at work with respect to his organizational membership. Table 7.26 was constructed on the basis of
this information. In interpreting the data which
appear in this table, the following two points
should be kept in mind. First, where the respondent mentioned membership in more than one organization, either before or after his involvement with
the community action program, analysis was made on
the basis of the one with which he indicated the
greatest degree of involvement. Second, in those
cases where, either before or after the program,
the respondent indicated no organizational membership, his behavioral orientation was classified as
particularistic, since in the context of this study
and from the point of view of authorities, a lack
of organizational activity was tantamount to acceptability.

The most significant feature of Table 7.26
lies in the fact that, whereas 4.6 percent of all
respondents had indicated continued acceptable socialization with respect to value orientation, almost one-half, or 49.4 percent of the total 87 in
the sample, evidenced such a process in terms of
behavioral orientation as reflected in organizational affiliation (Row 1a). Conversely, whereas
59 respondents, or 67.8 percent, had indicated

---

on what was known of the units' activities through
the data yielded throughout the study: 8 of the
Delegate Agencies were counted as following a particularistic strategy (TC Council, Federation,
Monterey, NAPRA, WFV, ETNA, Cadets, and Bronco),
while the Tremont Community Corporation and the
other 5 Delegate Agencies (THC, WANA, ETAC, Elsmere, and UBP) were considered as having at least
attempted to utilize a pluralistic approach or
strategy.

TABLE 7.26

Respondents' Behavioral Orientation, with Respect to
Organizational Membership, Before and After
Involvement with the Tremont Community
Action Program, by Type of Socialization-
Resocialization Occurring

Type of Socialization-Resocialization	P's	PB's	NPB's	Total	Percentage
1. Continued Acceptable Socialization:					
(a) particularistic to particularistic strategy	20	13	10	43	49.4
2. Deviant Resocialization:					
(a) particularistic to pluralistic strategy	12	10	0	22	25.3
(b) particularistic to status group strategy	2	1	7	10	11.5
3. Continued Deviant Socialization:					
(a) pluralistic to pluralistic strategy	3	0	0	3	3.5
(b) status group to status group strategy	2	0	0	2	2.2
(c) pluralistic to status group strategy	2	0	0	2	2.2
(d) status group to pluralistic strategy	3	0	0	3	3.5
4. Acceptable Resocialization:					
(a) pluralistic to particularistic strategy	1	0	0	1	1.2
(b) status group to particularistic strategy	0	0	1	1	1.2
Total	45	24	18	87	100.0

Source: Compiled by the authors.

continued deviant socialization in terms of value
orientation, only 10 individuals--all P's and comprising 11.4 percent of the sample--showed such socialization with regard to behavioral orientation
(Rows 3 a, b, c, and d). Thus, quite clearly the
picture emerging from an analysis of respondents'
behavioral orientations differs significantly from
that yielded through a consideration of their
stated value orientations.

In order to compare values and behavior on an
individual basis, the data presented in summary
form in Table 7.27 was then analyzed. Most significantly, of the 33 P's who indicated deviant values
both before and after involvement with the community action program in Tremont, 15 maintained acceptable organizational affiliations, 10 changed
from acceptable to deviant organizations, one
changed from a deviant to an acceptable organization, and only 7 continued, in keeping with their
stated values, to belong to deviant organizations.
Of the 16 PB's who were included in the category of
continued deviant socialization on the basis of
their value orientation, 9 evidenced continued acceptable socialization, and 7 showed deviant resocialization in terms of behavioral orientation.
Four of the 10 NPB's in the category of continued
deviant socialization with respect to values, evidenced continued acceptable socialization in organizational membership, 5 individuals showed deviant resocialization, and one showed acceptable resocialization. Significantly, none of the PB's or
NPB's here considered gave evidence of continued
deviant socialization on the basis of their behavioral orientation.

Overall, then, with reference to Table 7.27,
the following conclusions may be stated with respect to the variable of resocialization:

1. Four persons, all NPB's, indicated continued acceptable socialization in both values and
behavior, comprising Category #1.

2. Nine persons, 3 P's, 4 PB's, and 2 NPB's,
indicated deviant resocialization in both values
and behavior, comprising Category #2.

TABLE 7.27

Summary of Relationship Between Respondents' Value
Orientation and Behavioral Orientation

Type of Socialization-Resocialization Affecting Value Orientation	Type of Socialization-Resocialization Affecting Behavioral Orientation											
	P's				PB's				NPB's			
	Cont. Acc. Soc.	Dev. Resoc.	Cont. Dev. Soc.	Acc. Resoc.	Cont. Acc. Soc.	Dev. Resoc.	Cont. Dev. Soc.	Acc. Resoc.	Cont. Acc. Soc.	Dev. Resoc.	Cont. Dev. Soc.	Acc. Resoc.
Continued Acceptable Socialization	0	0	0	0	0	0	0	0	4	0	0	0
Deviant Resocialization	5	3	3	0	4	4	0	0	2	2	0	0
Continued Deviant Socialization	15	10	7	1	9	7	0	0	4	5	0	1
Acceptable Resocialization	0	1	0	0	0	0	0	0	0	0	0	0

Source: Compiled by the authors.

3. Seven persons, all P's, indicated continued deviant socialization in both values and behavior, comprising Category #3.

4. No one fell into Category #4 indicating acceptable resocialization in both values and behavior.

5. Eleven persons, 5 P's, 4 PB's, and 2 NPB's, indicated deviantly resocialized values and continued acceptable behavior. Since behavior was felt to be more indicative of overall orientation than expressed values, these 11 were placed in Category #1.*

6. Three persons, all P's, indicated deviantly resocialized values and continued deviant behavior, and thus were placed in Category #3.

7. Twenty-eight persons, 15 P's, 9 PB's, and 4 NPB's, indicated continued deviant values and continued acceptable behavior. Following the reasoning in conclusion (5) above, these individuals were placed in Category #1.

8. Twenty-two persons, 10 P's, 7 PB's, and 5 NPB's, indicated continued deviant values and deviantly resocialized behavior, and were thus placed in Category #3.

---

*Throughout the observational phase of the study, the often sharp discrepancy between the program participants' words and actions was repeatedly seen. In numerous informal conversations it was learned that, to a significant extent, such qualities as "leadership" were measured in the community-at-large by reference to one's ability to talk "radical." However, many of those who spoke the most "deviantly" conceded privately that they had no real intention of acting upon these expressed values. In light of this finding, and in considering the fact that as far as authorities are concerned it is deviant actors--rather than deviant talkers--who constitute a real--rather than merely potential threat--care was taken to characterize as truly deviant only those whose behavior supported their values.

9.   Two persons, one P and one NPB, indicated
continued deviant values and acceptable resocialized
behavior, and were placed in Category #4.
10.   One person, a P, indicated acceptably resocialized values and deviantly resocialized behavior, and was placed in Category #2.
These conclusions are recorded in Table 7.28.

TABLE 7.28

Classification of Respondents According to Overall
Type of Socialization-Resocialization Occurring
as Result of Involvement with Tremont
Community Action Program, Year "E"

Type of Socialization-Resocialization	P's	PB's	NPB's	Total	Percentage
Continued Acceptable Socialization	20	13	10	43	49.4
Deviant Re-socialization	4	4	2	10	11.5
Continued Deviant Socialization	20	7	5	32	36.9
Acceptable Re-socialization	1	0	1	2	2.2
Total	45	24	18	87	100.0

Source: Compiled by the authors.

Table 7.28 indicates that 43 individuals, or
49.3 percent of the sample, continued to be acceptably socialized as a result of their involvement
with the Tremont community action program.   In this

group we find 20 P's, 13 PB's, and 10 NPB's. The
second largest group, consisting of 32 individuals--
20 P's, 7 PB's, and 5 NPB's--or 36.9 percent of the
sample, continued to be deviantly socialized as a
result of the program. Only 12 persons gave evidence of having been resocialized--10 of these in a
deviant direction, and only 2 toward acceptability.

Thus, it appears quite clearly that during Program Year "E," the community action program in the
Tremont poverty area did not evidence social control in the sense of having acceptably resocialized
those individuals who became involved. However, it
does appear that a sizable proportion (almost half)
of those who directed, administered, worked in, and
received the services of the program, were acceptable in orientation both before and after having
become involved. This fact points most definitely
to a type of social control mechanism which may
well have operated to determine exactly who was
reached by and let into the program, the mechanism
of exemption or creaming. This mechanism may have
affected the 11.5 percent of our sample who, prior
to involvement with the program indicated acceptability, but who became deviant as a result of that
involvement. Nevertheless, if such a process of
social control was at work, it was not totally effective, as more than one-third (36.9 percent) of
the sample indicated deviance of one degree or another before becoming involved with the community
action program, and maintained that deviant orientation throughout. Also at the time of the study,
some 48.4 percent of the respondents (including
those who were deviantly resocialized as well as
those who continued in their deviance) reflected
orientations which would have been considered deviant by the authorities, indicating a substantial
group that could potentially serve as a basis for
the development of influence by the partisan group
in the Tremont community.

Unsuccessfuls and the Youth

In concluding our analysis of the respondents'
overall views on the community action program in

the Tremont poverty area, we should look very briefly at the views of the 3 Unsuccessfuls and 6 Youth
involved in the sample. These individuals have not
been included in the analysis provided in this chapter since it was found that neither of the groups
was able to provide as specific information concerning the operation of the program in Tremont as were
the P's, PB's, and NPB's. This is to be expected
considering the relative lack of involvement of
either the U's or the Youth in the program during
this time period. Nevertheless, their responses
with regard to each of the six variables measured
through the interviewing phase of the study supported the conclusions reached through the analysis
which has been presented.

Specifically, concerning the variables of separation and separateness, all 3 Unsuccessfuls and
all 6 Youth primarily identified with the poor, although 8 of the 9 indicated that their involvement
with the community action program had not brought
about these feelings. In their responses regarding
separation, all indicated the presence of a high
degree of antagonistic ethnic identity and fragmented interest group identity in the community;
and while admitting a lack of specific knowledge,
all 6 Youth and 2 of the U's judged that a policy
of containment characterized the overall program in
Tremont. The additional Unsuccessful was not able
to answer this question. None of the 9 had ever
heard of any one-step bargaining by the Delegate
Agencies in the area; while the only two-step bargaining attempt mentioned was the Washington antipoverty funds cutback demonstration. Finally, 5 of
the 6 Youth and one of the Unsuccessfuls indicated
deviant resocialization in terms of both value and
behavioral orientation; whereas the remaining Youth
and one other Unsuccessful were categorized as having evidenced continued deviant socialization, and
the final Unsuccessful was counted as having shown
continued acceptable socialization.

CONCLUSIONS

Our analysis of the data yielded through the
interviewing process has provided considerable

additional evidence in support of the major hypothesis of the study, that despite the stated goals of
the city-wide community action program which imply
that the neighborhood level program should be an
influence output, the actual operation of the program in the Tremont area may best be described as a
social control output. Two of the operational indicators of the concept of social control which
were developed for the purpose of the study--separa-
tion and containment--were seen to have been operative in the area to a significant extent. While the
third indicator, that of resocialization, was not so
clearly indicated, the extensive evidence in support
of a lack of occurrence through the Tremont community action program of the two major indicators of
influence--collaboration and bargaining--should allow us to conclude, on the basis of both the observational and interview data collected for this
study, that our hypothesis has been substantiated.

8

This research began with the aim of evaluating
the community action program in New York City--
which had previously been described as a "participatory output"--in terms of the actual consequences
of the programs for the poor and for the alleviation
of the stress brought about by poverty. Specifically, it was felt that what needed to be determined
was whether or not participation in such a program
had worked to the advantage of the poor. Utilizing
a conceptual framework based upon the recent work
of William Gamson, the study sought to classify the
community action program at one particular neighborhood level of the city, the Tremont poverty area,
as primarily constituting an "influence output" or
a "social control output," these two terms having
been defined as follows: An influence output is a
decision or set of decisions by authorities which
brings the potential partisans--the poor--or their
legitimate representatives into the political system
and gives them the necessary resources to make a
reasonable attempt to alleviate the stress coming
from the objects of discontent.* A social control
output, on the other hand, is a decision or set of
decisions by which the authorities primarily attempt
to alleviate the stress coming from the sources of
pressure.

*See Gamson's use of "potential partisans" on
p. xviii.

In terms of these two key concepts the study's major hypothesis was formulated and stated as follows: Although the stated goals of the community action program in New York City imply that the program on the neighborhood level should be an influence output, with the community action bureaucracy serving as an advocate of the potential partisans, the poor, the actual operation in the Tremont poverty area can best be described as a social control output, with the community action bureaucracy functioning as a social control agent and as another authority with which the poor must cope.

The terms "influence" and "social control outputs" were then further conceptualized through reference to Gerald Shattuck's six strategies of social order and conflict, yielding the following two subhypotheses:

1. To the extent that separateness, bargaining, and collaboration have taken place as a result of the Tremont community action program, this program can be described as an influence output.

2. To the extent that separation, containment, and resocialization have taken place as a result of the Tremont community action program, this program can be described as a social control output.

Finally, Shattuck's six variables were transformed into empirical indicators of influence and social control. Data on each variable were collected through observation, participant observation, content analysis, and interviewing; and centered on examining three major aspects of the community action program:

1. the resources and operation of the various neighborhood level units;

2. the most crucial relationships between the neighborhood level units and the community action bureaucracy, as reflected in the cycle of the funding process; and

3. the perceptions of a sample of those individuals who directed, administered, worked in, and received the services of the Tremont area program. During the various stages of data collection,

Gamson's "influence attempts" and "subjective probability" approaches to the measurement of the concept of influence were incorporated where appropriate.*

SUMMARY OF OBSERVATIONAL
AND INTERVIEW DATA

The observational and interview data yielded
through employing the theoretical and methodological frameworks described above may now be briefly
summarized in terms of the study's six major variables. In interpreting these findings, it should
be kept clearly in mind that through any program
such as the one under study, both influence and social control may well be occurring simultaneously;
and that the major goal of this research was to determine whether the influences variables, or those
of social control, were predominant.

1. Separateness and separation--The interviewing phase of the study yielded the conclusion that,
while little if any coalitional ethnic identity or
solid interest group identity was evidenced in the
Tremont area, a significant proportion (about 75
percent) of all respondents indicated firm identification with either the poor as a whole or with a
specific ethnic group. However, whereas only one-
third of the feelings of separateness expressed by
respondents was attributed to the community action
program, over 75 percent of those interviewed indicated that the program had resulted in heightening
conflict and antagonism among the various ethnic
groups in the area (type-two separation, or antagonistic ethnic identity), as well as destructive competition among the neighborhood level units of the

---

*It should be noted that neither of these ap-
proaches yielded significant data which were not
also uncovered through the measurement of the six
major variables.

community action program (type-three separation, or
fragmented interest group identity). Observational
data--particularly that resulting from examination
of the functioning of the Tremont Community Corporation and the various Delegate Agencies--supported
the finding that both types of separation were being fostered through the program in the Tremont
area; allowing the conclusion to be formulated that
the program had not developed the potential for influence which was present prior to its existence,
but rather had used the participants' feelings of
separateness as a basis for creating group conflict.

2. Collaboration and containment--Examination
of the functioning of the 13 Delegate Agencies in
Tremont showed that, at the time of the study, only
two possessed the necessary resources (in the form
of funds, trained personnel, and technical assistance) to operate the type of relevant and effective programs which could be taken as evidence of
collaboration; while an additional three agencies
appeared to possess the potential for building up
successful programs, given better trained personnel
or more meaningful technical assistance. The remaining eight Delegate Agencies provided rather
firm evidence of containment, insofar as their programs were clearly nonrelevant, unsuccessful or ineffective. These findings were generally supported
by the perceptions of program participants and recipients, less than 10 percent of whom saw the community action program in Tremont as having resulted
in collaboration.

3. Bargaining--Observational data indicated
that only three Delegate Agencies had, during the
time under consideration, undertaken bargaining attempts, in the sense of utilizing collective action
to engage a dominant target system; and that only
one of these agencies had experienced any meaningful degree of success. Here it was further seen
that no "two-step bargaining," or joint actions by
two or more agencies, had occurred. Knowledgeable
respondents (those closely associated with Delegate
Agency activities) provided evidence in general ac-
cord with these findings, with only one-third indicating knowledge of any bargaining attempts whatsoever. Those in this latter group generally supported

the finding that such attempts as did take place experienced a relatively low degree of success, while
describing only five collective actions as having
been very successful. Again, no real two-step bargaining was evidenced through the interview data.

    4. Resocialization--While little meaningful
data on this variable was obtained through the observational phase of the study, interview data indicated that as a result of the Tremont program,
almost one-half of the respondents evidenced continued acceptable socialization, while over one-
third continued a pattern of deviant socialization.
About 12 percent had become resocialized in a deviant direction, whereas only slightly more than 27
percent of all respondents indicated having been
acceptably resocialized.

    On the basis of the data summarized above, it
may be seen quite clearly that two of the social
control variables--separation and containment--were
operative in the Tremont community action program
to a very significant extent during Program Year
"E." As was noted at the end of Chapter 7, while
the third social control variable--resocialization--
was not nearly so clearly indicated, the extensive
evidence in support of a lack of occurrence through
the program of the two major indicators of influ-
ence--collaboration and bargaining--should allow us
to conclude that the social control variables were
clearly predominant. Most importantly, the analysis
undertaken of the role of the community action bureaucracy in structuring, assisting, and guiding
the program in Tremont, has placed primary responsibility for the occurrence and development of these
variables on the bureaucratic agencies themselves,
particularly on the Community Development Agency;
indicating that the community action bureaucracy
may be described much more accurately as a social
control agent and as another authority with whom
the poor must cope, rather than as an advocate of
the poor in their attempt to gain influence vis-à-
vis those individuals or groups which are perceived
to dominate their interests in the local area. The
research has substantiated the major hypothesis
that the community action program in the Tremont
poverty area is primarily a social control output,
as opposed to one of influence.

MAJOR IMPLICATIONS OF THE STUDY

At this point it would be well to turn our attention to several major implications inherent in the substantiation of this hypothesis, which should aid in interpreting the conclusions which have been drawn in the preceding few pages. While the Tremont program at the time of the study could not be considered a vehicle for having significantly increased the influence of area residents, certain factors suggest a potential for the program to be transformed in this direction. Among the most significant of these are the following:

1. Several of the Delegate Agencies examined showed the potential for building up meaningful and effective programs. If these agencies were to acquire the necessary resources to enable them to actualize this potential, they could perhaps serve, together with those two agencies already operating relevant and effective programs, as a significantly large focal group for the development of a strong constituency among area residents, and thus as a means of acquiring increased influence for those whom they represent.

2. Almost half of the interview respondents indicated value orientations which would be viewed as "deviant" by any authority attempting to control them. If these values were to be translated into behavior in keeping with the strategies of pluralistic or status group politics, and directed against perceived dominant, controlling groups, such persons could well serve as a basis for the development of influence on the part of the partisan group, the poor.

3. Over three-quarters of those interviewed indicated feelings of separateness in the sense of either poor or ethnic identity. Such feelings could conceivably be channeled into a significant force for the exercising of influence, given the existence of a unifying and centralizing group or program in the Tremont area.

In light of current policies operative in the community action bureaucracy, it appears unlikely that such potential as described above, will be

actualized through the program on the neighborhood
level in the relatively near future.* Nevertheless,
these factors should not be discounted in assessing
the long-term relationship between the poor in the
Tremont area and those who presently control their
interests.

A second important point which should be mentioned here is that what influence as was seen to
be occurring in Tremont as a result of the community
action program--both actual and potential--appeared
to be a result of social service programs controlled
by the poor and their legitimate representatives in
the area, as opposed to large-scale collective action. Most notably, with only one real exception
(East Tremont Action Committee), even those Delegate Agencies whose program functions implied group
action were much more successful in the provision
of services. This suggests additional support for
Michael Lipsky's contention[1] that the tactic of
mass protest does not carry the promise of a high
probability of success for relatively powerless
groups such as the minority poor; and that the social service strategy is more likely in the long
run to bring about influence for such groups, insofar as strong service programs can provide the
type of "stable political resources" which allow
for the development of a substantial constituency
among the poor. Again, it is at present unclear as
to whether the Tremont community action program
will be able to actualize the potential which it
appears to possess in this regard.

A third significant implication of this research lies in the fact that the community action
program in the Tremont area has undoubtedly provided
some individual participants--especially certain

----

*Continued contact and observation of the com-
munity action program in the Tremont area from October 1970 to June 1971 reinforces the conclusions
of the study since the Community Development Agency
has not, from all appearances, significantly modified its social control role at the neighborhood
level.

members of the Community Corporation Staff and
Board of Directors, as well as a very limited number of Delegate Agency Directors--the opportunity
to develop the kind of skills necessary for moving
themselves and those they represent into a position
of influence. Some evidence has recently come to
light that supports this finding and suggests that
it is occurring throughout the city-wide program.
In a recent New York Times article it was noted
that the Puerto Ricans in particular have used the
neighborhood level community action programs as a
"training ground for political leadership . . .
much as earlier waves of immigrants used [political]
clubhouses."[2] In the words of a former program participant and the first Puerto Rican elected to the
New York State Legislature, Louis Nine from Morrisania, "The Community Corporations are training
young Puerto Ricans to speak out in meetings, to
organize. They are in their neighborhoods twenty-
four hours a day. In the future, I think more and
more candidates for political office will come from
antipoverty programs."[3]

However, one must be careful not to overempha-
size the significance of this situation in terms of
bringing about increased influence for the poor,
because of the following two points:

1. A very real question exists as to whether
the Community Corporation and key figures in the
neighborhood level community action programs are in
fact legitimate representatives of the poor. First-
hand observation of the functioning of the Tremont
Community Corporation, undertaken for this study,
clearly pointed up the ability of this unit to play
a significant role in contributing to the community
action bureaucracy's overall process of social control, through its key position as an intermediary
between the bureaucracy and the ranks of the poor.
Also, from the analysis of the interview data gathered for the study, a significant number of persons
indicated to one degree or another that they regarded the Corporation itself as a major "target
system" against which the Delegate Agencies and
area residents had to struggle. That the situation
giving rise to such an attitude is quite common

throughout the city was attested to in another recent New York Times article which stated that, "Many
of the professional antipoverty organizers have become a new class in the slums, apart from and above
the poor, who are supposed to be the beneficiaries
of the programs."[4] The article further noted that
some critics have coined the term "povertycrats" to
describe these newly emerging professionals, many
of whom are neither poor (according to bureaucratic
definitions) nor indigenous to the areas in which
they are employed and which they claim to represent.
Thus, what may well be occurring here, rather than
the training of new legitimate leadership for the
poor, is the development of a new elite around the
issue of controlling antipoverty monies on the
neighborhood level.

    2. Given the existence of such a "new class"
in poverty areas, it is to be expected that the
antipoverty or community action program responsible
for its creation has likewise generated significant
conflict over who will comprise the "povertycrats"
in the local community. In the Tremont area, it
has been seen that this conflict has been manifested
primarily along racial and ethnic lines, a situation
which appears to be widespread throughout the city's
community action program. Representative Herman
Badillo, terming the antipoverty program in New York
City a "mechanism for patronage along ethnic lines"
and a "political spoils system," has provided support for this contention through his recent testimony before the Congressional Subcommittee on Poverty and Manpower that the operations of the Community Corporations are "an open scandal that in-
cubate violence between the Blacks and the Puerto
Ricans."[5] Even more recently, testimony has been
heard from Jewish spokesmen that the community action program in the city has likewise served as a
"mechanism to foment ethnic conflict between Blacks
and Jews."[6] Interestingly, in the eyes of almost
all who appeared before the Subcommittee, including
the current Chairman of the Council Against Poverty,
the "inevitable struggle" among the city's ethnic
groups could only be eased by increasing Federal
funds for antipoverty programs.[7]

Certainly, such a situation is most destructive in terms of the development of a strong coalition among the poor, and serves primarily as a means of channeling the efforts of program participants away from confrontation with dominant and controlling groups.

SIGNIFICANCE OF THE STUDY

Having looked at the major conclusions and implications of the study, a few brief remarks should be included concerning what is seen to be its major significance. Of first importance, the research undertaken has provided a body of data concerning the community action program at a particular neighborhood level, on the basis of which a concrete evaluation can be made as to the consequences of the program for the poor themselves. The study has clearly established the necessity of empirically examining such programs as community action on their most basic level of operation and in terms of the actual, rather than the stated goals to which participation of the poor is aimed as well as the quality of that participation, as reflected in concrete instances of program operation.

Secondly, this research has pointed out once again the necessity for community action outputs to be evaluated in terms of a solid theoretical framework--a position which has been so emphasized by various critics of recent antipoverty efforts. In developing such a framework, William Gamson's concepts of influence and social control have proven to be highly applicable, particularly insofar as these have been more concretely conceptualized through Gerald Shattuck's six strategies of social order and conflict (separateness and separation, collaboration and containment, bargaining, and resocialization).

Thirdly, and perhaps most significantly, it is felt that the study has contributed to the efforts of sociologists in recent years to develop empirical indicators of such concepts as influence and social control; and relatedly, those of social

conflict and order. The operational indicators of
Shattuck's six variables (as well as the further
subtypes of each variable spelled out for the purposes of this study), which have been developed in
connection with this research, provided a significant extension of Gamson's own approaches to measurement. According to the operational definitions
utilized here, the variables of collaboration and
containment emerged, respectively, as the key indicators of influence of influence and social control; while separateness was seen as most valuable
in terms of establishing the preliminary conditions
for the occurrence of influence, and the variable
of bargaining provided a useful check on the "group
action" aspect of the influence concept.

While the significance of the study is felt to
lie in the above respects, any interpretations made
on the basis of the conclusions formulated here
should heed the limitations inherent in the fact
that this research has consisted essentially of a
case study of only one of the 26 poverty areas
which make up the total community action program in
New York City. The Tremont poverty area was chosen
as the focus for the study primarily because of its
median position, according to its "poverty index,"
as defined by the city-wide bureaucracy, and the
amount of funds received for program operation during the 1969-70 year. While it has been clearly established that the community action program in this
area has not resulted in significantly increasing
the influence of the poor, it is quite possible
that a very different picture would emerge in an
area such as Bedford Stuyvesant which, according to
bureaucracy criteria, contained about three-and-one-
half times as many residents as did Tremont, but
which received almost seven-and-one-half times as
much money during the program year under consideration in this study. Implied is the possibility
that the city-wide bureaucracy may be forced to
concede to the development and influence in those
communities where, even prior to the existence of
the community action program, such factors as separateness, bargaining, and collaboration were already present to some significant degree; while

tightly controlling the large majority of poverty
areas which, like Tremont, reflect fairly widespread
fragmentations and a minimal degree of prior organization.

FUTURE RESEARCH

The need for the study to be replicated in
other areas is suggested so that more substantive
data may be made available to base firm conclusions
concerning the overall operation of the community
action program in New York City. Additional suggestions for research come to mind as a result of
this study: First, the operational definitions of
Shattuck's six variables developed for this study
need to be tested under a wide range of situations
and applied to various issue areas in order that
their value as a tool in evaluative research may be
further enhanced and established. Special attention should be directed to a possible reformulation
of the definition constructed for the variable of
resocialization, which in this study did not yield
data totally consistent with those resulting from
an examination of the community action program with
respect to the two other operational indicators of
social control.

Second, further attention needs to be directed
to the views of those who are receiving the services
of the various Delegate Agency programs in the local
poverty areas--those who, in this study, have been
characterized as the "Nonparticipant Beneficiaries."
Especially significant here would be the determination, to a much fuller extent, of this group's attitudes toward the program's administrators, directors, and employees; especially in view of the preceding discussion of the recent emergence of "povertycrats" in poverty areas throughout the city.
Finally, as a most necessary means of establishing
whether or not the emergence of such "a new class
in the slums" carries the potential for the development of increased influence on behalf of the partisan group, the poor, additional research needs to
be undertaken concerning the povertycrats themselves;

especially around such questions as their back-
grounds, their qualifications, and most importantly,
their own political stakes in the poor communities
in which they are becoming powerful.[8]

This research has shown that community action
programs, such as the one in the Tremont poverty
area, are now at a point where their development
could well proceed either in the direction of continued social control by the city-wide community
action bureaucracy, or of increased influence for
the poor, given the existence of legitimate leadership and a unifying program. Either way, such a
group as the povertycrats may well be playing the
key role in the years to come.[9]

APPENDIX

Separateness and Separation

General Identity

1. Some people that I've talked to in the Tremont area feel that they identify with other people. Who do you feel that you identify with?
   (IF MORE THAN ONE RESPONSE, ASK RESPONDENT TO RANK TOP THREE IN TERMS OF IMPORTANCE: 1 EQUALS FIRST, 2 EQUALS SECOND, 3 EQUALS THIRD. ASK: Who do you feel you identify with the most? Who next? Who next?)

RANK   COMMENTS:

_____ 0. NR
_____ 1. DK
_____ 2. no one (skip to question 5)
_____ 3. the poor
_____ 4. the people working in this Delegate Agency or in other Delegate Agencies
_____ 5. the people involved with the Tremont Community Corporation
_____ 6. Blacks
_____ 7. Puerto Ricans
_____ 8. Coalition of Blacks and Puerto Ricans
_____ 9. community leaders
_____ 10. church
_____ 11. other (SPECIFY)

Poor Identity

2. (IF ANSWERED #3 ABOVE, ASK) Do you feel that the poor in Tremont have to unite as a group to bring about changes in their living conditions?

_____ 0. NR   COMMENTS:
_____ 1. DK
_____ 2. yes
_____ 3. no (SKIP TO QUESTION 3)
_____ 4. other (SPECIFY)

215

2.1 (IF YES ABOVE, ASK)   Against whom do you think
    the poor have to unite as a group to bring
    about change?
    (IF MORE THAN ONE RESPONSE, ASK RESPONDENTS TO
    RANK TOP THREE OBSTACLES IN IMPORTANCE: 1 EQUALS
    FIRST, ETC. ASK: Who do you think is the main
    obstacle to change? Who next? Etc.?) (FIRST
    ASK, PAUSE, THEN SHOW CARD)

RANK   RANK
_____ 0. NR   _____   6. established
_____ 1. DK   bureaucracies
_____ 2. middle or upper   (welfare,
           class (SPECIFY)   housing, em-
_____ 3. Delegate Agencies   ployment agen-
           or Tremont Commu-   cies, etc.)
           nity Corporation   _____   7. police
           (SPECIFY)   _____   8. school systems
_____ 4. CAP-CDA (SPECIFY)   and policies
_____ 5. political struc-   _____   9. slum landlords
           tures (local,   _____ 10. others (SPECIFY)
           state, national)
           (SPECIFY)   COMMENTS:

2.2. (IF ANSWERED ABOVE, ASK) Did you feel this way
     before getting involved with the Tremont commu-
     nity action program, i.e., feel that the poor
     have to unite as a group against _____?
_____ 0. NR
_____ 1. DK or DR   COMMENTS:
_____ 2. yes
_____ 3. no
_____ 4. other (SPECIFY)

2.21 (IF NO ABOVE, ASK) Did you come to feel this
     way because of the Tremont community action
     program?
_____ 0. NR   COMMENTS:
_____ 1. DK or DR
_____ 2. yes
_____ 3. no

ETHNIC IDENTITY
3. (IF ANSWERED #6 or 7 TO QUESTION 1, ASK) Do you
   feel that the _____(ETHNIC GROUP OF RESPONDENT)

have to unite as a group to bring about changes
in their living conditions?

_____ 0. NR   COMMENTS:
_____ 1. DK
_____ 2. yes
_____ 3. no (SKIP TO QUESTION 4)
_____ 4. other (SPECIFY)

3.1 (IF YES ABOVE, ASK) Against whom do you think
    the _____ (ETHNIC GROUP OF RESPONDENT) have to
    unite as a group to bring about change?
    (IF MORE THAN ONE RESPONSE, ASK RESPONDENTS TO
    RANK TOP THREE OBSTACLES IN IMPORTANCE: 1
    EQUALS FIRST, ETC. ASK: Who do you think is
    the main obstacle to change? Who next? Etc.?)
    (FIRST ASK, PAUSE, THEN SHOW CARD)

RANK   RANK
_____ 0. NR   _____ 6. established
_____ 1. DK   bureaucracies
_____ 2. middle or upper   (welfare,
           class (SPECIFY)   housing, em-
_____ 3. Delegate Agencies   ployment agen-
           or Tremont Commu-   cies, etc.)
           nity Corporation   _____ 7. police
           (SPECIFY)   _____ 8. school systems
_____ 4. CAP-CDA (SPECIFY)   and policies
_____ 5. political struc-   _____ 9. slum landlords
           tures (local,   _____ 10. others (SPECIFY)
           state, national)
           (SPECIFY)   COMMENTS:

3.2 (IF ANSWERED ABOVE, ASK) Did you feel this way
    before getting involved with the Tremont commu-
    nity action program, i.e., feel that the _____
    have to unite as a group against the _____?
_____ 0. NR   COMMENTS:
_____ 1. DK or DR
_____ 2. yes
_____ 3. no
_____ 4. other (SPECIFY)

3.21 (IF NO ABOVE, ASK) Did you come to feel this
     way because of the Tremont community action
     program?

_____ 0. NR   COMMENTS:
_____ 1. DK or DR
_____ 2. yes
_____ 3. no
_____ 4. other (SPECIFY)

Interest Group Identity

4. (IF ANSWERED #4 or 5 TO QUESTION 1, ASK) Do you
   feel that the various agencies of the Tremont
   community action program have to unite as a
   group to bring about changes in the Tremont community?
_____ 0. NR   COMMENTS:
_____ 1. DK
_____ 2. yes
_____ 3. no
_____ 4. other (SPECIFY)

4.1 (IF YES ABOVE, ASK) Against whom do you think
    these agencies of the Tremont community action
    program have to unite to bring about changes?
    (IF MORE THAN ONE RESPONSE, ASK RESPONDENT TO
    RANK TOP THREE OBSTACLES IN IMPORTANCE: 1
    EQUALS FIRST, ETC. ASK: Who do you think is
    the main obstacle to change? Who next? Etc.?)
    (FIRST ASK, PAUSE, THEN SHOW CARD)

RANK   RANK
_____ 0. NR   _____ 6. established
_____ 1. DK   bureaucracies
_____ 2. middle or upper   (welfare,
           class (SPECIFY)   housing, em-
_____ 3. Delegate Agencies   ployment agen-
           or Tremont Commu-   cies, etc.)
           nity Corporation   _____ 7. police
           (SPECIFY)   _____ 8. school systems
_____ 4. CAP-CDA (SPECIFY)   and policies
_____ 5. political struc-   _____ 9. slum landlords
           tures (local,   _____ 10. others (SPECIFY)
           state, national)
           (SPECIFY)   COMMENTS:

5. (IF ANSWERED #2 to QUESTION 1, GIVE SHEET AND
   PENCIL) Please check the blank that describes
   how you feel about these statements.

1) Sometimes I feel all alone in the world.
__Strongly Agree __Agree __Uncertain __Disagree
__Strongly Disagree
2) I don't get invited out by friends as often as
   I'd really like.
__Strongly Agree __Agree __Uncertain __Disagree
__Strongly Disagree
3) Most people today seldom feel lonely.
__Strongly Agree __Agree __Uncertain __Disagree
__Strongly Disagree
4) Real friends are as easy as ever to find.
__Strongly Agree __Agree __Uncertain __Disagree
__Strongly Disagree
5) One can always find friends if he shows himself
friendly.
__Strongly Agree __Agree __Uncertain __Disagree
__Strongly Disagree
6) The world in which we live is basically a
   friendly place.
__Strongly Agree __Agree __Uncertain __Disagree
__Strongly Disagree
7) There are few dependable ties between people
   any more.
__Strongly Agree __Agree __Uncertain __Disagree
__Strongly Disagree
8) People are just naturally friendly and helpful.
__Strongly Agree __Agree __Uncertain __Disagree
__Strongly Disagree
9) I don't get to visit with friends as often as
   I'd really like.
__Strongly Agree __Agree __Uncertain __Disagree
__Strongly Disagree

Antagonistic Ethnic Identity
6. (IF ANSWERED #6 or 7 TO QUESTION 1, ASK) Do you
   feel that the blacks and Puerto Ricans in Tremont
   are able to work together toward common goals, or
   that there's conflict and antagonism between the
   two groups?
_____ 0. NR   COMMENTS:
_____ 1. DK
_____ 2. able to work together toward
           common goals
_____ 3. there's conflict and antagonism
           between the two groups
_____ 4. other (SPECIFY)

7. Would you say that you have come to feel this way through your involvement with the Tremont community action program?

_____ 0. NR
_____ 1. DK
_____ 2. yes
_____ 3. no
_____ 4. other (SPECIFY)

8. Do you see a united coalition of blacks and Puerto Ricans in Tremont as possible at this time?

_____ 0. NR
_____ 1. DK
_____ 2. yes
_____ 3. no
_____ 4. other (SPECIFY)

Fragmented Interest Group Identity

9. (IF ANSWERED #4 or 5 TO QUESTION 1, ASK) Do you feel that the community action program in Tremont has resulted in the various Delegate Agencies uniting together and cooperating with each other, or that the Delegate Agencies are too much in competition with one another for such things as funds and clients?

_____ 0. NR   COMMENTS:
_____ 1. DK
_____ 2. unite together and cooperate
          with each other
_____ 3. in too much competition with
          one another
_____ 4. other (SPECIFY)

10. Do you see a united coalition of all the Delegate Agencies in the Tremont area as possible at this time?

_____ 0. NR   COMMENTS:
_____ 1. DK
_____ 2. yes
_____ 3. no
_____ 4. other (SPECIFY)

Collaboration and Containment

1. Here are four statements describing what the community action program is accomplishing in

Tremont. Which one of these statements <u>best</u>
describes what is really happening through the
program. (SHOW CARD)

_____ 0. NR
_____ 1. DK
_____ 2. Middle-class people are setting up programs
           in Tremont and are trying to help the poor
           with the problems they're having with such
           things as jobs, landlords, and not enough
           education.
_____ 3. Middle-class people are giving some of the
           poor people in Tremont the chance to step
           up into the middle class through things
           like getting them into training programs
           and good jobs and helping them to go back
           to school.
_____ 4. Some of the poor people in Tremont are get-
           ting money to set up programs which try to
           help the rest of the people in the commu-
           nity with the problems they're having with
           things like jobs, landlords, and not enough
           education.
_____ 5. Some of the poor people in Tremont are get-
           ting the chance to set up programs which
           are trying to get the people in the commu-
           nity organized into real power groups so
           they can stand up against those who are
           controlling them and trying to keep them
           poor.
_____ 6. other (SPECIFY)
<u>COMMENTS</u>:

2. Overall, do you feel that the community action
   program in Tremont has enough resources--espe-
   cially enough funds, trained personnel and technical assistance from the community action bu-
   reaucracy--to allow it to operate in an effective manner and in a way that the poor are actually helped?

_____ 0. NR   <u>COMMENTS</u>:
_____ 1. DK
_____ 2. yes
_____ 3. no
_____ 4. other (SPECIFY)

Bargaining

A) One-step Bargaining:
Now I'd like to ask you some questions about collective action. By collective action I mean people
getting organized and doing something as a group in
order to try and get power for themselves and take
away power from the groups who are controlling them.
(Give examples of collective action: labor strikes,
sit-ins, demonstrations, etc.)

1. Have you ever heard about any collective action
   sponsored by _____(Delegate Agency of RESPONDENT)?
   _____ 0. NR
   _____ 1. DK or DR
   _____ 2. yes
   _____ 3. no (SKIP TO QUESTION 1 OF TWO-STEP BAR-
            GAINING)

2. (IF ANSWERED YES ABOVE, ASK) Now, please think
   of the one collective action which had the best
   results. Who was this collective action aimed
   against and what was the specific issue involved?
   (ADD TARGET TO APPROPRIATE CATEGORY)
   _____ 0. NR   COMMENTS:
   _____ 1. DK or DR
   _____ 2. housing
   _____ 3. education
   _____ 4. social services, including
            welfare
   _____ 5. jobs
   _____ 6. action aimed at TCCorporation
   _____ 7. action aimed at CAP-CDA
   _____ 8. action aimed at City Hall
   _____ 9. action aimed at Washington, D.C.
   _____10. other (SPECIFY)

3. How successful would you say this collective action was as far as getting some power for the
   poor in Tremont is concerned?
   _____ 0. NR   COMMENTS:
   _____ 1. DK or DR
   _____ 2. very unsuccessful
   _____ 3. slightly unsuccessful
   _____ 4. slightly successful
   _____ 5. very successful

3.1 (IF SUCCESSFUL ABOVE, ASK)   Can you give me
    some concrete examples of what was actually
    changed?

3.2 (IF UNSUCCESSFUL ABOVE, ASK)   Why do you think
    that it was unsuccessful?

4. Besides the collective action which you just
   mentioned, how many other collective actions
   would you say _____(DELEGATE AGENCY OF RESPONDENT)
   sponsored?

_____ 0. NR   COMMENTS:
_____ 1. DK or DR
_____ 2. none
_____ 3. 1
_____ 4. 2
_____ 5. 3-4
_____ 6. 5-7
_____ 7. 8-10
_____ 8. more than 10 (SPECIFY NUMBER)

5. (IF MORE THAN ONE COLLECTIVE ACTION, ASK)   On
   the whole, how successful do you feel these other
   collective actions were?   (SHOW CARD)

_____ 0. NR   COMMENTS:
_____ 1. DK or DR
_____ 2. very unsuccessful
_____ 3. slightly unsuccessful
_____ 4. slightly successful
_____ 5. very successful

B) Two-step Bargaining
Now I'd like to ask you some questions about joint
collective action. By joint collective action I
mean the various Delegate Agencies uniting and acting together in order to try and get power for the
poor and take power away from the groups who are
controlling them.

1. Have you ever heard about any joint collective
   actions in the Tremont area sponsored by _____
   (DELEGATE AGENCY OF RESPONDENT)?

_____ 0. NR
_____ 1. DK or DR
_____ 2. yes
_____ 3. no

2. (IF YES ABOVE, ASK) Now, please think of the
   one _joint_ collective action which had the best
   results. Who was this joint collective action
   aimed against and what was the specific issue
   involved?   (ADD TARGET TO APPROPRIATE CATEGORY)
   _____   0. NR   COMMENTS:
   _____   1. DK or DR
   _____   2. housing
   _____   3. education
   _____   4. social services, including
                welfare
   _____   5. jobs
   _____   6. action aimed at TCCorporation
   _____   7. action aimed at CAP-CDA
   _____   8. action aimed at City Hall
   _____   9. action aimed at Washington, D.C.
   _____ 10. other (SPECIFY)

3. How successful would you say this joint collective action was as far as getting some power for
   the poor in Tremont is concerned? (SHOW CARD)
   _____   0. NR   COMMENTS:
   _____   1. DK or DR
   _____   2. very unsuccessful
   _____   3. slightly unsuccessful
   _____   4. slightly successful
   _____   5. very successful

3.1 (IF SUCCESSFUL ABOVE, ASK) Can you give me
    some concrete examples of what was changed?

3.2 (IF UNSUCCESSFUL ABOVE, ASK) Why do you think
    that it was unsuccessful?

4. Besides the joint collective action you just described, how many other _joint_ collective actions
   would you say _____(DELEGATE AGENCY OF RESPONDENT)
   sponsored?
   _____   0. NR   _____ 5. 3-4
   _____   1. DK or DR   _____ 6. 5-7
   _____   2. none   _____ 7. 8-10
   _____   3. 1   _____ 8. more than 10
   _____   4. 2   (SPECIFY NUMBER)

COMMENTS:

5. (IF MORE THAN ONE JOINT COLLECTIVE ACTION, ASK)
   On the whole, how successful do you feel these
   other joint collective actions were?   (SHOW CARD)
   _____ 0. NR   COMMENTS:
   _____ 1. DK or DR
   _____ 2. very unsuccessful
   _____ 3. slightly unsuccessful
   _____ 4. slightly successful
   _____ 5. very successful

Resocialization

A) Value Orientation:
1. Now I'm going to show you three statements that
   describe three different ways to help the poor
   get out of poverty. Which of these do you feel
   is the best way?
A. Each poor person should vote for the candidate
   that will best represent him and leave it up to
   that official to find ways of getting the poor
   the help that they need.
   (PARTICULARISTIC STRATEGY)
B. Each poor person should join groups formed
   around some problem that the poor face--such as
   poor housing or lack of jobs. The leaders of
   these groups would then represent the members in
   trying to solve these problems and in fighting
   against those in power.
   (PLURALISTIC STRATEGY)
C. Each poor person should join with large groups
   of other poor people to develop leadership among
   the poor themselves. The members of these groups
   themselves, under their leaders, would then
   openly confront the people in power.
   (STATUS GROUP STRATEGY)
   _____ 0. NR   COMMENTS:
   _____ 1. DK
   _____ 2. A is best
   _____ 3. B is best
   _____ 4. C is best

2. Before you got involved with the Tremont community action program, which of these three ways
   did you feel was the best way to help the poor
   get out of poverty?   (SHOW CARD)

_____ 0. NR   <u>COMMENTS</u>:
_____ 1. DK or DR
_____ 2. A
_____ 3. B
_____ 4. C

2.1 (IF CHANGE INDICATED ABOVE, ASK) Did you come
    to feel the way you do <u>now because</u> of your in-
    volvement with the Tremont community action
    program?
_____ 0. NR   <u>COMMENTS</u>:
_____ 1. DK or DR
_____ 2. yes
_____ 3. no
_____ 4. other (SPECIFY)

B) <u>Behavioral Membership and Orientation</u>:
1. <u>Before</u> the community action program came into
   Tremont, were you involved with any group or organizations who were trying in some way to help
   the poor get out of poverty?
_____ 0. NR   <u>COMMENTS</u>:
_____ 1. DK or DR
_____ 2. yes
_____ 3. no
_____ 4. other (SPECIFY)

2. (IF YES ABOVE, ASK) Would you please tell me
   which groups or organizations you belonged to
   then?
   (IF MORE THAN ONE RESPONSE, ASK RESPONDENT TO
   RANK THEM IN TERMS OF GREATEST DEGREE OF IN-
   VOLVEMENT: 1 EQUALS FIRST, ETC.)
<u>RANK</u>   <u>COMMENTS</u>:
_____ 0. NR
_____ 1. DK or DR
_____ 2. organized group #1 (SPECIFY)
_____ 3. organized group #2 (SPECIFY)
_____ 4. organized group #3 (SPECIFY)
_____ 5. organized group #4 (SPECIFY)
_____ 6. other (SPECIFY)

3. (IF ONE OR MORE GROUPS MENTIONED, ASK) Could
   you describe the type of activities in which each
   of these groups or organizations was involved.

(PROD FOR PARTICULARISTIC, PLURALISTIC, AND
STATUS GROUP STRATEGIES, AND ADD THIS ORIENTA-
TION TO APPROPRIATE GROUP IN QUESTION 2)
Pa=Particularistic; Pl=Pluralistic; SG=Status
Group

4. At this time, are you involved with any group or
   organizations who are trying in some way to help
   the poor get out of poverty?
   (INCLUDE ANY AFFILIATION WITH THE TREMONT COMMU-
   NITY ACTION PROGRAM)
   _____ 0. NR   COMMENTS:
   _____ 1. DK
   _____ 2. yes
   _____ 3. no
   _____ 4. other (SPECIFY)

5. (IF YES ABOVE, ASK) Would you please tell me
   which groups you belong to?
   (IF MORE THAN ONE RESPONSE, ASK RESPONDENT TO
   RANK THEM IN TERMS OF GREATEST DEGREE OF INVOLVE-
   MENT: 1 EQUALS FIRST, ETC.)
   RANK   COMMENTS:
   _____ 0. NR
   _____ 1. DK
   _____ 2. Delegate Agency #1 (SPECIFY)
   _____ 3. Delegate Agency #2 (SPECIFY)
   _____ 4. Delegate Agency #3 (SPECIFY)
   _____ 5. Tremont Community Corporation
               (SPECIFY)
   _____ 6. organized group #1 (SPECIFY)
   _____ 7. organized group #2 (SPECIFY)
   _____ 8. organized group #3 (SPECIFY)
   _____ 9. organized group #4 (SPECIFY)

6. (IF ONE OR MORE GROUPS MENTIONED, ASK) Could
   you describe the type of activities which each
   of these groups or organizations is involved in?
   (PROD FOR PARTICULARISTIC, PLURALISTIC, AND
   STATUS GROUP STRATEGIES, AND ADD THIS ORIENTATION
   TO APPROPRIATE GROUP IN QUESTION 5)
   Pa=Particularistic; Pl=Pluralistic; SG-Status
   Group

Subjective Probability Approach
(For Participants and Participant Beneficiaries only)
1. Before the community action program came into
   Tremont, what chance of influencing existing in-
   stitutions did the people in Tremont have? (SHOW
   CARD)

_____ 0. NR   COMMENTS:
_____ 1. DK
_____ 2. no chance
_____ 3. a slight chance
_____ 4. a good chance
_____ 5. other (SPECIFY)

2. What chance of influencing existing institutions
   do the people in Tremont now have because of the
   Tremont community action program? (SHOW CARD)

_____ 0. NR   COMMENTS:
_____ 1. DK
_____ 2. a much worse chance
_____ 3. a slightly worse chance
_____ 4. same as before
_____ 5. a slightly better chance
_____ 6. a much better chance
_____ 7. other (SPECIFY)

2.1 (IF A BETTER CHANCE, ASK) Why do they now have
    a better chance than before? (LOOK FOR EXAMPLES
    AND COMMENTS)

2.2 (IF A WORSE CHANCE, ASK) Why do they now have
    a worse chance than before? (LOOK FOR EXAMPLES
    AND COMMENTS)

2.3 (IF SAME AS BEFORE, ASK) Why is their chance
    now the same as before? (LOOK FOR EXAMPLES AND
    COMMENTS)

Influence Attempts Approach
(For Directors only)
1. I understand that technical assistance was
   available last year. How often did you get
   technical assistance from the Tremont Community
   Corporation?

_____ 0. NR   <u>COMMENTS</u>:
_____ 1. DK or DR
_____ 2. never
_____ 3. a few times
_____ 4. frequently

1.1 How would you describe the quality of the
     technical assistance from the Corporation:
     very poor, poor, good, or very good?   (LOOK
     FOR EXAMPLES AND COMMENTS)
_____ 0. NR
_____ 1. DK or DR
_____ 2. very poor
_____ 3. poor
_____ 4. good
_____ 5. very good

2. How often did you get technical assistance from
   CDA?
_____ 0. NR
_____ 1. DK or DR
_____ 2. never
_____ 3. a few times
_____ 4. frequently

2.1 How would you describe the quality of the tech-
    nical assistance from CDA: very poor, poor,
    good, or very good?   (LOOK FOR EXAMPLES AND
    COMMENTS)
_____ 0. NR
_____ 1. DK or DR
_____ 2. very poor
_____ 3. poor
_____ 4. good
_____ 5. very good

3. Besides technical assistance, I understand that
   both the Corporation and CDA evaluate your program. What do they evaluate when they come?
_____ 0. NR   <u>LOOK FOR EXAMPLES AND COMMENTS</u>
_____ 1. DK or DR
_____ 2. actual impact of program
_____ 3. the formalities--books, files,
           personal appearance, etc.
_____ 4. both impact and formalities
_____ 5. other (SPECIFY)

4. What do you think about the procedures for the
   way program proposals are made and handed in?
   Are they good and fair, or are they just formalities?
   _____ 0. NR   COMMENTS:
   _____ 1. DK or DR
   _____ 2. good and fair
   _____ 3. just formalities
            (lots of forms)
   _____ 4. other (SPECIFY)

5. Do you feel that the Tremont Corporation was
   primarily supporting, hindering, or indifferent
   to your Delegate Agency work last year?
   _____ 0. NR   LOOK FOR EXAMPLES AND COMMENTS
   _____ 1. DK or DR
   _____ 2. supporting
   _____ 3. hindering
   _____ 4. indifferent

6. Do you feel that the community action bureaucracy
   (CAP-CDA) was primarily supporting, hindering,
   or indifferent to your Delegate Agency work last
   year?
   _____ 0. NR   EXAMPLES AND COMMENTS
   _____ 1. DK or DR
   _____ 2. supporting
   _____ 3. hindering
   _____ 4. indifferent

7. How often would you say your agency directly
   intervened (not just referred) in the person's
   problems and tried to get help for his or her
   problem by contacting someone?
   _____ 0. NR   COMMENTS:
   _____ 1. DK or DR
   _____ 2. never
   _____ 3. sometimes
   _____ 4. many times
   _____ 5. almost always
   _____ 6. always

8. Specifically, who do you contact directly in
   order to help people with their problems? (GET
   SPECIFIC NAMES AND ADDRESSES: IF NEED MORE
   SPACE, USE OPPOSITE PAGE)

_____ 0. NR   COMMENTS:
_____ 1. DK or DR
_____ 2. housing:
_____ 3. manpower:
_____ 4. economic development:
_____ 5. education: /
_____ 6. senior citizens:
_____ 7. welfare:
_____ 8. other (SPECIFY):

9. Of all the groups you just mentioned, which one
    helped you the most? Which next? Finally,
    which next? (GET TOP THREE)
_____ 0. NR   COMMENTS:
_____ 1. DK or DR
_____ 2. (FIRST RANKED: SPECIFY)
_____ 3. (SECOND RANKED: SPECIFY)
_____ 4. (THIRD RANKED: SPECIFY)

10. How satisfied are you with each one of the
    above?   (SHOW CARD)
    (very dissatisfied, dissatisfied, slightly
    satisfied, very satisfied)
_____ 0. NR   COMMENTS:
_____ 1. DK or DR
_____ 2. (FIRST RANKED) _____
_____ 3. (SECOND RANKED) _____
_____ 4. (THIRD RANKED) _____

11. Overall, how successful do you feel that you
    are in getting the help you seek for the people
    who need it: very unsuccessful, slightly un-
    successful, slightly successful, very success-
    ful) (SHOW CARD)
_____ 0. NR   EXAMPLES AND COMMENTS:
_____ 1. DK or DR
_____ 2. very unsuccessful
_____ 3. slightly unsuccessful
_____ 4. slightly successful
_____ 5. very successful

11.1 (IF OTHER THAN VERY SUCCESSFUL, ASK) Why do
     you think your efforts at influence don't meet
     with greater success?

_____ 0. NR   COMMENTS:
_____ 1. DK
_____ 2. too much bureaucracy
_____ 3. impossible to change city, state
         and private service agencies
_____ 4. the poor aren't willing to fight
_____ 5. other (SPECIFY)

Influence Attempts Approach
(For Nonparticipant Beneficiaries only)
1. Do you happen to remember why you first contacted _____(DELEGATE AGENCY OF RESPONDENT)?
_____ 0. NR   COMMENTS:
_____ 1. DK or DR
_____ 2. needed money
_____ 3. for recreation
_____ 4. was looking for a job
_____ 5. had a housing problem
_____ 6. wanted educational help
_____ 7. was referred to this group
         (BY WHOM?)
_____ 8. was told to join this group
         (BY WHOM?)
_____ 9. wanted welfare help
_____10. other (SPECIFY)

2. What did you expect _____(DELEGATE AGENCY OF RE-
   SPONDENT) could do in your case?
_____ 0. NR   COMMENTS:
_____ 1. DK or DR
_____ 2. didn't know what to expect
_____ 3. didn't really expect help
_____ 4. expected agency to make referral
         to a source of assistance
_____ 5. expected agency to give individual
         help for my own problem
_____ 6. expected agency to help organize
         group action which would help my
         problem
_____ 7. other (SPECIFY)

3. What did you actually get from _____(DELEGATE
   AGENCY OF RESPONDENT) on this occasion?

_____ 0. NR   <u>EXAMPLES AND COMMENTS:</u>
_____ 1. DK or DR
_____ 2. nothing
_____ 3. specific individual help
           (SPECIFY)
_____ 4. referral to another agency
           (SPECIFY)
_____ 5. big run around with no help
_____ 6. was brought into group with
           similar problems (SPECIFY)
_____ 7. agency provided the opportunity
           for collective action (SPECIFY)
_____ 8. other (SPECIFY)

4. How many times have you had or do you now have
   contact with this agency? (SHOW CARD)
_____ 0. NR
_____ 1. DK or DR
_____ 2. just once
_____ 3. several times (SPECIFY)
_____ 4. other (SPECIFY)

5. Overall, how satisfied were you with what you
   got? (SHOW CARD)
_____ 0. NR   <u>EXAMPLES AND COMMENTS:</u>
_____ 1. DK or DR
_____ 2. very dissatisfied
_____ 3. slightly dissatisfied
_____ 4. slightly satisfied
_____ 5. very satisfied

<u>Personal Data</u>
1. Sex (RECORD ONLY)
_____ 1. male
_____ 2. female

2. How many years of school did you finish?
   (INDICATE CATEGORY AND CIRCLE)
_____ 0. NR
_____ 1. DK or DR
_____ 2. 0 1 2 3 4 5 6 7 (did not finish
                                    grade school)
_____ 3. 8 9 10 11 (finished grade but not high
                          school)

_____ 4. 12 (finished high school)
_____ 5. 13 14 15 (started college)
_____ 6. 16 (finished college)
_____ 7. more than 16 (SPECIFY) _____

3. How old were you on your last birthday?
_____ 0. NR
_____ 1. DK or DR
_____ 2. 16-21
_____ 3. 22-29
_____ 4. 30-44
_____ 5. 45-64
_____ 6. 65 and over

4. (CROSS-CHECK) When were you born?
_____ 0. NR
_____ 1. DK or DR
_____ 2. year _____
_____ 3. month _____

5. How would you describe yourself in terms of race
   or ethnic group?
_____ 0. NR
_____ 1. DK or DR
_____ 2. Puerto Rican
_____ 3. Black or Negro
_____ 4. Jewish
_____ 5. Italian
_____ 6. Irish
_____ 7. Mexican American
_____ 8. other white (SPECIFY)

6. What is your present address? _____

7. Is your present address within Tremont's bound-
   aries? (TELL RESPONDENT ABOUT TREMONT'S BOUND-
   ARIES)
_____ 0. NR
_____ 1. DK
_____ 2. yes
_____ 3. no

7.1 (IF YES ABOVE, ASK) How long have you lived
    within these boundaries?

_____ 0. NR
_____ 1. DK or DR
_____ 2. less than 6 months
_____ 3. 6 months to 1 year
_____ 4. 1 to 2 years
_____ 5. 2 to 3 years
_____ 6. 3 to 4 years
_____ 7. 4 to 5 years
_____ 8. 5 to 6 years
_____ 9. 7 or more years (SPECIFY)

7.2 (IF NO ABOVE, ASK) Have you ever lived within
    these boundaries/
_____ 0. NR
_____ 1. DK or DR
_____ 2. yes
_____ 3. no

7.21 (IF YES ABOVE, ASK) What was your address
     then _____

7.22 Roughly, from when to when did you live at
     that address?
     (SPECIFY DATES) From _____ to _____.

8. What is your or your family's economic position
   like compared to other people in the area?
   (SHOW CARD)
_____ 0. NR   _____ 4. average
_____ 1. DK or DR   _____ 5. above average
_____ 2. near the bottom _____ 6. near the top
_____ 3. below average   _____ 7. other (SPECIFY)
COMMENTS:

9. Before getting involved with the Tremont community action program, what was your or your
   family's economic position like compared to
   other people in the area? (SHOW CARD)
_____ 0. NR   _____ 4. average
_____ 1. DK or DR   _____ 5. above average
_____ 2. near the bottom _____ 6. near the top
_____ 3. below average   _____ 7. other (SPECIFY)
COMMENTS:

10. Where did you work immediately before getting
    involved with the Tremont community action pro-
    gram? (IF DID NOT WORK, ASK: How did you man-
    age to live then?)
    _____ 0. NR   COMMENTS:
    _____ 1. DK or DR
    _____ 2. welfare
    _____ 3. social security
    _____ 4. pension
    _____ 5. occupation (SPECIFY)
    _____ 6. other (SPECIFY)

11. If you don't mind my asking, what was your
    yearly income at that time? (IF CONFUSION, ASK:
    Monthly _____; Weekly _____)
    _____ 0. NR   _____ 8. 6,000-6,999
    _____ 1. DK or DR   _____ 9. 7,000-7,999
    _____ 2. under 1,000   _____ 10. 8,000-8,999
    _____ 3. 1,000-1,999   _____ 11. 9,000-9,999
    _____ 4. 2,000-2,999   _____ 12. 10,000-14,000
    _____ 5. 3,000-3,999   _____ 13. more than 14,000
    _____ 6. 4,000-4,999   (SPECIFY) _____
    _____ 7. 5,000-5,999

12. Finally, may I ask for your yearly income last
    year? (IF CONFUSION, ASK: Monthly _____;
    Weekly _____)
    _____ 0. NR   _____ 7. 5,000-5,999
    _____ 1. DK or DR   _____ 8. 6,000-6,999
    _____ 2. under 1,000   _____ 9. 7,000-7,999
    _____ 3. 1,000-1,999   _____ 10. 8,000-8,999
    _____ 4. 2,000-2,999   _____ 11. 9,000-9,999
    _____ 5. 3,000-3,999   _____ 12. 10,000-14,000
    _____ 6. 4,000-4,999   _____ 13. more than 14,000
                                         (SPECIFY)

INTRODUCTION

    1. These terms are used in the sense presented in William A. Gamson, <u>Power and Discontent</u> (Homewood, Ill.: Dorsey Press, 1968).

    2. Particularly significant in this regard was Jewel Bellush and Stephen M. David, eds., <u>Race and Politics in New York City</u> (New York: Praeger Publishers, 1971), pp. 3-24.

CHAPTER 1

    1. William O. Douglas, <u>Points of Rebellion</u> (New York: Vintage Books, 1970), pp. 88-89.

    2. Lewis A. Coser, "The Sociology of Poverty," <u>Social Problems</u>, XIII, 2 (1965), 140-48.

    3. Peter Marris and Martin Rein, <u>Dilemmas of Social Reform: Poverty and Community Action in the United States</u> (New York: Atherton Press, 1967); Martin Rein, "Community Action Programs: A Critical Reassessment," <u>Poverty and Human Resources Abstracts</u>, III, 3 (May-June 1968), 2-8.

    4. Richard Blumenthal, "The Bureaucracy: Antipoverty and the Community Action Program," in Allan P Sindler, ed., <u>American Political Institutions and Public Policy</u> (Boston: Little, Brown and Company, 1969), pp. 129-79. For other sources on the origin of the Public Law 88-454 and the role of Congress in passing the law popularly known as the Economic Opportunity Act of 1964: John F. Biddy and Roger Davidson, <u>On Capitol Hill</u> (New York: Holt, Rinehart and Winston, 1967), Chapter 7; John C. Donovan, <u>The Politics of Poverty</u> (New York: Pegasus, 1967), Chapters 1-2; Sar A. Levitan, <u>The Design of the Federal Antipoverty Strategy</u> (Ann Arbor: Institute of Labor and Industrial Relations, 1967); Daniel P. Moynihan, <u>Maximum Feasible Misunderstanding</u> (New York: Free Press, 1969), Chapters 1-5; Adam Yarmolinsky, "The Beginnings of OEO," in James Sundquist, ed., <u>On Fighting Poverty: Perspectives from Experience</u> (New York: Basic Books, 1969), pp. 34-51.

5.   Blumenthal, op. cit., p. 166.

6.   Ibid., p. 167.

7.   U.S. Congress, An Act to Mobilize the Human and Financial Resources of the Nation to Combat Poverty in the United States, Public Law 88-454, 88th Congress, 2d. Session, 1964; Joseph A. Kershaw, Government Against Poverty (Chicago: Markham Publishers, 1970).

8.   David Easton, A Systems Analysis of Political Life (New York: John Wiley, 1965), pp. 406-7.

9.   Blumenthal, op. cit., passim.

10.   Stephen M David, "Leadership of the Poor in Poverty Programs," Urban Riots: Violence and Social Change, Proceedings of the Academy of Political Science, XXIX (July 1968), 86-100.

11.   David Easton's analysis of political systems provides an appropriate theoretical framework for this discussion of the emergence and development of community action outputs. See Easton, op. cit., p. 33.

12.   Paul E. Peterson, "City Politics and Community Action: The Implementation of the Community Action Program in Three American Cities" (unpublished Ph.D. dissertation, Department of Political Science, University of Chicago, 1967).

13.   Paul E. Peterson, "Forms of Representation: Participation of the Poor in the Community Action Program," American Political Science Review, LXIV, 2 (June 1970), 26.

14.   Ibid., p. 21.

15.   Stephen M. David, "Welfare: The Community Action Program Controversy," in Jewel Bellush and Stephen M. David, eds., Race and Politics in New York City (New York: Praeger Publishers, 1971), pp. 25-58; Bertram M. Beck, "Organizing Community Action," in Robert H. Connery and Demetrios Caraley, eds., Governing the City: Challenges and Options for New York (New York: Praeger Publishers, 1969), pp. 162-78; Howard W. Hallman, Neighborhood Control of Public Programs (New York: Praeger Publishers, 1970), pp. 12-20; Martin Hockbaum, "The Decision-Making Process in New York City's Council Against Poverty" (unpublished Ph.D. dissertation, Department of Political Science, Hunter College, City University of New York, 1971), Chapter 2, pp. 1-84.

16. In the 1965 election, 60 percent of the
city's blacks and 68 percent of its Puerto Ricans
voted for Beame, while Lindsay received 40 percent
of the black vote and somewhat less than 32 percent
of the Puerto Rican vote. In a phenomenal 1969 reversal, Lindsay captured 80 percent of the black
vote and 63 percent of the Puerto Rican vote. New
York Times, Nov. 4, 1965, p. 26, and Nov. 6, 1969,
p. 28.

17. City of New York, Council Against Poverty,
An Introduction to the New York City Council Against
Poverty, March 1969, pp. 2-3.

18. City of New York, Community Development
Agency, PY F Versatile Program Guidelines, April
1970, pp. 2-3.

19. City of New York, Community Development
Agency, Versatile Program Guidelines 1969/70, April
1969, pp. 2-3.

20. Tremont Community Corporation, Tremont
Community Corporation Year-Round Project, Program
Year "F" 1970-71, 1970, p. 3.

21. It may be noted that some evidence exists
that questions whether it is in fact possible for
such goals as have been described above to be fulfilled. In "Functions of a Bureaucratic Ideology:
'Citizen Participation,'" Social Problems, XVI, 2
(1968), 129-43, Elliot A. Krause notes that the
idea of maximum participation by the poor adopted
by the early community action programs implicitly
places a "positive evaluation of 'citizen participation' as a good and desirable activity." However,
he adds that, "at the local level, if participation
works in any oppositional, conflict-producing, or
boat-rocking sense, the local action bureaucracy
has come to expect trouble from their own federal
headquarters. [Thus] the policy in fact used by
the bureaucracies has been to avoid conflict at all
costs." The result is that such action bureaucracies adopt a state of ambivalence toward their own
ideology of citizen participation. Furthermore,
such an ideology presents a very real dilemma for
the poor themselves. For if they choose to participate, they assume the substantial risk of being
negatively coopted; while if they reject the ideology, and do not participate, they lose one of the

few legal channels open to them for presenting demands, knowing all the while that their places in
the community action program will always be filled
with other spokesman.

22.   William A. Gamson, Power and Discontent
(Homewood, Ill.: Dorsey Press, 1968).

23.   Ibid., p. 113.

24.   Ibid., pp. 37-7. All of these terms will
be explained in detail at the beginning of Chapter 2.

25.   Gamson, op. cit., pp. 135-42; Peterson,
"City Politics and Community Action," pp. 48-9;
Peter Bachrach and Morton S. Baratz, Power and Poverty: Theory and Practice (New York: Oxford University Press, 1970), pp. 201-13, especially on the
concept of "cooptative participation"; Philip Selznick, TVA and the Grass Roots (Berkeley: University
of California Press, 1953); Sidney Verba, Small
Groups and Political Behavior (Princeton: Princeton
University Press, 1961); Thomas C. Schelling, The
Strategy of Conflict (New York: Oxford University
Press, 1963), pp. 84-5, on the concept of "collaboration."

26.   For a concise argument supporting the
characterization of social service programs as a
means of achieving and exercising influence, see
Michael Lipsky, Protest in City Politics: Rent
Strikes, Housing and the Power of the Poor (Chicago:
Rand McNally, 1970), pp. 163-203. Lipsky argues
that relatively powerless groups cannot use the
tactic of protest (mass action) with a high probability of success, since, by definition, they lack
organizational resources. "Rather," he states,
"long-run success will depend upon the acquisition
of stable political resources which do not rely on
the use of third parties." In this sense, social
service programs controlled by the poor may provide
them with the necessary resources to build a future
constituency--which may, at a later date, result in
the poor gaining more influence.

27.   Kenneth B. Clark and Jeannette Hopkins,
A Relevant War Against Poverty (New York: Harper
Torchbooks, 1970), pp. 14-5; Terry N. Clark, "On
Decentralization," Polity, II, 4 (1970), 508-14;
Ralph M. Kramer, Participation of the Poor

(Englewood Cliffs, N.J.: Prentice-Hall, 1969), p.
270; Louis A. Zurcher, Poverty Warriors (Austin:
University of Texas Press, 1970), p. 381.

28.   Edgar S. Cahn and Barry A. Passett, Citizen Participation: Effecting Community Change (New
York: Praeger, 1971), especially pp. 69-89.

29.   Krause, op. cit.

CHAPTER 2

1.   William A. Gamson, Power and Discontent
(Homewood, Ill.: Dorsey Press, 1968), p. 21. It
should be noted that with respect to certain decisions, authorities may function as potential partisans. For a further discussion on this point, see
ibid., pp. 28-31.

2.   Sar A. Levitan, "What's Happening, Baby?
Essential Research for the War on Poverty," The Use
of Social Research in Federal Domestic Programs
(Part II). U.S. Congress Committee on Governmental
Operations (Washington, D.C.: U.S. Government
Printing Office, 1967), p. 260.

3.   Peter H. Rossi, "Practice, Methods and
Theory in Evaluating Social-Action Programs," in
James Sundquist, ed., On Fighting Poverty: Perspectives from Experience (New York: Basic Books,
1969), pp. 217-34.

4.   Daniel P. Moynihan, Maximum Feasible Misunderstanding (New York: Free Press, 1969), p. 203.

5.   Levitan, op. cit., p. 261.

6. Edward A. Suchman, "Principles and Practice
of Evaluative Research," in John T. Doby, ed., An
Introduction to Social Research (New York: Appleton-
Century-Crofts, 1967), p. 338; and more importantly,
Edward A. Suchman, Evaluative Research (New York:
Russell Sage Foundation, 1967).

7.   Howard E. Freeman and Clarence C. Sherwood, Social Research and Social Policy (Englewood
Cliffs, N.J.: Prentice-Hall, 1970), p. 39.

8.   Ibid., p. 40.

9.   Gamson, op. cit., pp. 2-19, summarizes
some of this material in attempting to integrate
the two perspectives. The literature on these contrasting models is so well known and documented in
other writings that we will only add the following:

Joseph S. Roucek, <u>Social Control Theory</u> (New York: D. Van Nostrand, 2d ed., 1956); Kurt H. Wolff, "Social Control," in Joseph S. Roucek, ed., <u>Contemporary Sociology</u> (New York: Philosophical Library, 1958), pp. 110-31; Jesse R. Pitts and Amitai Etzioni, "Social Control," in David L Sills, ed., <u>International Encyclopedia of the Social Sciences</u> (New York: Macmillan and Free Press, 1968), pp. 381-402.

10. Harry C. Bredemier and Richard M. Stephenson, <u>The Analysis of Social Systems</u> (New York: Holt, Rinehart, and Winston, 1962), pp. 146-76.

11. <u>Ibid</u>., p. 146.

12. Gamson, <u>op. cit</u>., pp. 116-43.

13. Gerald M. Shattuck, "Structural Change and Social Work Intervention: Relationships Between Policy and Theory" (unpublished paper, Fordham University, 1969), pp. 1-16.

14. Gamson, <u>op. cit</u>., pp. 60-1.

15. <u>Ibid</u>., p. 61.

16. <u>Ibid</u>., pp. 65-6.

17. <u>Ibid</u>., p. 67.

18. For the stages in the development of group formation, see Gamson, <u>op. cit</u>., pp. 33-6; Ralf Dahrendorf, <u>Class and Class Conflict in Industrial Society</u> (Stanford, Calif.: Stanford University Press, 1959), pp. 179-89; Robin M. Williams, <u>Strangers Next Door</u> (Englewood Cliffs, N.J.: Prentice-Hall, 1964), pp. 17-21.

19. Lewis A. Coser, "The Sociology of Poverty," <u>Social Problems</u>, XIII, 2 (1965), 142.

20. Paul E. Peterson, "City Politics and Community Action: The Implementation of the Community Action Program in Three American Cities" (unpublished Ph.D. dissertation, Department of Political Science, University of Chicago), pp. 48-9.

21. Philip Selznick, <u>TVA and the Grass Roots</u> (Berkeley: University of California Press, 1953), p. 13.

22. Gamson, <u>op. cit</u>., p. 137.

23. Peter Bachrach and Morton S. Baratz, <u>Power and Poverty: Theory and Practice</u> (New York: Oxford University Press, 1970), pp. 206-7.

24. For an examination of the concept of exemption, see Williams, <u>op. cit</u>., pp. 337-8; and

for a discussion of the related concept of "creaming," see S. M. Miller, Pamela Roby, and Alwine A.
de Vos van Steenwijk, "Creaming the Poor," <u>Transac-
tion</u>, VII, 8 (June 1970), 39-45. After defining
creaming as "the process by which mainly the least
poor are included in poverty programs," the latter
authors state that "creaming can also serve to
maintain the <u>status quo</u> of the larger society. It
coopts the potential or actual leaders of the poor
and leaves untouched those poor who may be too mis-
erable to pressure for change," p. 44.

    25. Paul E. Peterson, "The Politics of Wel-
fare: Public Policy and Changing Policy-making
Processes" (unpublished paper, Department of Political Science, University of Chicago, June 1968), pp.
3-5.

CHAPTER 3
    1. City of New York, Council Against Poverty,
<u>Charter and By-Laws</u>, Article IV, Section 4.
    2. See Martin Hockbaum, "The Decision-making
Process in New York City's Council Against Poverty"
(unpublished Ph.D. dissertation, Department of
Political Science, Hunter College, City University
of New York, 1971), Chapter IV, Section 2, pp. 5-8,
for background material on how the Mayor fills
these positions.
    3. City of New York, Council Against Poverty,
<u>Charter and By-Laws</u>, Article IV, Section 6.
    4. City of New York, Council Against Poverty,
<u>An Introduction to the New York City Council Against
Poverty</u>, March 1969, p. 2.
    5. Hockbaum, <u>op. cit.</u>, Chapter I, pp. 43-44.
    6. <u>Ibid.</u>, Chapter V, p. 28.
    7. <u>Ibid.</u>, p. 26.
    8. City of New York, Council Against Poverty,
<u>An Introduction</u>, p. 4.
    9. See Howard W. Hallman, <u>Neighborhood Con-
trol of Public Programs</u> (New York: Praeger Publishers, 1970), pp. 28-31, 145-48, for information
concerning the other Bronx poverty areas.
    10. City of New York, Council Against Poverty,
<u>New York City Poverty Area Maps</u>, 1967, p. 33.

11.   See Hockbaum, op. cit., Chapter I, pp.
39-42, for a detailed discussion of the series of
steps in setting up a Community Corporation.

12.   There are at present 62 Community Planning
Districts, each having a Community Planning Board
whose members are appointed solely by the Borough
President. Their function is to be spokesmen for
their neighborhoods in dealing with all city problems by providing for the planning and service needs
of the area. For a discussion of their present
structure and proposed reorganization, see Mayor
John V. Lindsay, A Plan for Neighborhood Government
for New York City (New York City: The Office of
the Mayor, June 1970); Robert Abrams, A Plan for
Borough and Neighborhood and Neighborhood Government in New York City (New York City: The Office
of the President of the Borough of the Bronx, October 1970).

13.   City of New York, Council Against Poverty,
Annual Report of the New York City Council Against
Poverty, 1966-67, 1967, p. 13.

14.   Tremont Area Master Plan, July 1, 1968,
p. 5. At this time, the Tremont Planning Committee
was located at 927 East 180th Street.

15.   Information obtained from the files of
the Corporation.

16.   City of New York, Community Development
Agency, Guidelines for the Formation of Community
Corporations, 1966, Section I, Paragraph G.

17.   City of New York, Council Against Poverty,
Summary: Major Decisions of the New York City Coun-
cil Against Poverty: Nov. 7, 1968--Aug. 7, 1969,
August 1969, p. 1.

18.   City of New York, Community Development
Agency, Community Corporation Election Master Plan,
March 1969, p. 35.

19.   City of New York, Community Development
Agency, Community Corporations Elections Manual,
1969, p. 22.

20.   Edgar Litt, Ethnic Politics in America
(Glenview, Ill.: Scott, Foresman, and Company,
1970), pp. 20-1.

21.   See Hockbaum, op. cit., Chapter III, Section 1, pp. 14-25, for a brief history of the problems and reasons leading up to this plan.

22. *Minutes* of the Tremont Community Corporation, July 11, 1969, p. 5 (in the files of the Corporation).

23. City of New York, Community Development
Agency, *Versatile Program Guidelines 1969/70*, April
1969, p. 14.

24. Public Affairs Office, Human Resources
Administration, *Community Development in New York
City*, 1969, pp. 14-15; plus personal observation.

25. Hockbaum, *op. cit.*, Chapter IV, Section
2, pp. 18-21, for more detailed information on
steps 11 and 12.

26. City of New York, Community Development
Agency, *Memo*: Recommendations for the Disposition
of the Tremont Community Corporation 1970/71 Council Against Poverty Versatile Grant Request, August
17, 1970, pp. 1, 7.

CHAPTER 4

1. For information on this trial, especially
concerning the Delegate Agency of Elsmere Tenants
Council, see the following articles in the *New York
Times*: Oct. 20, 1970, p. 1; Dec. 23, 1970, p. 28;
Jan. 6, 1971, p. 33; Jan. 27, 1971, p. 41; Feb. 17,
1971, p. 43; April 8, 1971, p. 47; and finally, May
14, 1971, p. 1, when the "13" Panthers were found
not guilty on all twelve counts.

2. Peter Bachrach and Morton S. Baratz, *Power
and Poverty: Theory and Practice* (New York: Oxford University Press, 1970), p. 212.

3. City of New York, Community Development
Agency, *Guidelines for Youth Development Programs,
Program Account No. 59, FY 1970-71*, 1969, especially
the Appendix, "Development of Meaningful and Realistic Guidelines for Youth Programs," pp. 1-10.

4. *New York Times*, Nov. 3, 1970, p. 34. This
article concerns Bronco-Self-Improvement Association, which sponsored a program in Education Action
during Program Year "E."

CHAPTER 5

1. Information obtained from Delegate Agency
Manning Tables in the files of the Tremont Community Corporation.

2. City of New York, Manpower Career Development Agency, <u>The Neighborhood Manpower Service Centers: Tremont Budget FY 1970-71</u>, 1969, pp. 13-4.

3. Interview, April 20, 1970, with a Delegate Agency community organizer who worked in two of the better functioning agencies and eventually became an important figure in the Tremont community action program.

4. From a Community Corporation Board of Directors' meeting held on May 12, 1970, as recorded on page five of a diary kept during the field work phase of the study, hereafter referred to as <u>Diary</u>. This manuscript provides the only known record of the Board's transactions for the two-month period of March-May 1970, which followed the firing of the Executive Secretary, and thus became rather significant for the research.

5. <u>Diary</u>, p. 24, a telephone call to Ron Craig of CDA, on July 21, 1970.

6. <u>Delegate Agency Evaluation Forms</u> created by the Information and Evaluation Specialist, both long and short forms, on file at the Tremont Community Corporation.

7. <u>Minutes</u> of the Tremont Community Corporation Board of Directors, Dec. 19, 1969, and March 17, 1970.

8. <u>Diary</u>, p. 22, a conversation with a Puerto Rican Board member who was "in" with the most powerful clique. This fact was also confirmed by some top-level Corporation Staff members.

9. <u>Ibid</u>., p. 25.

10. <u>Ibid</u>., p. 14, a conversation with an extremely knowledgeable Puerto Rican CDA District Office worker who previously worked in the Tremont Community Corporation. This sentiment was repeatedly corroborated by other program participants.

11. <u>Ibid</u>., p. 17, the Specialist stated that he got no cooperation whatsoever from the Executive Director and added, "This man wants to control everything."

12. The Community Corporation elections at the end of Program Year "E"--Sept. 15, 1970--provide further evidence of the Corporation not removing the barriers of isolation: only 1,041 residents

voted, which was exactly 12 fewer voters than the
year before. People, Nov. 1970, No. 4, New York
City: Human Resources Administration, p. 3.

13. Diary, p. 16, a conversation with one of
the CDA District Office field workers.

14. Ibid., p. 29. These figures were provided
by the Acting Director of the Manpower Center.

15. A recent article in the New York Times,
April 22, 1971, p. 54, demonstrates clearly that
the Tremont Manpower Center is typical of those
throughout the city. In a study of the 1969-70
fiscal year, reported in this article, it was found
that 45,674 applications for assistance had been received at Neighborhood Centers. Of these, 40 percent or 18,693 persons were referred directly to
jobs. However, only 11 percent of the original
group, or 6,037, actually got these jobs. Nineteen
percent, or 8,937, were placed in training programs,
with 2,900 of these later placed in jobs. The total
cost of the city-wide Neighborhood Manpower Service
Center program, which succeeded in placing fewer
than 8,000 persons in jobs during 1969-70, was $38
million. Significantly, the article notes that because of the emphasis placed on proper qualifications for referral, those in direst economic need
of work were systematically excluded because such
individuals generally failed to meet necessary
standards.

16. S. M. Miller, Pamela Roby, and Alwine A.
de Vos van Steenwijk, "Creaming the Poor," Transaction, VII, 8 (June 1970), 39.

17. As the Evaluation Specialist put it,
"Over $43,000 to make $24 a month--some economic
development!"

18. This attempt was short-lived and, as the
West Farms Villagers' Director stated, "eventually
the whole thing fell apart because the Corporation
Board felt threatened by an economic program developed by 'whitey'" (referring to himself).

19. Diary, May 20, 1970, p. 19: a discussion
with the Director at the Agency location during one
of several visits.

20. Evaluation Reports of the Tremont Community Corporation, prepared by the Evaluation

Specialist. These documents are utilized by the Corporation Board, CDA, and the Tremont Area Panel in their deliberations concerning funding decisions.

21. _Diary_, June 11, 1970, from a conversation with a Corporation Board member.

22. _Monthly Narrative Reports_ submitted by WANA to the Corporation, _passim_.

23. _Narrative Report No. 7_, April 30, 1970, from ETAC to Community Corporation.

24. _Diary_, April 28, 1970, p. 28, a conversation with the most active community organizer of the ETAC.

25. _Ibid._, p. 28, same conversation with same person.

26. The incident was related by an employee of the Tremont Housing Clinic that once, when he attempted to assist someone living in ETAC's assigned area, a warning to "stay out of our territory" was given to him. This attitude appeared to characterize the relationships of all three Agencies in this program category.

27. For example, when a student from Fordham University worked on a volunteer basis in the agency, he confirmed that the agency personnel would only visit a few people in the building and not try to organize all of them. The personnel would return to the office, document their visits, and most often, only return to the building when another complaint was received at the agency.

28. Monthly _Narrative Report_ of the Tremont Housing Clinic, Jan. 1970, pp. 6-8. On file at the Corporation.

29. _New York Post_, Sept. 22, 1970, p. 19.

30. _Diary_, May 18, 1970, a three-hour informal conversation with the Director concerning her lengthy experience in the program.

CHAPTER 6

1. City of New York, Community Development Agency, _Guidelines for Youth Development Programs, Program Account No. 59, FY 1970-71_, 1969.

2. Mary Mitchell, _Umbrella Project: Summer 1970, Program Account No. 59_ (Bronx: Tremont Community Corporation, 1969), p. 1.

3. Ibid., p. 2.

4. City of New York, Community Development Agency, Special Youth Programs Review and Analysis Department, Panel Presentation Form, 1969, p. 1.

5. City of New York, Community Development Agency, PY F Versatile Program Guidelines, 1970-71, April 1970, p. 2.

6. Ibid., p. 3.

7. Elliot A. Krause, in his article, "Functions of a Bureaucratic Ideology: 'Citizen Participation,'" Social Problems, XVI, 2 (1968), pp. 140-41, observes that the community action program will always find some way to insure "participation," making very difficult the "boycotting" of such programs by the poor.

8. City of New York, Community Development Agency, PY F Versatile Guidelines, pp. 12-25.

9. Diary, June 9, 1970, p. 13.

10. Ibid., p. 15.

11. Ibid., p. 18.

12. Minutes of the Tremont Community Corporation, April 28, 1970. A meeting was held at the Corporation that involved six Human Resources Administration officials along with the Exective Director and another Board member.

13. Diary, p. 19.

14. Ibid.

15. Minutes of Tremont Community Corporation, June 24, 1970, p. 3.

16. Diary, p. 22.

17. Ibid.

18. Ibid., p. 24.

19. Ibid., p. 28.

20. Ibid., at the time of the CAP Areal Panel meeting only one black agency had been approved for Program Year "F," whereas in Year "E" four black programs had been funded.

21. This letter and WANA's 40-page report are in the possession of the authors.

22. Diary, p. 33, besides receiving a copy of all the pertinent documents of this case, periodic contact was maintained with the Director of WANA in order to keep up with the case.

CHAPTER 7

1.   Kenneth B. Clark and Jeannette Hopkins, A
Relevant War Against Poverty (New York: Harper
Torchbooks, 1970), pp. 26-27.

2.   According to both members and nonmembers
of the PRCDP, this group engaged in what is defined
as status group strategies. For instance, Puerto
Rican protestors from the PRCDP and other groups
took control of a capital budget hearing in City
Hall on Feb. 24, 1970, to protest that the city's
poverty program favored the blacks, often at the expense of the Puerto Ricans--see New York Times, Feb.
25, 1970, p. 36; as another example, on Sept. 10,
1970, 300 Puerto Rican supporters of PRCDP demonstrated against the Council Against Poverty's proposed cuts in antipoverty money for Puerto Rican
programs, including PRCDP, causing Human Resources
Administrator Jules M. Sugarman to defer the cuts--
see New York Times, Sept. 11, 1970, p. 83.

CHAPTER 8

1.   Michael Lipsky, Protest in City Politics:
Rent Strikes, Housing and the Power of the Poor
(Chicago: Rand McNally, 1970), especially pp.
163-203.

2.   New York Times, March 27, 1971, p. 31.
3.   Ibid., p. 43.
4.   New York Times, March 29, 1971, p. 26.
5.   New York Times, April 4, 1971, p. 38.
6.   New York Times, June 26, 1971, p. 27.
7.   Ibid.
8.   It is interesting to note that the black
and Puerto Rican povertycrats in the Morrisania Community Corporation of the Bronx recently decided to
settle their two-year-old conflict over poverty
funds rather than see social services to the commu-
nity--and their positions--terminated. New York
Times, April 27, 1972, p. 1.

9.   There is some evidence to indicate that
the number of "povertycrats" will become larger.
See New York Times, April 10, 1972, p. 1, where
Edward C. Burks analyzes the rapid spread of poverty which has mushroomed far beyond the 26 officially designated poverty areas that this study
has been concerned with.

SELECTED BIBLIOGRAPHY

SELECTED BIBLIOGRAPHY

BOOKS

Bachrach, Peter, and Morton S. Baratz. Power and Poverty: Theory and Practice. New York: Oxford University Press, 1970.

Banfield, Edward. Political Influence: A New Theory of Urban Politics. New York: Free Press, 1964.

Biddy, John F., and Roger Davidson. On Capitol Hill. New York: Holt, Rinehart and Winston, 1967.

Bredemier, Harry C., and Richard M. Stephenson. The Analysis of Social Systems. New York: Holt, Rinehart and Winston, 1962.

Clark, Kenneth B., and Jeannette Hopkins. A Relevant War Against Poverty. New York: Harper Torchbooks, 1970.

Dahrendorf, Ralf. Class and Class Conflict in Industrial Society. Stanford, Calif.: Stanford University Press, 1959.

Donovan, John C. The Politics of Poverty. New York: Pegasus, 1967.

Douglas, William O. Points of Rebellion. New York: Vintage, 1970.

Easton, David. A Systems Analysis of Political Life. New York: Wiley, 1965.

Etzioni, Amitai, ed. Complex Organizations: A Sociological Reader. New York: Holt, Rinehart and Winston, 1964.

Freeman, Howard E., and Clarence C. Sherwood. Social Science and Social Policy. Englewood Cliffs, N.J.: Prentice-Hall, 1970.

Gamson, William A. Power and Discontent. Homewood, Ill.: Dorsey Press, 1968.

Hallman, Howard W. Neighborhood Control of Public Programs. New York: Praeger Publishers, 1970.

Kershaw, Joseph A. Government Against Poverty. Englewood Cliffs, N.J.: Prentice-Hall, 1969.

Kramer, Ralph M. Participation of the Poor. Englewood Cliffs, N.J.: Prentice-Hall, 1969.

Levitan, Sar A. The Design of the Federal Antipoverty Strategy. Ann Arbor, Mich.: Institute of Labor and Industrial Relations, 1967.

Lipsky, Michael. Protest in City Politics: Rent
    Strikes, Housing and the Power of the Poor.
    Chicago: Rand McNally, 1970.
Litt, Edgar. Ethnic Politics in America. Glenview,
    Ill.: Scott, Foresman and Co., 1970.
Marris, Peter, and Martin Rein. Dilemmas of Social
    Reform: Poverty and Community Action in the
    United States. New York: Atherton Press, 1967.
Mogulof, Melvin B. Citizen Participation: A Review
    and Commentary of Federal Policies and Prac-
    tices. Washington, D.C.: The Urban Institute,
    1970.
_____. Citizen Participation: The Local Perspec-
    tive. Washington, D.C.: The Urban Institute,
    1970.
Moynihan, Daniel P. Maximum Feasible Misunderstand-
    ing. New York: Free Press, 1969.
Roucek, Joseph S. Social Control Theory. New York:
    D. Van Nostrand, 1956.
Schelling, Thomas C. The Strategy of Conflict.
    New York: Oxford University Press, 1963.
Selznick, Philip. TVA and the Grass Roots. Berke-
    ley: University of California Press, 1953.
Suchman, Edward A. Evaluative Research. New York:
    Russell Sage Foundation, 1967.
Williams, Robin M. Strangers Next Door. Englewood
    Cliffs, N.J.: Prentice-Hall, 1964.
Zurcher, Louis A. Poverty Warriors. Austin: Uni-
    versity of Texas Press, 1970.

ARTICLES

Beck, Bertram M. "Organizing Community Action," in
    Robert H. Connery and Demetrios Caraley, eds.,
    Governing the City: Challenges and Options
    for New York. New York: Frederick A. Praeger,
    1969, pp. 162-78.
Blumenthal, Richard. "The Bureaucracy: Antipoverty
    and the Community Action Program," in Alan P.
    Sindler, ed., American Political Institutions
    and Public Policy. Boston: Little, Brown and
    Co., 1969, pp. 129-79.
Clark, Terry N. "On Decentralization," Polity, II,
    4 (1970), 508-14.

Coser, Lewis A.   "The Sociology of Poverty," Social
     Problems, XIII, 2 (1965), 30-35.
David, Stephen M.   "Leadership of the Poor in Pov-
     erty Programs," Urban Riots: Violence and So-
     cial Change. Proceedings of the Academy of
     Political Science, XXIX (July 1968), 86-100.
_____. "Welfare: The Community Action Program Con-
     troversy," in Jewel Bellush and Stephen M.
     David, eds., Race and Politics in New York
     City. New York: Praeger Publishers, 1971,
     pp. 25-58.
Dean, Dwight G.   "Index: Dean's Alienation Scale,"
     in Delbert C. Miller, ed., Handbook of Research
     Design and Social Measurement, 2d ed. New
     York: David McKay, 1970.
Krause, Elliot A.   "Functions of a Bureaucratic
     Ideology: 'Citizen Participation,'" Social
     Problems, XVI, 2 (1968), 129-43.
Levitan, Sar A.   "What's Happening, Baby? Essen-
     tial Research for the War on Poverty," in The
     Use of Social Research in Federal Domestic
     Programs (Part II). U.S. Congress Committee
     on Governmental Operations. Washington, D.C.:
     U.S. Government Printing Office, 1967, pp.
     260-70.
Miller, S. M., Pamela Roby, and Alwine A. de Vos
     van Steenwijk. "Creaming the Poor," Transac-
     tion, VII, 8 (June 1970), 39-45.
The New York Post, Sept. 22, 1970, p. 19.
The New York Times, Nov. 4, 1965, p. 26; Nov. 6,
     1969, p. 28; Feb. 25, 1970, p. 36; Sept. 11,
     1970, p. 83; Sept. 17, 1970, p. 13; Sept. 23,
     1970, p. 55; Oct. 20, 1970, p. 1; Dec. 23,
     1970, p. 28; Jan. 6, 1971, pp. 33,41; Jan. 27,
     1971, p. 41; Feb. 17, 1971, p. 43; April 8,
     1971, p. 47; May 14, 1971, p. 1; April 9,
     1972, p. 67; and April 10, 1972, p. 1.
People, Nov. 1970, No. 4. New York City: Human
     Resources Administration.
Peterson, Paul E.   "Forms of Representation: Par-
     ticipation of the Poor in the Community Action
     Program," American Political Science Review,
     LXIV, 2 (June 1970), 491-507.
Pitts, Jesse R., and Amitai Etzioni. "Social Con-
     trol," in David L. Sills, ed., International

Encyclopedia of the Social Sciences. New York:
Macmillan and Free Press, 1968, Vol. 14, pp.
381-402.

Rein, Martin. "Community Action Programs: A Critical Reassessment," _Poverty and Human Resources
Abstracts_, III, 3 (May-June 1968), 2-8.

Rossi, Peter H. "Practice, Methods and Theory in
Evaluating Social-Action Programs," in James
Sundquist, ed. _On Fighting Poverty: Perspectives from Experience_. New York: Basic Books,
1969, pp. 217-34.

Sherril, Robert. "De-escalator of the War on Poverty," _New York Times Magazine_, Dec. 13, 1970,
p. 23.

Wolff, Kurt H. "Social Control," in Joseph S.
Roucek, ed. _Contemporary Sociology_. New York:
Philosophical Library, 1958, pp. 110-31.

Yarmolinsky, Adam. "The Beginnings of OEO," in
James Sundquist, ed., _On Fighting Poverty:
Perspectives from Experience_. New York:
Basic Books, 1969, pp. 34-51.

UNPUBLISHED WORKS

Hockbaum, Martin. "The Decision-making Process in
New York City's Council Against Poverty." Unpublished Ph.D. dissertation, Department of
Political Science, Hunter College, City University of New York, 1971.

Peterson, Paul E. "City Politics and Community Action: The Implementation of the Community Action Program in Three American Cities." Unpublished Ph.D. dissertation, Department of Political Science, University of Chicago, 1967.

_____. "The Politics of Welfare: Public Policy and
Changing Policy-making Processes." Unpublished
paper, Department of Political Science, University of Chicago, June 1968.

Shattuck, Gerald M. "Structural Change and Social
Work Intervention: Relationships Between
Policy and Theory." Unpublished paper, Department of Sociology, Fordham University,
1969.

REPORTS

Evaluation Reports of the Tremont Community Corpora-
      tion, prepared by the Evaluation Specialist.
Letter of Washington Avenue Neighborhood Associa-
      tion's Director to OEO Regional Director, Sept.
      28, 1971.
Minutes of the Tremont Community Corporation: July
      11, 1969, p. 5; Dec. 19, 1969; March 17, 1970;
      April 28, 1970; June 24, 1970.
Monthly Narrative Reports of the Tremont Community
      Corporation's Delegate Agencies.
Report of the Acting Director of the Tremont Neigh-
      borhood Manpower Service Center, Oct. 24, 1970.
Tremont Community Corporation and Delegate Agency
      Manning Tables.

DOCUMENTS

Abrams, Robert. A Plan for Borough and Neighborhood
      Government in New York City. New York City:
      The Office of the President of the Borough of
      the Bronx, October 1970.
City of New York, Community Development Agency:
      Community Corporation Election Master Plan,
          March 1969.
      Community Corporations Elections Manual, 1969.
      Guidelines for Youth Development Programs, Pro-
          gram Account No. 59, FY 1970-71, 1969.
      Guidelines for the Formation of Community Cor-
          porations, 1966.
      PY F Versatile Program Guidelines, 1970-71,
          April 1970.
      Versatile Program Guidelines 1969/70, April 1969.
City of New York, Council Against Poverty:
      An Introduction to the New York City Council
          Against Poverty, March 1969.
      Annual Report of the New York City Council
          Against Poverty, 1966-67, 1967.
      Charter and By-Laws, 1966.
      New York City Poverty Area Maps, 1967.
      Summary: Major Decisions of the New York City
          Council Against Poverty: Nov. 7, 1968--
          Aug. 7, 1969, August 1969.

Lindsay, John V. A Plan for Neighborhood Government
    for New York City. New York City: The Office
    of the Mayor, June 1970.
Mitchell, Mary. Umbrella Project: Summer 1970,
    Program Account No. 59. Bronx, N.Y.:   Tremont
    Community Corporation, 1969.
Public Affairs Office, Human Resources Administra-
    tion. Community Development in New York City.
    New York City: Human Resources Administration,
    1969.
The Neighborhood Manpower Service Centers: Tremont
    Budget FY 1970-71. New York City: Manpower
    Career Development Agency, 1969.
Tremont Area Master Plan. Bronx, N.Y.: Tremont
    Community Corporation, July 1, 1968.
Tremont Community Corporation Year-Round Project,
    Program Year "F" 1970-1971. Bronx, N.Y.:
    Tremont Community Corporation, 1969.
U.S. Congress. An Act to Mobilize the Human and
    Financial Resources of the Nation to Combat
    Poverty in the United States. Public Law
    88-454. 88th Congress, 2d Session, 1964.

ABOUT THE AUTHORS

KENNETH J. POLLINGER, Assistant Professor of Sociology at the University of Bridgeport, Connecticut, teaches Sociological Statistics and Methodology, on both the undergraduate and graduate levels. His present interests revolve around Urban Sociology, with specific emphasis on the Community, from an evaluative and policy research perspective.

Dr. Pollinger was formerly on the faculty of both Fordham University and Herbert H. Lehman College. Before that, he traveled widely in Latin America and taught there for two years. He received the masters and doctoral degrees in Sociology from Fordham University.

ANNETTE C. POLLINGER, Acting Chairman of the Department of Sociology at Manhattanville College, Purchase, New York, specializes in Sociological Statistics, Methodology, and Juvenile Delinquency. Her current interests center around research in the suburbs of the Greater New York Metropolitan Region.

Ms. Pollinger, an ex-Peace Corps Community Developer in Turkey, is a doctoral candidate at Fordham University.

DATE DUE

3/20			
GAYLORD			PRINTED IN U.S.A.